For Declan and Mark

Multiculturalism without Culture

Multiculturalism without Culture

Anne Phillips

PRINCETON UNIVERSITY PRESS

PRINCETON AND OXFORD

Copyright © 2007 by Princeton University Press
Published by Princeton University Press, 41 William Street,
Princeton, New Jersey 08540
In the United Kingdom: Princeton University Press, 6 Oxford Street,
Woodstock, Oxfordshire OX20 1TW

Third printing, and first paperback printing, 2009
Paperback ISBN: 978-0-691-14115-2

The Library of Congress has cataloged the cloth edition of this book as follows

Phillips, Anne, 1950–
Multiculturalism without culture / Anne Phillips.
p.   cm.
Includes bibliographical references and index.
ISBN-13: 978-0-691-12944-0 (alk. paper)
ISBN-10: 0-691-12944-4 (alk. paper)
1. Feminism. 2. Multiculturalism. 3. Cultural conflict. 4. Sex discrimination
against women. I. Title.
HQ1161.P452 2007
305.4809182′1—dc22
2006025980

British Library Cataloging-in-Publication Data is available

This book has been composed in Sabon

Printed on acid-free paper. ∞

press.princeton.edu

Printed in the United States of America

10   9   8   7   6   5   4   3

Contents

Acknowledgments

THE WORK for this book was supported by two grants from the Nuffield Foundation, research leave from the London School of Economics, and a period as adjunct professor at the Research School of Social Sciences, Australian National University. I am grateful to all of these organisations.

The ideas evolved over a number of years, and I became indebted to many people en route. I particularly wish to thank Moira Dustin and Oonagh Reitman, who worked with me on the first Nuffield-funded project, *Sexual and Cultural Equality*; Sawitri Saharso, whose writings on autonomy were a major spur to my thinking, and who read and commented on an early draft of the book; and all the contributors to the two conferences on Gender Equality, Cultural Diversity: European Comparisons and Lessons, held in London and Amsterdam, that Sawitri and I organised. I also benefited enormously from my participation in the Minorities within Minorities conference at the University of Nebraska in 2002, and the Sexual Justice, Cultural Justice conference at the University of British Columbia at Vancouver in 2004, as well as from helpful questioning in a number of seminars over the years. My thanks, in addition, to the late and much missed Iris Young and an anonymous reader for comments on the first draft, and to Ian Malcolm for his expert editing.

Some portions of the book have appeared elsewhere in different forms. I am grateful to the publishers for permission to make use of the following material:

"What Is Culture?" in *Sexual Justice/Cultural Justice*, ed. Barbara Arneil, Monique Deveaux, Rita Dhamoon, and Avigail Eisenberg. (London: Routledge, 2006), for some of the material in chapters 1 and 2.

"When Culture Means Gender: Issues of Cultural Defence in the British Courts," *Modern Law Review* 66 (2003): 510–31, for some of the material in chapter 3.

(with Moira Dustin) "UK Initiatives on Forced Marriage: Regulation, Dialogue, and Exit," *Political Studies* 52 (October 2004): 531–51, for material on forced marriage scattered throughout the book.

Multiculturalism without Culture

THIS BOOK AROSE out of two preoccupations. The first was my feeling that feminism was becoming prone to paralysis by cultural difference, with anxieties about cultural imperialism engendering a kind of relativism that made it difficult to represent *any* belief or practice as oppressive to women or at odds with gender equality. The feeling became especially acute after Susan Moller Okin published her essays on the tension between feminism and multiculturalism, including an abbreviated version, under the title she later regretted, "Is Multiculturalism Bad for Women?"[1] One might have thought Okin's contentions would be rapidly incorporated into the common sense of feminism; indeed, Katha Pollittt commented that "coming in late to this debate, I have to say I've had a hard time understanding how anyone could find these arguments controversial."[2] Okin noted that most cultures are suffused with gendered practices and ideologies that disadvantage women relative to men. For a feminist, this is not an especially controversial claim. She asserted that while most cultures are patriarchal, some are more so than others, and that cultural minorities claiming group rights or multicultural accommodation are often more patriarchal in their practices than the surrounding cultures. It would be easy to get into arguments about how to define patriarchy and whether it remains a useful term; but again, it seems uncontroversial to say that some practices are better for women than others, and hard to see why all cultures would turn out to be equally good or bad on the woman question. Nor is it hugely contentious to suggest (as Okin did) that a practice like polygamy is less popular among women than men, or to point out that it is no longer regarded as an acceptable form of marriage in legal systems across Europe and North America. Okin also maintained that when claims are made on behalf of cultures, they should be carefully interrogated to see who is going to benefit, and that the "requirements"

---

[1] Susan Moller Okin, "Feminism and Multiculturalism: Some Tensions," *Ethics* 108 (1998): of 661–84; Susan Moller Okin, "Is Multiculturalism Bad for Women?" in *Is Multiculturalism Bad for Women?* ed. Joshua Cohen, Matthew Howard, and Martha C. Nussbaum (Princeton, NJ: Princeton University Press, 1999); Susan Moller Okin, " 'Mistresses of Their Own Destiny': Group Rights, Gender, and Realistic Rights of Exit," *Ethics* 112 (January 2002): 205–30.

[2] Katha Pollitt, "Whose Culture?" in *Is Multiculturalism Bad for Women?* ed. Joshua Cohen, Matthew Howard, and Martha C. Nussbaum (Princeton, NJ: Princeton University Press, 1999), 27.

of the culture will often turn out to be the interests of the more powerful men. This is a view almost any feminist could endorse.

Okin made her arguments, however, in a way that gave many hostages to fortune, drawing her examples eclectically from sometimes sensationalist newspaper sources, and offering a much-criticised formulation about some women perhaps being better off if the culture they were born into were "to become extinct."[3] As the debate developed, Okin came to be regarded as representing a hegemonic Western discourse that considered non-Western cultures as almost by definition patriarchal. Like many feminists, I had problems with what she argued, but I also had problems with what seemed to be a backing away from normative judgment among those most hostile to her analysis. As the critics identified implicit hierarchies of culture and rejected what they saw as the arrogant assertion of one true road to gender equality, they often found themselves unable to articulate criticisms of female genital cutting, child marriage, or religious conventions that gave men, but not women, the unilateral right to divorce. Cultural difference had become overlaid with too many distorting assumptions and stereotypes, to the point where any criticism of a cultural practice evoked the image of the "do-gooder" outsider, secure in the superiority of her own culture, telling the insiders what they ought to do. Faced with this unattractive proposition, it looked for a while as if feminists would abandon the language of universals and give up on normative critique.

My second preoccupation—almost the mirror image—was the perception that outside of feminist circles, principles of gender equality were being deployed as part of a demonisation of minority cultural groups. Overt expressions of racism were being transformed into a more socially acceptable criticism of minorities said to keep their women indoors, marry their girls off young to unknown and unwanted partners, and force their daughters and wives to wear veils. People not previously marked by their ardent support for women's rights seemed to rely on claims about the maltreatment of women to justify their distaste for minority cultural groups, and in these claims, cultural stereotypes were rife. It was, of course, partly this perception that made Okin's critics so determined not to give sustenance to views about minority cultures that could be abused in this way. But with the equality agenda seemingly hijacked to promote cultural stereotypes, and feminists curbing their criticisms in order not to support this move, it looked as if things were going badly wrong.

In embarking on this book, I hoped to cut through these dilemmas with an unashamed normative commitment to the principle of equality, and a demonstration that this implied support for both multiculturalism *and*

---

[3] Okin, "Is Multiculturalism Bad for Women?" 22. The sentence continues: "or, preferably, to be encouraged to alter itself so as to reinforce the equality of women."

women's equality and rights. Much of my previous work had explored the relationship between equality and difference, and the viability of group representation as a way of redressing imbalances of power between women and men as well as minority and majority ethnic groups. I saw myself drawing on insights from this work in ways that would mediate the stark opposition between either feminism or multiculturalism, and make it possible to pursue these important components of equality together. I began with an understanding of feminism as a politics of gender equality that sometimes requires policies treating women differently from men, and multiculturalism as a policy agenda designed to redress the unequal treatment of cultural groups and the "culture-racism" to which members of minority cultural groups are often exposed. My initial take on conflicts between these two was to see them in terms of competing equality claims: to say that multiculturalism addresses the inequalities experienced by cultural minorities and feminism the inequalities experienced by women; that both projects draw on a shared commitment to equality; and the two must therefore be balanced in circumstances where they appear to collide. I was not, that is, happy with the notion that one project could simply trump the other. Since both deal with compelling issues of inequality, it could not be appropriate to declare one more fundamental than the other.

In the course of writing the book, things took a different course, both because my ideas changed, and because the world did. Writing in the late 1990s, Okin thought she was dealing with an uncritical consensus, at least among those regarding themselves as progressives, in favour of multiculturalism. Against the backdrop, however, of increasing domestic worries about the economic and social integration of ethnocultural minorities, and rising world tensions over terrorism, the failure of the peace process in the Middle East, and the invasion of Iraq, this rapidly metamorphosed into a retreat. Multiculturalism became the scapegoat for an extraordinary array of political and social evils, a supposedly misguided approach to cultural diversity that encouraged men to beat their wives, parents to abuse their children, and communities to erupt in racial violence. In Australia, a country that declared itself multicultural as far back as 1982 and drew up the *National Agenda for a Multicultural Society* in 1989, a decade of right-wing populism pretty much reversed attempts to define the nation through its multiplicity of cultural groups, and ushered in a more strident assertion of those so-called Australian values that must be upheld against the influx of migrants from Southeast Asia. In the United States, where multiculturalism had become associated with the revision of curriculum and college admissions policies to reflect the diverse experiences of more marginal groups, there was a reaction against what came to be seen as excesses, and a reaffirmation of the supposedly core values of freedom, democracy, and (a Christian) god. In Europe, where multiculturalism had come to involve a range of legislative and administrative adjustments to meet the needs of the ethnically diverse populations brought together by postcolonial migration, there was a sharp retreat from the rhetoric of multiculturalism—with as yet unknown consequences for the practice. Dating this from the beginning of this century, Christian Joppke noted a "seismic shift" from a language of multiculturalism to one of civic integration.[4]

Here are just two examples. Over the years, Britain had stumbled onto a relatively robust version of multiculturalism, with minority religious groups able to apply for state funding to finance denominational schools, wide-ranging accommodations of dress codes and diets in schools, colleges, and places of work, and a significant number of laws or legal judgments that exempt members of certain ethnocultural groups from requirements that are at odds with their religion or culture.[5] In a much-cited speech from 1966, Home Secretary Roy Jenkins had rejected the melting pot ideal that would "turn everybody out in a common mould, as one of a series of carbon copies of someone's misplaced vision of the stereotyped Englishman," and defined integration "not as a flattening process of assimilation but as equal opportunity, coupled with cultural diversity, in an atmosphere of mutual tolerance."[6] The subsequent evolution of multicultural policy was never codified in official statements, and many citizens would probably be surprised to discover the number of small accommodations permitting Sikhs to wear turbans instead of crash helmets, modifying the regulations governing slaughterhouses to allow for halal and kosher meat, or splitting a pension between two widows of a polygamous marriage.[7] (It is, in fact, rare to see Sikhs taking advantage of their right to wear turbans instead of crash helmets when riding a motorbike, so presumably concerns about road safety have prevailed.) Critics have suggested that the "managers of ethnic diversity" deliberately avoided public debate, preferring to negotiate the practical fixes of multi-

---

[4] Christian Joppke, "The Retreat of Multiculturalism in the Liberal State: Theory and Policy," *British Journal of Sociology* 55, no. 2 (2004): 249. See also Christian Joppke and Eva Morawska, eds. *Towards Assimilation and Citizenship: Immigrants in Liberal Nation-States* (Basingstoke, UK: Palgrave, 2003).

[5] For a survey of the last, see Sebastian Poulter, *English Law and Ethnic Minority Customs* (London: Butterworth, 1986).

[6] Roy Jenkins, *Essays and Speeches* (London: Collins, 1970), 267.

[7] The UK National Health Service (Superannuation) (Amendment) Regulation 1989, SI 1989/804, allows for the splitting of the widow's pension between two widows of a polygamous marriage. Yet since no one domiciled in the country can legally contract a polygamous marriage, and second and subsequent wives of polygamous marriages contracted in other jurisdictions have no entitlement to join husbands in the United Kingdom for settlement purposes, it is now virtually impossible for this situation to arise.

culturalism "behind closed doors."[8] The more accurate reading is probably a process of "multicultural drift"[9]—a series of smallish adjustments and accommodations that added up to a quite substantial practice of multiculturalism. Though not underpinned by any very conscious philosophy, the result was relatively robust. In contrast to some other parts of Europe, for example, there was never much of an issue about Muslim schoolgirls wanting to wear headscarves to school. In most cases where this arose, school governors agreed alternative uniforms that met religious and cultural concerns.

More recently, there has been much talk of the death of multiculturalism, the bigotries of multiculturalism, or multiculturalism turning into "a dangerous form of benign neglect and exclusion." (This last is from a speech by the chair of the Commission for Racial Equality in 2004.)[10] The events of September 11, 2001, undoubtedly played a part in this. A more local impetus was civil unrest in spring and summer 2001 in the towns of Burnley, Oldham, and Bradford, where young Asians fought in the streets with white racists, and police and property were attacked. In a significant marker of a new approach towards cultural diversity, the Community Cohesion Review Team set up to review the events was charged with identifying good practice on social cohesion. Though its report reaffirmed the vision of Britain as a multiracial society and rejected nostalgia for the "supposedly halcyon days of a mono-cultural society," it also expressed deep disquiet at the degree of social and residential segregation uncovered in the course of the enquiry, noting that "separate educational arrangements, community and voluntary bodies, employment, places of worship, language, social and cultural networks, means that many communities operate on the basis of a series of parallel lives."[11] It might be thought geographic segregation was the real problem here, and the report did recommend new housing strategies to promote a greater mixing of ethnic groups while ensuring effective support against harassment and intimidation. But despite many useful recommendations, the main message was the need for a "greater sense of citizenship, based on (a few) common principles which are shared and observed by all sections of the community."[12] Subsequent policy discussions focused on this common core of citizenship values, perceived as the necessary ingredient holding a multi-

[8] Brian Barry, *Culture and Equality: An Egalitarian Critique of Multiculturalism* (Cambridge, UK: Polity Press, 2001), 95.

[9] Runnymede Trust Commission, *The Future of Multi-Ethnic Britain* (London: Profile Books, 2000), 14.

[10] Trevor Phillips to the Civil Service Race Equality Network, London, 26 April 2004.

[11] *Community Cohesion: Report of the Independent Review Team* (London: Home Office, 2001), chapter 2, sec. 2.1.

[12] *Community Cohesion*, chap. 2, sec. 2.13.

cultural society together. Incidentally, it is interesting to contrast the rising anxieties concerning cultural segregation with the relative complacency regarding class segregation. The latter has intensified over recent decades, as the gap between rich and poor widens, and the rich increasingly insulate themselves in separate neighbourhoods and schools. Egalitarians worry about this, but it does not seem to evoke the same kind of public hysteria.

The new take on multiculturalism was reflected in the 2004 introduction of a citizenship ceremony for new nationals, involving an oath of allegiance to the queen along with a pledge to respect the rights, freedoms, and democratic values of the United Kingdom—which is not something that existing citizens have to do. A year later, the government introduced a citizenship test, requiring applicants to demonstrate a working knowledge of the English language and life in the United Kingdom, and failing that, complete a lengthy language and citizenship course. In a form of argument that surfaces again and again, advocates of compulsory language classes promoted them in explicitly gendered terms, claiming that they would be particularly valuable in freeing older women from domestic seclusion and their enforced dependence on male family members. The rhetorical retreat from multiculturalism was therefore well under way before July 7, 2005, when four British citizens—three from Pakistani Muslim families but born and brought up in England, and the fourth born in Jamaica and converting to Islam in his teens—killed themselves and fifty-two others on London's public transport system At this point, the prime minister declared that "the rules of the game" had definitively changed, introduced wide-ranging discretionary powers to deport nonnationals believed to be promoting or glorifying terrorism, and announced plans for a major review of multiculturalism. Too much toleration of difference, it was suggested, was leaving young Muslims outside the mainstream of society, refusing all loyalties to Britain, available as terrorist fodder.

The reversal in the Netherlands has been even more striking. Respect for cultural identity, including a right to be taught one's mother tongue in primary schools, had been a notable part of public policy from the mid-1970s. Initially, this reflected the belief that immigrants were only temporary visitors, but when the Dutch government finally acknowledged in 1980 that most migrants would stay for good, similar principles continued to shape policy.[13] The 1983 Minorities Memorandum marked out the Netherlands as Europe's most explicitly multicultural regime, committed to addressing socioeconomic disadvantage, but also recognising the right of minority groups to retain and develop their cultural and religious iden-

---

[13] Details of the Netherlands are taken from Han Entzinger, "The Rise and Fall of Multiculturalism: The Case of the Netherlands," in *Towards Assimilation and Citizenship: Immigrants in Liberal Nation-States* (Basingstoke, UK: Palgrave, 2003), 59–86.

tity, and representing this as an enrichment of the entire society. Institutionally, this was reflected in generous subsidies to ethnic organisations and media, the creation of consultative councils at both the local and national level, and an obligation on the part of local and national governments to consult these councils in the development of policy plans. (For those familiar with Iris Marion Young's proposals for the political representation of oppressed groups, these mechanisms come close to meeting her suggestions, with the important difference that the consultative councils were set up at the initiative of the authorities rather than arising out of the self-organisation of minority groups.)[14] Children from specified minority groups were offered five hours a week of instruction in their mother tongue in the public schools, missing, in the process, lessons in core subjects. Access to housing, employment, and education was to be guided by principles of proportionality, though people from minority ethnic groups continued to experience higher rates of school dropout and unemployment along with lower rates of pay.

The emphasis was already shifting by 1994, when the government published a new policy, the Integration of Ethnic Minorities, describing the preservation of minority cultures as a responsibility of each specific community and no longer a public commitment. As in the case of the United Kingdom, the shift in language is important, for the term integration was previously regarded as having unacceptable overtones of assimilation. In 1998, a new law, Civic Integration for Newcomers, gave local authorities the power to require migrants from outside the European Union to attend five hundred hours of language training and one hundred hours of training in social and civic skills. Again, the justification was partly gendered. Han Entzinger, one of the proponents, argued that mandatory courses made it easier "to include categories that otherwise can be difficult to reach, such as traditional Muslim women or school dropouts."[15]

Over the next few years, reservations about Dutch multiculturalism continued to be linked to the treatment of women in Islam. Ayaan Hirsi Ali, a young Dutch Somali woman elected to Parliament in 2003, became a particularly prominent voice, representing Islam as responsible for forced marriages, female genital mutilation, and honour killings. In 2004, she worked with filmmaker Theo Van Gogh on the film *Submission I*, which denounced violence against Muslim women. Van Gogh was subsequently killed by a young Dutch Moroccan, who left a letter warning that Hirsi Ali was his real target, and anti-Muslim violence temporarily erupted across this previously model multicultural country. By December

---

[14] Iris Marion Young, *Justice and the Politics of Difference* (Princeton, NJ: Princeton University Press, 1990).

[15] Entzinger, "The Rise and Fall of Multiculturalism," 76.

2005, a majority of Dutch parliamentarians supported a motion calling for a ban on women wearing the niqab or burka in public spaces—not just a ban on teachers or pupils wearing it in schools (at least debatable, on the grounds that teaching depends on face-to-face communication), and not just a ban on public officials wearing it in courtrooms (again, at least debatable, on the basis of secularism or security), but a ban on *any* female walking down the streets dressed in a burka. Inspired by this, the minister for immigration and integration said she favoured the introduction of a code of conduct to emphasise Dutch identity, which would include an expectation that citizens speak Dutch in public. This was retreating from multiculturalism with a vengeance.[16]

The retreat forms the political context for my book, which should be read as arguing for a different kind of multiculturalism—but for multiculturalism nonetheless. Neither the one-sided assimilation that preceded talk of multiculturalism nor the more generous cosmopolitanism that has followed it satisfactorily address the power inequalities that provide the normative case for multiculturalism, while the strident assertions of national identity that have characterised the post–September 11 world make the case more urgent than ever. My object, however, is a multiculturalism without culture: a multiculturalism that dispenses with the reified notions of culture that feed those stereotypes to which so many feminists have objected, yet retains enough robustness to address inequalities between cultural groups; a multiculturalism in which the language of cultural difference no longer gives hostages to fortune or sustenance to racists, but also no longer paralyses normative judgment. I maintain that those writing on multiculturalism (supporters as well as critics) have exaggerated not only the unity and solidity of cultures but the intractability of value conflict as well, and often misrecognised highly contextual political dilemmas as if these reflected deep value disagreement. Though there are important areas of cultural disagreement, most do not involve a deep diversity with respect to ethical principles and norms, and many are more comparable to the disputes that take place *within* cultural groups.

In developing this argument, I query what I see as one of the biggest problems with culture: the tendency to represent individuals from minority

---

[16] At the time of writing, it seems there will not be a ban on the niqab or burka in public spaces. In May 2006, a television documentary "revealed" that Hirsi Ali had given false information at the time of her application for asylum in 1992. Though Hirsi Ali had openly acknowledged this when she at entered national politics, she was told (by the same minister of immigration and integration who had previously suggested a ban on the niqab) that she was not, therefore, a Dutch citizen. Hirsi Ali resigned her parliamentary seat and announced that she was moving to the United States. The minister of immigration came under heavy criticism from other members of the political elite, and in June 2006, the government announced that Hirsi Ali would retain her Dutch citizenship.

or non-Western groups as driven by their culture and compelled by cultural dictates to behave in particular ways. Culture is now widely employed in a discourse that denies human agency, defining individuals through their culture, and treating culture as the explanation for virtually everything they say or do. This sometimes features as part of the case for multicultural policies or concessions, but it more commonly appears in punitive policies designed to stamp out what have been deemed inappropriate or unacceptable practices. When, for example, European governments decide that the best way to protect young Moroccan, Turkish, or Bangladeshi women from being forced into unwanted marriages with strangers from their parents' country of origin is to ban marriages with overseas partners for anyone under the age of eighteen, twenty-one, or twenty-four, they represent young women from these groups as incapable of agency. They operate on the (highly stereotypical) assumption that all parents from these cultural groups are coercive and all young women are submissive, and hence, that any marriage arranged with an overseas partner should be regarded as forced. I argue that a more careful understanding of culture provides a better basis for multicultural policy than the overly homogenised version that currently figures in the arguments of supporters and critics alike. A defensible multiculturalism will put human agency much more at its centre; it will dispense with strong notions of culture.

I focus on areas of contestation where a sensitivity to cultural traditions has been employed to deny women their rights or principles of gender equality have been used as a reason to ban cultural practices, and I draw on a growing feminist literature that sees the deconstruction of culture as the way forward in addressing tensions between gender equality and cultural diversity. My own approach is closest to those who have noted the selective way culture is employed to explain behaviour in non-Western societies or among individuals from racialised minority groups, and the implied contrast with rational, autonomous (Western) individuals, whose actions are presumed to reflect moral judgments, and who can be held individually responsible for those actions and beliefs. This binary approach to cultural difference is neither helpful nor convincing. The basic contention throughout is that multiculturalism can be made compatible with the pursuit of gender equality and women's rights so long as it dispenses with an essentialist understanding of culture. I have somewhat polemically described my project as a multiculturalism without culture.

Chapter 1 sets out the main themes by reference to the notions of culture employed in the political theory and feminist literatures, and identifies the main normative issues. Chapter 2 provides a more detailed exploration of the concept of culture, drawing on arguments in the anthropological literature of the last twenty years, and confronts the most obvious alternative—cosmopolitanism. Chapter 3 focuses on cultural defence, based primarily on cases from the English and U.S. courts. Chapter 4 addresses notions of culture as constraint that figure in the case both for and against multiculturalism. A central part of the argument in both chapters 3 and 4 is that culture needs to be treated in the more nuanced way that has become available for class and gender: that is, as something that influences, shapes, and constrains behaviour, but does not determine it. Chapter 5 looks at questions of exit, suggesting that the right to leave an oppressive family or group does not provide enough protection for "at-risk members" partly because it does not attach *enough* significance to cultural belonging. Chapter 6 pulls together the various threads of my argument as regards the relationship between the individual and the group, and spells out in more detail what this means in terms of some specific policy questions.

A final note on style. My first draft was liberally sprinkled with scare quotes in order to distance myself from conventional usages of terms such as race, culture, ethnicity, and so on. Given that culture is the most overused word in the book, this made for untidy reading. I came to the conclusion that it was also unnecessary. Since the explicit claim is that culture is a problematic term, it was a bit patronising to feel I had to remind the reader of this every time I employed the word. Having decided to drop the scare quotes for culture, there seemed no good reason to retain them for ethnicity or race.

CHAPTER ONE

Multiculturalism without Culture

IN A 2001 book, Will Kymlicka declared that the long battle to establish the justice of minority rights was over.[1] Those concerned with the rights of ethnocultural minorities had successfully redefined the terms of public debate. It was now widely recognised that states can harm their citizens by trivialising or ignoring their cultural identities, and that this harm (commonly described, following Charles Taylor's work, as a failure of recognition)[2] can be as damaging to people as denying them their civil or political rights. It was also widely accepted that laws, rules, and institutions are likely to be biased towards the identities and interests of majority cultural groups, even when they have been crafted in ways that are supposed to make them culture blind. "If we accept either or both of these points," Kymlicka continued, "then we can see minority rights not as unfair privileges or invidious forms of discrimination, but as compensation for unfair disadvantages and so as consistent with, and even required by, justice."[3] In conditions of cultural diversity, what the majority supports does not guarantee citizen equality, and it may be necessary to supplement majority decisions by a stronger regime of minority rights. In some circumstances—most notably those involving the rights of indigenous peoples—justice may mean devolving authority to subnational groups. In others, it may be more a matter of reviewing the society's institutions to see whether and where its rules and symbols disadvantage minority groups. In many cases, insisting that everyone must abide by identical rules will turn out to be unfair to minorities. Sometimes it is more equitable to have different rules for different groups.

In making what subsequently proved a premature declaration of victory, Kymlicka was not suggesting that the cultural wars were over. He predicted, however, that future critics of multiculturalism would spend less time challenging the intrinsic justice of minority rights and more querying the perverse effects of particular multicultural policies. There would be fewer arguments about whether it was possible to be a liberal and yet

[1] Will Kymlicka, *Politics in the Vernacular: Nationalism, Multiculturalism, and Citizenship* (Oxford: Oxford University Press, 2001), 32.

[2] Charles Taylor, "The Politics of Recognition," in *Multiculturalism and the Politics of Recognition*, ed. Amy Gutmann (Princeton, NJ: Princeton University Press, 1992).

[3] Kymlicka, *Politics in the Vernacular*, 33.

support something that smacked of group rights, or to be an egalitarian and still condone differential treatment. Future critics of multiculturalism would be more likely to dwell on the way policies defended in the name of all members of a disadvantaged cultural group end up favouring some over others, creating a new kind of injustice in the course of redressing an old. Or they would worry about multicultural policies corroding the common core of citizenship, undermining the bases of social unity, and making it impossible for citizens to sustain a strong sense of national identity. In either case, they might be willing to accept that cultural recognition matters to people, and that some of the society's rules and institutions have been biased against minority cultural groups. They would still question whether multicultural policies were the best way of dealing with this.

Kymlicka's prediction has been largely borne out, though with more devastating consequences for multiculturalism than he anticipated at the time. In the theoretical literature, much of the attention has shifted to what are seen as the perverse effects of multicultural policies on the members of minority cultural groups—on those, in other words, who the policies are most supposed to benefit. There is a large and growing body of feminist writing exploring the damage that can be done to women in minority groups when the societies they live in adopt multiculturalism, the main contention being that multicultural policies shore up the power base of the older men within the community and encourage the public authorities to tolerate practices that undermine women's equality. This criticism forms part of a wider "minorities within minorities" literature that draws attention to the way groups can oppress their own internal minorities—which might be women, but could also be children, homosexuals, or the poor—and the risk that policies of multiculturalism will reinforce the inequities of power.[4] Those writing in this vein do not necessarily take issue with what might be described as the defining principles of multiculturalism: the notion that minority cultural groups *are* disadvantaged vis-à-vis majority ones; and that remedying this can involve significant changes in the society's institutions and rules. Rather, the question is who carries the costs? Ayelet Shachar notes that "well-meaning accommodations aimed at mitigating power inequalities between groups may end up reinforcing power hierarchies within them."[5] Where this happens, "some categories of at-risk group members are being asked to shoulder a disproportionate share of the costs of multiculturalism."[6]

---

[4] Avigail Eisenberg and Jeff Spinner-Halev, eds., *Minorities within Minorities: Equality, Rights, and Diversity* (Cambridge: Cambridge University Press, 2005).

[5] Ayelet Shachar, *Multicultural Jurisdictions: Cultural Differences and Women's Rights* (Cambridge: Cambridge University Press, 2001), 4.

[6] Ibid., 17.

A second arm of criticism represents multiculturalism as undermining social cohesion, dissipating national identity, and emptying citizenship of much of its content. There were a number of early versions of this (particularly in the United States) that talked of the "disuniting" or "fraying" of America;[7] but the criticism has resurfaced in recent years and been especially effective when linked to a broadly redistributive politics. David Miller, for example, argues that radical multiculturalism emphasises group difference at the expense of what people have in common, and in doing so, weakens the bonds of solidarity that lead citizens to support the redistributive policies of the welfare state.[8] In an era when welfare spending is being scaled down under the combined pressures of global markets and tax-resistant voters, this looks a serious concern. Fears about social unity have been further heightened by the spread of terrorist activities into the heartlands of the West. In Europe, worries about what are described as homegrown terrorists have prompted a major review of multiculturalism, with commentators asserting that an excess of cultural toleration is preventing minority groups from integrating and thus creating a breeding ground for Islamist militants. In the words of one journalist, writing after the 2005 suicide bombs in London, "These British bombers are a consequence of a misguided and catastrophic pursuit of multiculturalism."[9] "Misguided" ways of practising multiculturalism are seen as promoting a separatism that makes it harder for people to see themselves as belonging to the same national community. Where this happens, they may be less willing to support social justice programmes that involve a redistribution of resources from some parts of the society to others. More urgently still, they may be willing to kill their fellow citizens.

My original aim related closely to Kymlicka's first area of concern: the worry that multicultural policies could end up favouring some members of minority groups over others; and more specifically, end up disadvantaging women. It was inspired, in other words, by a feminist literature that examined the impact of multiculturalism on the rights of women, and the very real danger that women's freedom of choice or equality with men

---

[7] Arthur M. Schlesinger, *The Disuniting of America* (New York: W. W. Norton, 1992); Robert Hughes, *The Culture of Complaint: The Fraying of America* (New York: Oxford University Press, 1993), esp. chap. 2.

[8] David Miller, *On Nationality* (Oxford: Oxford University Press, 1995), chap. 5. For a response, specifically on the charge that multicultural policies undermine the prospects for a strong welfare state, see Kymlicka, *Politics in the Vernacular*; Keith Banting and Will Kymlicka, "Do Multiculturalism Policies Erode the Welfare State?" in *Cultural Diversity versus Economic Solidarity: Proceedings of the Seventh Francqui Colloquium*, ed. Philippe van Parijs (Brussels: De Boeck, 2004).

[9] William Pfaff, "A Monster of Our Own Making," *Guardian* (Manchester), 21 August 2005.

could be sacrificed in the name of what were deemed to be important cultural traditions. I look at the use of culture by defence lawyers seeking to mitigate acts of violence against women; the banning of Muslim head-scarves in schools or public institutions (officially defended as part of the secular separation of church from state, but often supported by additional arguments about protecting young women from oppression); and the introduction of age restrictions on marriages with overseas partners (frequently defended as a way of protecting young women in cultural minorities from gender oppression). But in addressing these issues, it became clear I had to step back from the supposed tension between the rights of women and the rights of cultures. I had to begin with a further objection to multiculturalism, touched on only briefly by Kymlicka, that strikes deep at the heart of the multicultural project.

This third objection takes issue with the notion of culture itself, representing it as a falsely homogenising reification. Multiculturalism considers itself the route to a more tolerant and inclusive society because it recognises that there *is* a diversity of cultures, and rejects the assimilation of these into the cultural traditions of the dominant group. Much recent literature claims that this exaggerates the internal unity of cultures, solidifies differences that are currently more fluid, and makes people from other cultures seem more exotic and distinct than they really are. Multiculturalism then appears not as a cultural liberator but as a cultural straitjacket, forcing those described as members of a minority cultural group into a regime of authenticity, denying them the chance to cross cultural borders, borrow cultural influences, define and redefine themselves. If the accusations are correct, they threaten to remove the very basis for multicultural policies, for if culture imputes a false stability to experiences that are intrinsically fluid, what exactly is left to be recognised, accommodated, or equalised?

Say we were to conclude that the boundaries between cultures are highly permeable, to the point where it becomes virtually impossible to identify individuals by discrete cultural tags. Would there be anything left for multicultural policy to do? Say we were to conclude that it is a patronising denial of human agency and responsibility to represent individuals from minority ethnic groups as compelled by their culture to behave in certain ways. Would it still be possible to argue that societies should exempt members of particular cultural groups from dress codes or health and safety regulations on the grounds that their cultures make it especially hard for them to meet these requirements? Say we were to conclude that what are represented as the traditions and practices of a minority culture are primarily the traditions and practices favoured by the old men who run the community. Would this sweep away all grounds for criticising a hegemonic monoculturalism? If culture is a misnomer, what is left of multiculturalism? Is it possible to have multiculturalism without culture?

My answer is a qualified yes. There has been too speedy a move from a problematic multiculturalism to a transnational cosmopolitanism; I see the latter as inadequate, even with the additions that turn it into a "rooted," "vernacular," or "critical" cosmopolitanism.[10] Culture matters, as part of the way we give meaning to our world, as an important element in self-ascribed identity, and as one of the mechanisms through which social hierarchies are sustained. Material inequality—measured in terms of income, education, employment, health, housing, and so on—continues to have a recognisable group quality. It correlates with differences of gender, race, ethnicity, and national origin, and does so in a structured manner that goes beyond questions of identity or choice. The individuals concerned may have no interest in defining themselves by reference to their sex, ethnicity, or supposed culture, but they cannot thereby escape all forms of discrimination or disadvantage visited on "their" group. As part of the way that people give meaning to their world, culture will always be inescapable. As part of what currently allocates us to unequal positions in society, it is also contingently so. This is not something that can be addressed by pretending cultural differences away.

The limits of sex- or race-blind approaches to gender and racial oppression have been widely canvassed over recent decades. Similar issues arise as regards culture. In all three cases, the category is problematic, but simply denying its validity is never enough to combat the hierarchies of power. Opponents of racism do not pack up their bags once they have demonstrated that *race* is an invalid category; indeed, many continue to support policies of affirmative action that employ the racial categorisations they know to be unsound. Nor do feminists retreat once they have demonstrated the slipperiness of notions of *women*. Many go on to argue that an effective challenge to the hierarchies of gender involves recognising women as a politically salient category—for example, in establishing some kind of quota mechanism to ensure that women are more adequately represented.[11] When critics take their category objections too literally—as did the French Socialist members of Parliament who proposed removing the "shocking" and "dangerous" term *race* from the constitutional guarantee of equality for all without distinction of race—this usu-

---

[10] Kwame Anthony Appiah talks of a rooted cosmopolitanism in his "Cosmopolitan Patriots" *Critical Inquiry* 23 (1997): 617–34. A number of the essays discuss a vernacular cosmopolitanism in Carol A. Breckenridge, Sheldon Pollock, Homi K. Bhabha, and Dipesh Chakrabarty, eds., *Cosmopolitanism* (Durham, NC: Duke University Press, 2002).

[11] I argue this more fully in *The Politics of Presence: The Political Representation of Gender, Ethnicity, and Race* (Oxford: Oxford University Press, 1995).

ally indicates a failure of political judgment.[12] Querying *race, culture,* and *women* does not mean excising these terms altogether from our vocabulary. It means, rather, a radical overhaul of the ways they are employed.

Culture in Political Theory

The critique of culture is most fully developed in the anthropological and sociological literature, where it often combines with a critique of ethnicity, community, and race. The idea that race is a misnomer—that there are no such things as races in the world—is by now widely recognised, to the point where many sociologists will only use the term with scare quotes around it. As a way of identifying populations that share a significant proportion of their genetic material, the folk division of the world into white, black, brown, yellow, and red is woefully mistaken. As Kwame Anthony Appiah notes, small intermarrying communities like the Amish in North America might be better candidates for the term race than African Americans, who are estimated to derive up to 30 percent of their genetic material from European and American Indian ancestors.[13] Scientists studying the heritability of characteristics have found the greatest concentration of shared genetic material in the populations of small island communities like Iceland or Sardinia, yet people rarely talk of the Icelandic or Sardinian people as constituting a distinct race. Human beings clearly vary in their skin colour and physiognomy, but it was only in the process of justifying slavery and colonialism that these characteristics were wrapped up in packages with qualities like strength, intelligence, creativity, or the capacity for hard work. What Paul Gilroy has described as "the rational irrationality of 'race'" is a political rather than scientific invention.[14]

Ethnicity—a politer hybrid that combines the notion of blood connection with a more historically mutable culture—has become the preferred term in recent decades, but is also widely attacked. It was criticised by Max Weber for its lack of conceptual rigour as far back as 1912.[15] Since then, it has been described as "an ambiguous concept referring to an

---

[12] Judith Ezekiel describes it as "a philosophically coherent, but politically dangerous, position" in "Magritte Meets Maghreb: This Is Not a Veil," *Australian Feminist Studies* 20, no. 47 (2005): 235.

[13] Kwame Anthony Appiah and Amy Gutmann, *Color-Conscious: The Political Morality of Race* (Princeton, NJ: Princeton University Press, 1996), 70–73.

[14] Paul Gilroy, *Against Race: Imagining Political Culture beyond the Color Line* (Cambridge, MA: Belknap Press, 2000), 69.

[15] Gerd Baumann and Thijl Sunier, eds), *Post-Migration Ethnicity: Cohesion, Commitments, Comparison* (Amsterdam: Het Spinhuis, 1995), 1.

identity that is sometimes national and sometimes religious or class-linked," and as "analytically impotent."[16] When coupled with community (as in ethnic community), it is regarded as misleading and even dishonest. In Michael Ignatieff's view, for example, "ethnic minorities are called 'communities' either because it makes them feel better, or because it makes the white majority feel more secure."[17] Even those who see ethnicity as a useful category of social analysis complain that it gets misread as if it described a real entity, thereby conjuring into existence some thing to which ethnicity is supposed to correspond. This commits what Rogers Brubaker considers the error of groupism: "the tendency to take discrete, sharply differentiated, internally homogeneous and externally bounded groups as basic constituents of social life, chief protagonists of social conflict, and fundamental units of social analysis."[18] Once a common error in relation to class (remember when the working class bestrode the stage of history?), this has persisted in relation to ethnic groups, nations, and races, which are still treated as if they were social protagonists with intentions and interests attached. Brubaker is not denying that people may identify themselves in terms of their ethnicity—and often identify those they see as their enemies in terms of theirs—yet he argues that the protagonists of most ethnic conflicts are not groups but organisations, and usually organisations with a vested interest in making people see themselves in ethnic terms. In terms that deliberately recall E. P. Thompson's analysis of the "making" of the English working class, he argues that it makes most sense to think of "groupness as an event, as something that 'happens,'" and ethnicity as a category that has been made to do (often disreputable) political work.[19]

The reservations about ethnicity are mirrored in similar ones about culture. Adam Kuper maintains that culture can become "a euphemism for race, fostering a discourse on racial identities while apparently abjuring racism."[20] Many have argued that the boundaries between cultures are themselves political creations: Riva Kastoryano, to give one example,

[16] Riva Kastoryano, *Negotiating Identities: States and Immigrants in France and Germany* (Princeton, NJ: Princeton University Press, 2002), 35; Gerd Baumann, *Contesting Culture: Discourses of Identity in Multi-Ethnic London* (Cambridge: Cambridge University Press, 1996), 19.

[17] Michael Ignatieff, "Why 'Community' Is a Dishonest Word," *Observer* (Manchester), 3 May 1993.

[18] Rogers Brubaker, "Ethnicity without Groups," *European Journal of Sociology* 43, no. 3 (2002), 164. See also Rogers Brubaker and Frederick Cooper, "Beyond 'Identity,'" *Theory and Society* 29 (2000): 1–47.

[19] Brubaker, "Ethnicity without Groups," 168.

[20] Adam Kuper, *Culture: The Anthropologists' Account* (Cambridge, MA: Harvard University Press, 1999), 14.

talks of the "invention of a culture that claims to be collective" as part of the process of constructing an ethnic group that can lay claim to public resources.[21] Feminists have stressed the tendency towards cultural essentialism, alleging that discourses of culture allow the more powerful members of a group to codify what are normally changing and contested practices, thereby establishing their own authoritative readings that they employ to enforce conformity among group members.[22] In these and other criticisms (discussed at greater length in chapter 2), people have registered considerable scepticism about *culture* and what the term is being deployed to do.

Those working in the field of political theory have mostly remained more trusting in their use of the term, offering perhaps a quick definition of cultural or ethnocultural group, but then continuing on as if *ethnicity* and *culture* had a clear and self-evident application. The influential collection on *Ethnicity and Group Rights*, published as part of the NOMOS series in 1997, takes as its starting point the existence of ethnocultural groups that have aspirations and make political claims.[23] Though a number of the contributors note that these groups are not internally homogeneous, or query the precise difference between so-called ethnic groups and others, no one seriously questions the existence of ethnic groups, the fact of ethnic diversity, or the idea that ethnic groups act. All the compelling issues begin from that point onwards, with what societies ought to do in response to ethnocultural claims. That this should be the case is neither surprising nor particularly blameworthy, for political theorists deal in normative questions of justice, equality, and autonomy, and in a period dominated by the discourse of human rights, have been particularly preoccupied by what rights, if any, can be claimed by minority groups. Culture enters the field of investigation not so much as difference (which might then direct attention to the boundaries between cultures and how fixed or indeterminate these are) but inequality (which presumes the existence of separate groups and focuses on the relationship between them). It was the recognition of unequal power relations between majority and minority groups, and the perception that states can unfairly disadvantage citizens from minority groups when they impose a unitary political and legal framework, that first gave impetus to the arguments for multiculturalism.

[21] Kastoryano, *Negotiating Identities*, 98.

[22] See, for example, Uma Narayan, *Dislocating Cultures: Identities, Traditions, and Third World Women* (London: Routledge, 1997); "Essence of Culture and a Sense of History: A Feminist Critique of Cultural Essentialism," *Hypatia* 13, no. 2 (1998): 86–106; "Undoing the 'Package Picture' of Cultures," *Signs* 25, no. 4 (2000): 1083–86.

[23] Ian Shapiro and Will Kymlicka, eds., *Ethnicity and Group Rights (NOMOS XXXIX)* (New York: New York University Press, 1997).

Political theorists are—to their credit—political. They think about inequality and power.

But this means culture crosses the horizon already attached to distinctions between majority and minority, and already linked to territorial or legal claims. Kymlicka is barely a paragraph into *Multicultural Citizenship* before remarking that "minorities and majorities increasingly clash over such issues as language rights, regional autonomy, political representation, education curriculum, land claims, immigration and naturalization policy, even national symbols, such as the choice of national anthem or public holiday."[24] These are the clashes Kymlicka seeks to resolve, as indicated in his decision to employ culture as virtually synonymous with nation or people, referring to "an intergenerational community, more or less institutionally complete, occupying a given territory or homeland, sharing a distinct language and history."[25] The definition conjures up a group of considerable solidity. It has its own institutions, territories, language and history, and by implication, its own potentially extensive claims on the loyalty of its members. It is not surprising to learn that such groups are often in conflict with one another. Shachar criticises Kymlicka for a theory of multiculturalism that provides too little protection for women and other vulnerable groups, but she operates with what might be considered an even stronger definition. She employs the term *nomoi* community to refer to a group that has "a comprehensive and distinguishable worldview that extends to creating a law for the community."[26] The groups that interest Shachar—those whose claims to accommodation she wants to consider and assess—are ones that are already staking extensive claims. They are distinguished not just by particular systems of meaning, or specific codes of conduct that teach their members what is considered appropriate or inappropriate behaviour. These are groups that seek to regulate the behaviour of community members through law.

In the political theorist's understanding of culture, cultural group then becomes associated with a quasi-legal entity that has historically enjoyed or is now claiming jurisdiction over its members. This solidifies the group into something very substantial. The group is presumed, moreover, to play a large role in the loyalties of its members—hence the emphasis, from

[24] Will Kymlicka, *Multicultural Citizenship: A Liberal Theory of Minority Rights* (Oxford: Clarendon Press, 1995), 1.

[25] Ibid., 18.

[26] Shachar, *Multicultural Jurisdictions*, 2n. Here she is quoting from Robert Cover, "The Supreme Court 1982 Term, Forward: *Nomos* and Narrative," *Harvard Law Review* 97 (1983): 4–68. Her own definition, later in the footnote, is that these are groups that share "a unique history and collective memory, a distinct culture, a set of social norms, customs and traditions, or perhaps an experience of maltreatment by mainstream society or oppression by the state."

Taylor onwards, on the responsibility states have to extend due respect and recognition to cultures. Taylor, in particular, has linked this to a strong sense of what distinguishes one group from another: "with the politics of difference," he argues, "what we are being asked to recognise is the unique identity of the individual or group, their distinctness from everyone else."[27] Sustaining that distinctness then becomes a large part of what cultural politics is about. People's loyalty to their group does not necessarily displace loyalty to a larger national community (both Kymlicka and Taylor have been rather reassuring on this score), but with distinctness so strongly emphasised, there is a tendency to see group identities as intrinsically oppositional.

Consider Jacob Levy's characterisation of ethnocultural identities, which links cultural belonging firmly to a demarcation between kin and strangers:

> Persons identify and empathize more easily with those with whom they have more in common than those with whom they have less. They rally around their fellow religionists; they seek the familiar comforts of native speakers of their native languages; they support those they see as kin against those they see as strangers. They seek places that feel like home, and seek to protect those places; they are raised in particular cultures, with particular sets of knowledge, norms and traditions, which come to seem normal and enduring. These feelings, repeated and generalized, help give rise to a world of ethnic, cultural and national loyalty, and also a world of enduring ethnic, cultural, and national variety.[28]

This is a pretty bounded notion of culture, presuming that we have both a clear sense of who counts as kin and a distinct preference for them, and it makes culture almost by definition oppositional. "My" culture means "not yours." Given this, it comes as no surprise that Levy does not share the optimistic take on cultural hybridity that sees this as dissolving the rigidity of ethnic and/or cultural boundaries and defusing the conflicts of the multiethnic world. A hybrid cultural community is still, for Levy, a cultural community, and therefore as much a basis for bounded and exclusionary loyalties as any more pristine cultural group. To have a culture is to find your ways of doing things more natural than any other and to feel greater allegiance to those you regard as your own.

These tendencies—reserving the term cultural group for quasi-legal entities, thinking of the problem of culture as intrinsically bound up with the status of minority groups, and associating cultural belonging with potentially exclusionary loyalties—reflect the political theorist's aware-

---

[27] Taylor, "The Politics of Recognition," 38.

[28] Jacob T. Levy, *The Multiculturalism of Fear* (Oxford: Oxford University Press, 2000), 6.

ness of inequality and conflict, and are not in themselves bad things. The downside is an overly solid representation of the cultural group: what Seyla Benhabib has characterised as a "reductionist sociology of culture" that reifies cultures as separate entities and overemphasises their internal homogeneity.[29] There are exceptions. Writing in the mid-1990s, James Tully already repudiated what he called the billiard-ball conception of culture, which represents each culture as "separate, bounded and internally uniform," and cited new developments in anthropology as informing his own more fluid understanding of the term.[30] But more commonly, political theorists have shown little interest in what other disciplines say about culture—David Scott says that most of them "are less interested in culture *per se* than in identifying a culture-concept that best suits their political theory of liberal democracy"[31]—and take the term too much at face value.

The Retreat from Multiculturalism

My worries about this are not just academic. There is not much to be gained from ticking off the practitioners of one discipline for their failure to read widely in the literatures of a neighbouring one; and anyway, political theory scores considerably better in this respect than many other fields of study. The reason the too-ready acceptance of culture matters is that it helps nourish cultural stereotypes. In the process, it not only subverts the object of multicultural policies; it also contributes to what is currently a marked retreat from multiculturalism.

I began the chapter with Kymlicka's claim that the battle to establish the justice of minority rights is over, and multiculturalism, by implication, now in the ascendant. Looking around the globe today, it seems more plausible to assert the opposite. In Europe, the flirtation with multiculturalism—which developed, in some cases, into quite a strong relationship—seems to have given way to a more strident insistence on national belonging and identity. Newspaper articles call on immigrants to make it clearer that they have opted for the values of their host society (usually assumed to be more liberal and democratic than those of the society they left), while governments require applicants for citizenship to take courses in the

---

[29] Seyla Benhabib, *The Claims of Culture: Equality and Diversity in the Global Era* (Princeton, NJ: Princeton University Press, 2002), 4.

[30] James Tully, *Strange Multiplicity: Constitutionalism in an Age of Diversity* (Cambridge: Cambridge University Press, 1995), 10.

[31] David Scott, "Culture in Political Theory," *Political Theory* 31, no. 1 (February 2003): 96.

national language and what are said to be the values of the host country as a condition for their naturalisation. Classes to promote the integration of new citizens might be regarded as a small sign of change and not intrinsically incompatible with multiculturalism. Citizenship tests and ceremonies have long been part of Canadian policy, and there is nothing inherently oppressive about making it easier for people to function in a new society by providing them with the necessary language tools. But the new language of integration and social or community *cohesion* is significant, as is the growing preoccupation in a number of European countries with identifying the core values said to characterise the nation. Where previous policy pronouncements had stressed respect for cultural diversity (implying, though not always stating, a degree of mutual adjustment between majority and minority groups), talk of integration or cohesion conjures up a preexisting set of values that distinguishes each host society, and urges people from minority cultural groups to adapt themselves more actively to this. The standard justification for citizenship training is the importance of familiarising new migrants with the core principles of democracy, toleration, and equality. There is a clear enough implication that such principles will not be familiar to the new migrants.

Christian Joppke represents the European retreat from multiculturalism in relatively benign terms, arguing that the national identities being affirmed in this process are not especially British or Dutch but comprise a generic liberal democracy that has been detached from any specifically ethnic identity. He notes that when a government document tried to spell out the fundamental tenets of British citizenship, it only managed to come up with respecting human rights and freedoms, upholding democratic values, observing laws faithfully, and fulfilling duties and obligations. A parallel attempt to define the dominant culture in Germany ended up with the norms of the constitution, the idea of Europe, and the equality of women.[32] This is not, Joppke insists, a retreat from a multi- to a monoculturalism. It no longer has much to do with the bugbear of the multicultural literature—an enforced and one-way assimilation into the substantive values and practices of a dominant group—but is better read as a new assertiveness by the liberal state of its own specifically liberal culture. While clearly marking a change from the language of cultural diversity, it should not, Joppke argues, be seen as the majority triumphant or a significant threat to minority rights. This is a de-ethnicised national identity that no longer rests on substantive cultural norms.

My own reading of the retreat is more troubled, for while I agree that this is not a return to "the supposedly halcyon days of a monocultural

---

[32] Christian Joppke, "The Retreat of Multiculturalism in the Liberal State: Theory and Policy." *British Journal of Sociology* 55, no. 2 (2004): 253.

society" it invokes a stereotypical contrast between Western and non-Western values that replays monoculturalism in a more political guise. Think about what is going on here. The generic values of respecting human rights, upholding democracy and constitutions, and faithfully observing the law cannot, as Joppke observes, be presented as peculiarly British, German, or Dutch. But neither can they be claimed as peculiarly liberal, European, or Western, as if migrants from India have never heard of a democratic constitution or asylum seekers escaping torture need to be taught about the value of human rights. The idea that support for these values might end at the borders of Europe—or that those whose families have lived in Europe for generations will have imbibed them from the atmosphere, while recent arrivals need to be taught them in civics classes—draws on and reinforces stereotypical distinctions between liberal and illiberal, modern and traditional, Western and non-Western cultures. It proclaims a world of "us" and "them," and makes it pretty clear that "our" values are superior. If this is what is emerging as the new paradigm of national identity across Europe, it is deeply problematic.

Cultural stereotypes provide the backdrop to this, helping secure such binary divisions. Consider just one example: an opinion poll carried out in France in 1989. When asked how they understood Islam, 76 percent of non-Muslim respondents associated it with the submission of women, 71 percent with fanaticism, 66 percent with regression, and 60 percent with violence. Among Muslim respondents, by contrast, 84 percent associated Islam with peace, 64 percent with progress, 62 percent with tolerance, and 61 percent with the protection of women.[33] Even allowing for the limited choice offered to the respondents (either the submission or protection of women; either peace or violence), this indicates a high level of cultural stereotyping. Differences of culture and religion are seen as suggestive of profound differences of value, and these are being mapped onto opposing sides of a liberal/illiberal divide. This way of understanding cultural difference has, I believe, played an important part in the hemorrhaging of support for multicultural policies.

It would be absurd to blame this on political theory. But the arguments theorists have developed in support of multiculturalism have not been particularly designed to challenge exaggerated representations of difference. More typically, the emphasis has been on getting people to recognise the scale, significance, and legitimacy of cultural diversity. Those working on questions of cultural and religious diversity have often preferred to test themselves on what they perceive to be the hard cases, arguing that it is easy enough to tolerate and accommodate difference when there is

[33] The poll was carried out by the French Institute for Opinion Polls; cited in Kastoryano, *Negotiating Identities*, 194.

not much at stake, but more problematic when a self-consciously liberal society is faced with a minority cultural group that engages in illiberal practices. It is relatively easy, for example, to agree that regulations about what can be disposed of in rivers or coastal waters should be modified to accommodate the wish of many Hindus to scatter the ashes of their dead in rivers.[34] It is much more testing to consider whether regulations should be modified to accommodate a cultural or religious preference for the circumcision of girls. Yet the pursuit of rigour in one area (focusing on hard, not easy cases) has meant a lack of rigour in another, for the degree of value divergence is sometimes overstated in order to heighten the conflict. Groups are then identified in a totalising way with either the liberal or illiberal camp. When this happens, the political theory of multiculturalism encourages precisely the kind of cultural stereotyping it was designed to dissolve.

Part of my contention, then, is that the failure to problematise culture has contributed to a radical otherness that represents people as profoundly different in their practices, values, and beliefs. This in turn has enabled critics of multiculturalism to represent it as more intrinsically separatist than most of its (rather moderate) proponents intended, and to misrepresent cultural difference as a major source of political instability. By contrast, the underlying assumption of this book is that people are not so very different from one another the world over. This is not to say that everyone is a liberal or supports equality between the sexes, any more than that everyone is kind to animals and nice to their parents. People differ enormously as individuals. They also differ in ways that reflect their gender, social class, and culture. But these differences do not map onto simple binaries like liberal or nonliberal, Western or non-Western, any more than they map onto simple distinctions between female and male. Anthropologist Lila Abu-Lughod once recommended an ethnography of the particular that brings out the similarities in people's lives. "The particulars," as she puts it, "suggest that others live as we perceive ourselves living, not as robots programmed with 'cultural' rules, but as people going through life agonizing over decisions, making mistakes, trying to make themselves look good, enduring tragedies and personal losses, enjoying others, and finding moments of happiness."[35] Recognising the similarities

---

[34] The UK Water Act (1989) allows this practice and the perhaps more contentious one of submerging a corpse in deep water, so long as a licence is obtained and certain rules are followed regarding which waters can be used in this way. Bhikhu Parekh argues that there is no reason why those Hindus who wish it should not also be allowed to cremate their dead on funeral pyres in officially designated places; see *Rethinking Multiculturalism: Cultural Diversity and Political Theory* (London: Palgrave Press, 2000), 273–74.

[35] Lila Abu-Lughod, "Writing against Culture," in *Recapturing Anthropology: Working in the Present*, ed. Richard G. Fox (Santa Fe, NM: School of American Research Press, 1991), 158.

does not mean discounting the differences: what we count as tragedy, for example, is likely to be inflected by our cultural norms, as is what we experience as moments of happiness. But it is one of the ironies of the multicultural project that in the name of equality and mutual respect between peoples, it has encouraged us to view peoples and cultures as more systematically different than they are. In the process, it has contributed to forms of cultural stereotyping that now help whip up opposition to multiculturalism.

Feminism and Multiculturalism

Equality between the sexes plays a complicated role in this. As Joppke's comments on definitions of the dominant culture in Germany indicate, the rights of women have come to figure as one of the elements delineating a modern liberal society, and gender equality as what distinguishes such a society from so-called traditional, non-Western, illiberal cultures. This focuses attention on practices that have long been the subject of debate within feminism and/or the object of activist campaigns—the veiling and seclusion of women, female genital cutting, honour killings, polygyny, and forced marriage—and employs these as the markers of backwardness. Activists have observed wryly that a lot of people not previously known for their support for gender equality now seem to get very agitated about the abuse of women, so long as it is abuse within minority or non-Western cultural groups.

Feminists have not been entirely innocent bystanders here, for while the feminist literature offers some of the most effective deconstructions of essentialised notions of culture, feminism has also generated strong binaries between liberal and illiberal groups. It is almost true by definition that feminists will suspect claims made on behalf of culture, for feminism involves a worldview that is particularly alert to differences of experience, perception, and interest between women and men, and is therefore unlikely to buy into the unity and homogeneity of cultures. Feminists are also going to be especially alert to the way prescriptions regarding women's behaviour get used to differentiate one culture from another. When Susan Moller Okin set out her criticisms of multiculturalism, she pointed out that the regulation of sexuality and reproduction was a central concern in most cultures, and that the prescriptions drawn up often involve a subordination of women to men. She noted that the women in the cultural group might be less enamoured of these prescriptions than the men.[36] This

---

[36] Susan Moller Okin, "Is Multiculturalism Bad for Women?" in *Is Multiculturalism Bad for Women?* ed. Joshua Cohen, Matthew Howard, and Martha C. Nussbaum (Princeton, NJ: Princeton University Press, 1999).

clearly suggests a sceptical view of culture. It says that what is presented by cultural spokespeople as a requirement of their culture—thus as something a good multiculturalist might want to accommodate and condone—is in reality what is preferred by the men, and that if anyone were to ask the women what they thought, they might get a very different point of view. When Okin considers how best to resolve the conflict between recognising the rights of minority cultural groups and recognising the rights of women within those groups, she therefore stresses the importance of giving women a voice. "Unless women—and, more specifically young women (since older women often are co-opted into reinforcing gender inequality)—are fully represented in negotiations about group rights, their interests may be harmed rather than promoted by the granting of such rights."[37] Clearly, she expects the inclusion of women in the negotiations to reveal that the culture's values are not as widely shared as its self-appointed guardians suggest. Many of the female members of the cultural group would prefer to live by different rules.

Yet Okin combines this scepticism about cultural claims with what many have seen as a static conception of culture, and an overly strong demarcation between cultures that are more egalitarian and those that are more patriarchal. In differentiating between cultures, she gives the impression that each reproduces itself in relative isolation, and in describing the power of men in traditional cultures, she seems to understate the extent of internal contestation and processes of cultural change. So while the dilemma Okin sets out—that policies designed to reduce inequalities between cultural groups can have the effect of increasing inequalities between women and men—is widely recognised in feminist circles, there has been considerable resistance to the way she makes her argument. As already noted, the least sympathetic to Okin's work associate her with a hegemonic Western discourse that views non-Western cultures as almost by definition patriarchal and the women in these cultures as victims in need of protection. Okin has been accused of imagining women in traditional societies as duped into a kind of false consciousness that leaves them incapable of noticing just how oppressive the traditions of their society are (as in her comments about older women being "co-opted into reinforcing gender inequality"); failing to recognise the many ways in which women already contest power hierarchies within their cultural groups; ignoring the value women in a minority or nondominant group actively attach to their cultural membership; and generally treating minority women, in Shachar's phrase, as "victims without agency."[38]

[37] Ibid., 24.
[38] Shachar, *Multicultural Jurisdictions*, 66.

Much of the criticism draws on de-essentialised notions of culture, stressing that cultures are not bounded, cultural meanings are internally contested, and cultures are not static but involved in a continuous process of change. The critique of essentialism has a long pedigree in feminism, although criticisms of an essential womanhood have sometimes combined with a cultural essentialism that reproduces binary divisions between the West and the rest. Indeed, as feminists became more alert to the dangers of presuming that other women's experiences coincided with their own, they sometimes fell into ways of talking about cultural difference that were equally problematic. As Uma Narayan puts it, "Seemingly universal essentialist generalizations about 'all women' are replaced by culture-specific essentialist generalizations that depend on totalizing categories such as 'Western culture,' 'non-Western cultures,' 'Indian women,' and 'Muslim women.' "[39] In her dissection of this cultural essentialism, Narayan identifies a "package picture of cultures" that represents each culture as neatly wrapped up, sealed off, and identifiable by core values and practices that separate it from all others. In a process she terms "selective labelling," certain changes in values and practices are then designated as consonant with cultural preservation, while others (funnily enough, usually the ones that would make life a bit better for women) are treated as threatening the entire survival of the culture. This portrait of culture is, of course, highly congenial to the more conservative members of the cultural group; but it may also be adopted by Western liberals whose anxieties about cultural imperialism lead them to exaggerate the otherness of cultures they see as different from their own.

This kind of argument figures large in assessments of Okin. Shachar charges her with making sweeping generalisations about the world's cultures and religions, ignoring their dynamism, malleability, and the substantial changes that have come about, partly because of women's resistance and agency. Leti Volpp sees the failure to recognise cultures as hybrid and contested as part of what leads Okin to set up feminism and multiculturalism as intrinsically opposed. Volpp also identifies a tendency to assume that people from racialised minority cultures are motivated by their culture, while others are motivated by choice.[40] Seyla Benhabib argues that even after recognising the divisions between women and men, Okin still falls into the "outsider" trap of treating cultures as "unified,

[39] Uma Narayan, "Undoing the 'Package Picture' of Cultures." *Signs* 25, no. 4 (2000): 1083.
[40] Leti Volpp, "Feminism and Multiculturalism," *Columbia Law Review* 101 (2001): 1190.

harmonious, seamless wholes that speak with one narrative voice."[41] Anne Norton maintains that Okin tends to read the principles of liberal cultures from their best practices and those of non-Western ones from their worst: "When men in the United States beat their wives, it is an aberration, counter to the liberal principles that govern here. When Muslim men beat their wives, it is an act representative of the principles of Islam—whatever Koran or hadith may say."[42]

The critics employ a more nuanced understanding of culture to refuse the stark opposition between either feminism or multiculturalism, but they do so in different ways. For Shachar (whose work I discuss in more detail in chapter 5), recognising the dynamism and malleability of culture is the first step towards strategies of internal reform. Instead of having to choose between accepting or denouncing a culture—between staying in or getting out—it becomes possible to think of working within the contours of one's own culture to promote more sexually egalitarian practices. This rejects the notion of cultures as static or unified (what might be described as a take it or leave it approach), but it does so out of a strong sense of the importance of cultural belonging and the distinctiveness of each cultural group. Shachar's nomoi communities are characterised by their comprehensive worldview (so there may be internal disagreement, but there is still something distinctive marking each one from the others), and she ends up allowing for a considerable level of group control over individual behaviour. Cultures are malleable, and with the right kind of incentive structure in place, there is a good chance of them changing in directions that are more favourable to women. But as cultures, they remain pretty bounded and strong.

For Benhabib, the impetus to reform comes primarily from what she describes as "complex cultural dialogue," from the engagement between different cultural traditions, out of which sexually egalitarian norms will hopefully emerge. It is important to her argument that cultures are not hermetically sealed—otherwise, how could individuals from one culture speak to and understand those from another?—and that they contain within them a variety of narratives and voices. Her point is not just that there are subgroups within each cultural group (young and old, women and men) but that the way any of us lives our belief system is not particularly systematic, and that when we participate in a culture, we experience it "as a set of competing as well as cohering accounts."[43] If the accounts

---

[41] Benhabib, *The Claims of Culture*, 102. Benhabib goes on to remark, "Although she recognizes gender as a cleavage, Okin writes as if cultures are unified structures of meaning in other respects" (103).

[42] Anne Norton, "Review Essay on Euben, Okin, and Nussbaum," *Political Theory* 29, no. 5 (2001): 741.

[43] Benhabib, *The Claims of Culture*, 103.

were all coherent, with no cracks or slippages, it would be difficult to see how dialogue could occur: to recall James Tully's image, cultures would be like billiard balls, bouncing off one another, unable ever to pause and get a grip. There would be little prospect of cultural dialogue and negotiation to, say, resolve disagreements about polygamy or how to divide property between women and men on divorce. The scope for moderating tensions between gender equality and cultural difference depends, for Benhabib, very much on the openness of one culture to another. It depends on challenging a holistic understanding of culture. But in her work, as in Shachar's, there remains a strong sense of the normative significance of culture. "Culture matters; cultural evaluations are deeply bound up with our interpretations of our needs, our visions of the good life, and our dreams for the future."[44]

Volpp and Norton are more concerned with questioning the binary between Western liberal cultures and non-Western or minority ones, and challenging the notion that gender subordination is peculiarly characteristic of the latter. Norton suggests opening up the critique to Western liberal cultures "on equal terms,"[45] while Volpp argues that the intense focus on other women's sexist cultures obscures the extent of violence against women within the United States. This can sound evasive, for even though there is inequality and oppression in all societies, it would be rather a coincidence if societies were all equally sexist, racist, and homophobic— and quite a blow to those campaigning on these issues if it turned out that all societies are doomed to remain in the same place. Moreover, while there is much to be said for sorting out one's own backyard before embarking on a mission to sort out everyone else's, there is also merit in a political activism that looks beyond one's immediate neighbourhood or reference group. The more compelling point, to my mind, is Volpp's about the selectivity that surrounds culture: the tendency to attribute all aspects of behaviour to culture when dealing with people from racialized minority groups, while regarding the behaviour of others as reflecting their personal choice. Culture, it seems, has been redefined as something that characterises non-Western or minority groups. It has become a prominent component in the stereotyping and disparagement of people from minority ethnic groups that everything they do is attributed to their culture.

Part of what is at stake here is a set of issues long familiar to feminists: how to challenge a disparaged identity without thereby reinforcing the stereotypes that surround it. As versions of what has come to be known as identity politics, both feminism and multiculturalism deal in stereotypes, dividing up the world through categories like sex, gender, culture, sexual-

---

[44] Ibid., 129.
[45] Norton, "Review Essay," 745.

ity, ethnicity, and religion. When employed by others, these labels are readily recognisable as the kind of stereotype we would prefer to avoid: most statements prefaced by "all women," "all black people," or "all Muslims" are likely to be both offensive and wrong. Yet even in criticising the labels, we may apply them on occasion to ourselves: "as a woman," "as a black person," or "as a Muslim," we might say. This is a less sweeping rendition that at least allows for the possibility that others in our category might think and act differently from us. But insofar as it attributes thoughts and actions to the fact of being a woman (or black or Muslim), it still conjures up a notion of *women* that can only be a stereotype: in some way formulaic, dealing in probabilities and typical features, and positing some defining characteristics. Joan Scott has described it as the constitutive paradox of feminism that women organised themselves to eliminate "sexual difference" in employment, education, and politics, but had to make their claims on behalf of women, who were discursively produced through the very sexual difference feminists were trying to eliminate.[46] It is, of course, entirely coherent to campaign against false stereotypes, or the way that what have been represented as your group characteristics are employed to deny you political, civil, or economic rights. But insofar as this involves organising as members of that group, you implicitly call the group back into existence.

Reams have been written about how to do feminism without women: about why gender essentialisms should be rejected, whether it is possible to maintain a vigorous feminist politics without invoking women, whether the solution lies in a strategic essentialism, and so on. Biological essentialism of the kind that derives personality and intelligence from the shape of one's genitals or the size of one's skull is about as much discredited these days as parallel claims about race. (That is to say, mostly discredited, but not yet entirely abandoned.) But while switching to a language of gender not sex, culture not race, takes us away from the most contested terrain, it still leaves room for concern about what it means to define something by reference to its essential characteristics, those things without which X would not be X. Some reject this kind of characterisation for Foucauldian reasons, arguing that policing the boundaries of who counts as a woman is an invidious act of power.[47] Others reject it because any way of defining women privileges gender over other vectors of difference.[48] Some nonetheless speak of a "strategic essentialism" or having "to

[46] Joan W. Scott, *Only Paradoxes to Offer: French Feminists and the Rights of Man* (Cambridge, MA: Harvard University Press, 1996).

[47] See, for example, Judith Butler, *Gender Trouble: Feminism and the Subversion of Identity* (London: Routledge, 1999).

[48] See, for example, Elizabeth Spelman, *Inessential Woman: Problems of Exclusion in Feminist Thought* (Boston: Beacon Press, 1988).

take the risk of essence" because otherwise it becomes impossible to do feminist politics.[49] But it probably helps here that essentialism is not such a compelling risk in relation to gender. Most women live and work alongside men, which makes it particularly hard to think of the group women as externally bounded, and half the world's population is female, which makes it virtually impossible to think of the group as internally homogeneous. So while developing a feminism without women remains high on the agenda for many, others have concluded that worrying about essentialised conceptions is a worry too far.

More pressing issues arise in relation to culture because there is a much stronger perception of cultures as bounded, distinct, and organised around essential defining values, and with culture, far more than with gender, there is a tendency to presume that individuals do what they do because of their culture. In a study of discourses of identity, Gerd Baumann observes a kind of ethnic reductionism—a way of talking about "the Asian," "the Irish," or "the Jews"—in which "all agency seemed to be absent, and culture an imprisoning cocoon or a determining force."[50] The perception of people as products of their culture, and culture as the all-encompassing explanation of what people do, is worryingly prevalent as a way of understanding people from minority or non-Western cultures. As I argue in chapter 4, it even surfaces in some of the arguments for multiculturalism. This way of thinking about culture makes it too solid an entity, far more definitive of each individual's horizon than is likely to be the case. In doing so, it also encourages an unhelpful distinction between traditional and modern cultures. "They" have cultural traditions; "I" have moral values.

At least part of the impetus for multiculturalism was the need to challenge dismissive and disparaging stereotypes of people from minority cultural groups, to contest the hierarchy of "us" and "them." But insofar as it starts from the unquestioned "fact" of cultural difference, multiculturalism tends to call up its own stereotypes, categorising people in ways that simplify differences, emphasise typical features, and suggest defining characteristics of each cultural group. This intentionally promotes a view of individuals from minority and non-Western cultural groups as guided by different norms and values, and inadvertently fuels a perception of them as driven by illiberal and undemocratic ones.

[49] Strategic essentialism is most associated with Gayatri Spivak, though she has repeatedly distanced herself from what she sees as misuses of the notion. See Gayatri Chakravorty Spivak, "Subaltern Studies: Deconstructing Historiography," in *Selected Subaltern Studies*, ed. Ranajit Guha and Gayatri Chakravorty Spivak (Oxford: Oxford University Press, 1988).

[50] Gerd Baumann, *Contesting Culture: Discourses of Identity in Multi-Ethnic London* (Cambridge: Cambridge University Press, 1996), 1.

Cultural Difference and Moral Norms

The critical deconstruction of culture promises to ease some of the normative difficulties surrounding the pursuit of gender equality in a context of cultural diversity; but intensifies others. On the plus side, it promises to defuse the tension between universalism and cultural relativism that has proved especially—perhaps unexpectedly—agonising for feminists. As already noted, one might expect feminists to be at the forefront in denouncing cultural relativism, for if anything defines feminism, it is surely the willingness to criticise existing patterns of relationships between women and men, and challenge cultural norms. Announcing her support for Okin, Katha Pollitt argues that "in its demand for equality for women, feminism sets itself in opposition to virtually every culture on earth. You could say that multiculturalism demands respect for all cultural traditions, while feminism interrogates and challenges all cultural traditions."[51] Yet feminists have also been at the forefront in querying the false universalisms of mainstream political and social theory: identifying the masculine figure lurking behind the disembodied individual of much contemporary liberalism; maintaining that the dichotomy between emotion and reason has been framed by and wrongly correlated with differences between women and men; and noting the many ways in which supposedly gender-neutral concepts incorporate a male bias.[52] This sensitivity to the ways the norms and perspectives of a dominant social group can come to claim the authority of universal truth has generated a larger scepticism about the status of all universal claims.

Anyone advocating policies of multicultural accommodation has to engage with the question of limits: Is there a limit to the practices and behaviours that can be condoned in any given society, and if so, what justifies this limit? Refusing to engage with the question—for example, refusing to make judgments on the permissibility of female genital cutting, or sex between a ten-year-old girl and a thirty-year-old man—invites criticism for abdicating moral responsibility. But answering with a supposedly universal principle that turns out to reflect more local norms invites criticism for privileging one group above others. The universalist ignores the con-

---

[51] Katha Pollitt, "Whose Culture?" in *Is Multiculturalism Bad for Women?* ed. Joshua Cohen, Matthew Howard, and Martha C. Nussbaum (Princeton, NJ: Princeton University Press, 1999), 27.

[52] There is a long literature here. Early examples include Carole Pateman, *The Sexual Contract* (Cambridge, UK: Polity Press, 1988); Genevieve Lloyd, *The Man of Reason: "Male" and "Female" in Western Philosophy* (London: Methuen, 1986); Jane Flax, "Beyond Equality: Gender, Justice, and Difference," in *Beyond Equality and Difference*, ed. Gisela Bock and Susan James (London: Routledge, 1992).

textual nature of principles of justice, the shaping of all norms of right and wrong by the historical circumstances in which they evolved. The relativist goes off in the other direction, presenting norms of justice as if they are always relative to the societies in which they emerge, and arguing that it is inappropriate to take the norms of one culture as the measure against which to assess the practices of another. Between the deception that dresses up the parochial concerns of one group as if these were universal requirements of justice and the relativism that suspends judgment in the face of oppression and harm, where on earth is one supposed to go?

This stark opposition is at least partially dissolved when we move away from a bounded understanding of culture. It then becomes less plausible to conceive of cultures as existing in mutual isolation, or to think of their value systems as evolving in unique and distinct ways. It is certainly a mistake, as Joseph Carens argues, to equate a moral community with a political one, as if the norms that regulate our lives begin and end at the borders of our state.[53] It is also a mistake to conceive of the larger society or culture as bounded in this way. Cultures are made up of people, and people and their ideas move. Trade, migration, the forcible removal of millions from one continent to another, and the more peaceful exchange of literatures and ideas (all long predating what is currently labelled globalisation) mean that there are few societies left in the world that can be described as insulated from contact with outside groups. Cultures are also made up of subcultures, each evolving its own norms of behaviour, which means there will always be a range of normative principles being debated (or squashed) within any single cultural group.

The idea that each culture evolves its own distinct norms of justice, with not much overlap and not much hope of mutual reconciliation, only makes sense if, first, there has been no exchange of people or ideas, and second, there is no great similarity in human experience that might lead people in different societies or cultures to formulate similar principles for regulating their collective life. Both assumptions seem misplaced. Gilroy talks of an overwhelming, "almost banal" human sameness, reflecting the predicaments of a common species life.[54] Bhikhu Parekh, more convinced than Gilroy of the salience of cultural difference, still observes the "genuinely universal feel" of the United Nations Declaration of Human Rights, and the way its notions of respect for human life, dignity, and equality of rights speak across cultural difference to human values and needs.[55] It would be too easy to leap to the conclusion that there are no major value

---

[53] Joseph H. Carens, *Culture, Citizenship, and Community: A Contextual Exploration of Justice as Evenhandedness* (Oxford: Oxford University Press, 2000), 27.

[54] Gilroy, *Against Race*, 29.

[55] Parekh, *Rethinking Multiculturalism*, 134.

differences: indeed, Parekh goes on to claim that some of the rights in the declaration are culturally specific, and offers the right to marriage based on "free and full consent" as an example. But when culture loses its solidity and force, so too do many of the assumptions about cultural difference. This makes it easier to argue for particular principles of justice or equality, without thereby inviting criticism for dressing up the prejudices of one society as universal principles for all.

Though I believe, along with many contemporary writers on multiculturalism, that the norms we live by should be subjected to continual scrutiny and can be expected to evolve and change when exposed to a wider variety of ideals, I also think there are some relatively straightforward limiting principles. These are not especially original: I believe that societies should act to protect minors from harm, prevent physical and mental violence, and ensure that men and women are treated as equals. Among those pressing for a more multicultural approach to policymaking, it is commonly alleged that cultural uncertainty stops at the point where a practice causes significant and irreversible harm to a minor. Although this is not usually how people put it, the underlying thought seems to be that it is irrelevant whether the prejudice against causing such harm is culturally induced, for this is one prejudice that is worth defending. Carens describes female genital cutting as a "relatively easy case" because it involves permanent and significant physical harm to young girls. "In the light of this fact, its local meaning and the degree to which that meaning is accepted by people subject to the practice . . . seem to me irrelevant."[56] Parekh also identifies the genital cutting of young girls as an simple case, while noting that it is harder to see why the practice should be banned for adult women.[57]

As Parekh's qualification indicates, we cannot simply extend the protections we regard as appropriate for children to apply equally to adults because of the well-rehearsed risks of paternalism; but cultural uncertainty should also stop at the point where people are being subjected to physical or mental violence. Definitions will always be problematic here, as will the implied distinction between a legitimate harm we inflict on ourselves and violence inflicted by others. But the contestability of definitions should not blind us to the effects of violence or cruelty, which speak

---

[56] Carens, *Culture, Citizenship, and Community*, 42.

[57] Parekh, *Rethinking Multiculturalism*, 278–80. Alison Renteln also employs the criterion of "irreparable physical harm" as the point at which it becomes illegitimate to use cultural arguments to defend a practice, but does not restrict this to minors, extending it rather to cover any practice using violence. She then finds herself ruling out male circumcision as well, while remaining open to persuasion on polygamy. Alison Renteln, *The Cultural Defense* (New York: Oxford University Press, 2004).

to a universal human vulnerability to pain. Nor should the frequent breaking of this norm lead us to think of it as peculiar to particular societies and cultures. Torture, to take one subset of the norm against violence, is employed by many regimes around the world, but the fact that it is so widely practiced does not undermine the basic intuition against it.

My third principle is equality, which I take to include equality between the sexes. When people say the principle of gender equality is culturally specific, they usually have in mind the fact that practices regarding the status of women vary greatly around the world. But again, variations in practice do not prove differences of principle, and if we are willing (as people increasingly are) to see equality as reflecting a widely shared intuition about all humans having the same rights to dignity and respect, it is incoherent to represent equality between the sexes as requiring separate or additional justification. It is, of course, depressingly apparent that women are not treated as equal to men, but it is also hard to envisage any social group in which no one raises a voice to object to women being treated as intrinsically inferior. Equality between the sexes is not to be regarded as something additional to equality. Nor is it something that can be claimed as the value of a particular kind of society or cultural group.

The ideal of equality is historically, but not geographically, specific. I incline to the view (derived broadly from Karl Marx) that as the evolution of market society made people more interchangeable, this made it more possible to conceive of them as composed of the same sort of stuff. New circumstances enabled new ways of thinking, and a notion that seemed bizarre at one point in time—that all humans are born equal—came to be regarded as relatively commonplace during another. The meaning of *human* equality then had to be fought over and extended via political contestations that spanned many centuries, and only slowly incorporated women as well as men, black people as well as white. The process has been extraordinarily slow, and its achievements remain fragile, but while the norm of equality is rightly understood as historically contingent and contextual, it cannot be seen as peculiar to Western societies. Indian notions of caste differences are sometimes cited as evidence that the idea of a fundamental human equality remains alien to many cultures. Amartya Sen notes, however, that dissident voices have spoken against caste differentiations at least as far back as the *Mahabharata*, as in Bharadvaja's comment that "we all seem to be affected by desire, anger, fear, sorrow, worry, hunger, and labour: how do we have caste differences then?"[58] I believe we can assert the principle of human equality and its subsequent elaboration to include sexual equality as a widely shared norm, and like

[58] Cited in Amartya Sen, *The Argumentative Indian: Writings on Indian History, Culture, and Identity* (London: Allen Lane, 2005), 11.

Sen, am unconvinced by suggestions that equality is culturally specific. And though this does not constitute proof of universality, it is worth remembering that equality is the official position in all countries that have endorsed the Universal Declaration of Human Rights, and a fortiori, all those that have signed up to the United Nations Convention on the Elimination of Discrimination against Women. That people should be treated as equals has become the default position in discourses around the globe—something from which people have to justify deviations, rather than something to be defended in its own right. This is now commonly said as regards the general principle of equality. In my view, the same also applies to the principle of gender equality.

Before the irritated reader throws this book across the room, I hasten to add that this rosy vision of the world, with everyone signed up to the same basic norms, does not mean everyone now endorses the same version of equality. There may be no great division at the level of official declarations, but there is still much disagreement between people; or there may be no great division between people on fundamental principles, but there is still almost endless scope for disagreement when it comes to interpretations. In the case of equality, it is evident that some of the endorsements are cynical, yet there are also heartfelt disagreements about meaning, even among those who genuinely support the ideal. It is often argued, for example, that equality means desegregation, and is at odds with separate spheres for women and men or separate enclaves for blacks and whites. But it is possible to make a plausible case about equality also requiring a degree of segregation. In the context of current gender relations, some have argued that girls will get more attention from their teachers or more opportunity to specialise in scientific subjects if they are taught in single-sex schools. In Britain, where pupils of African Caribbean origin may be stereotyped by their teachers and treated as an inherently disruptive influence, there has been discussion about whether separate classes or schools might provide better opportunities for educational advancement. In many countries, it is alleged that the division of cities between black and white neighbourhoods is a major obstacle to citizen equality. But it is also argued that in a context of racist violence and harassment, people may enjoy better security if they are able to concentrate in the same neighbourhood than if they are dispersed around the city. These disagreements cannot be settled by a simple invocation of the equality principle. The vexed questions start from that stage onwards, in the competing interpretations of what equality means.

Is a woman who believes that mothers, but not fathers, ought to stay at home to care for young children denying the principle of gender equality? Or is she expressing a version of equality I happen to disagree with—one that represents men and women as different but equal? Is a schoolgirl who believes that girls, but not boys, should cover their heads in public places denying the principle of gender equality? Or is she demonstrating her sense of her own equality by her willingness to defy the advice of her father and brothers? Is the mother who sends her daughter to a single-sex school, but her son to a coeducational one denying the principle of gender equality? Or is she trying to ensure that both her children get the best possible opportunities, regardless of their sex? Is the country that enters a reservation against the Convention on the Elimination of Discrimination against Women on the grounds of religion or culture demonstrating that it does not, after all, respect women's equality? Or is it expressing a legitimate reservation about the precise way in which equality should be interpreted? As individuals, we may have strong views on these questions, but it is not obvious that one interpretation can simply sweep the board. When it comes to content, equality remains a highly contested concept (which is why the global consensus is not such a great achievement).

Probably the most widely held understanding of gender equality in contemporary Europe and the United States takes it as referring to an equality of opportunity or choice—the idea being that men and women alike must have the same opportunities to choose their way of life, and not be prevented by sexist discrimination or excluded by sexist laws, but that they do not therefore have to end up performing the same social roles or earning the same levels of income. On this understanding, there would be nothing intrinsically inegalitarian about a woman being more likely than a man to become a full-time caregiver for the young, sick, or old, or a man being more likely than a woman to reach positions of high influence in the political and economic world or to earn an above-average wage. If men and women have the same opportunities, but systematically choose different occupations or roles, then according to this view, no one can really complain of inequality. Many feminists contest this, including Okin, who argued in much of her work that justice requires an equal division between the sexes not only in terms of incomes but also in relation to the time spent on housework, paid employment, and caring for children.[59] Yet the idea that men and women can be different but equal has continued to exert its appeal. Criticising Okin's "equal split" scenario, Richard Arneson probably speaks for many when he objects that differences in tastes and talents may make it more efficient for the one to specialise in child care and the other in paid employment (he suggests, somewhat disingenuously, that it might be the man whose tastes and talents lead him to be better at looking after the child and the woman who is the better bet on the job market), in which case surely it is better for everyone

[59] Susan Moller Okin, *Justice, Gender, and the Family* (New York: Basic Books, 1989).

if they divide things in this way.[60] Like Okin, I find this complacency about the sexual division of labour unsatisfactory. Like her, I incline to the view that men and women only "choose" systematically unequal outcomes because they live in gender regimes that make it hard for them to do otherwise.[61] But I suspect that Arneson's understanding of what is required by gender equality is closer to the dominant ones than either Okin's or mine, and my insouciance about asserting the general principle of gender equality does not carry over to the more specific contention that everyone must take equal shares. I am happy to assert, without further justification, a general principle of gender equality, but I have to argue, against much disbelief, my own interpretation of this. Simply saying "that's what equality means" cannot be expected to carry much weight.

Equality and Autonomy

At this point, we seem to come back to the questions that underpin much feminist thinking about cultural differences. Who is to say what counts as gender equality? And by what right does someone with one set of cultural experiences comment on and judge the practices and beliefs of someone from a different background? In challenging the distinction between what have been presented as distinct and separate cultures, we seemed to move towards a resolution, because this undermined the notion of distinct worldviews insulated from one another behind impenetrable cultural walls. But if a central part of that challenge is questioning the notion of individuals as driven by cultural dictates, this means taking more seriously than before what people represent as their own choice. Rejecting holistic understandings of culture then promises to ease some of the normative difficulties associated with value differences, but makes it harder to settle some others.

Previous discussions of this have largely revolved around two competing principles.[62] On the one hand, it seems plausible to think that insiders, those who share a belief or engage in a practice will be better able than

[60] Richard Arneson, "Feminism and Family Justice," *Public Affairs Quarterly* 11, no. 4 (1997): 345–63.

[61] See Anne Phillips, "Defending Equality of Outcome," *Journal of Political Philosophy* 12, no. 1 (2004): 1–19, Anne Phillips, "'Really' Equal: Opportunities and Autonomy," *Journal of Political Philosophy* 14, no. 1 (2006): 18–32.

[62] See Anne Phillips, "Multiculturalism, Universalism, and the Claims of Democracy," in *Gender Justice, Development, and Rights*, ed. Maxine Molyneux and Shahra Razavi (Oxford: Oxford University Press, 2002). See also Alison Jaggar, "Globalizing Feminist Ethics," in *Decentering the Center: Philosophy for a Multicultural, Postcolonial, and Feminist World*, ed. Uma Narayan and Sandra Harding (Bloomington: Indiana University Press, 2000).

outsiders to articulate its social meaning and significance. Of course, people do all sorts of things without even realising what they are doing, which is why the sociological observer might sometimes be in a better position to explain what is going on than those being observed. But we would be distinctly unimpressed by the sociologist who tried to arrive at an understanding of particular beliefs or practices without engaging with or listening to the people being studied. I, for one, would think this a guaranteed way to get things wrong. Lived experience matters, not as a uniquely privileged route to knowledge and understanding, but certainly as an important one. The weight attached to this lived experience is, however, commonly set against a second principle, which is that those unconstrained by a particular belief or practice will sometimes be in the better position to identify its limitations. At work here is the human tendency to make the best of a bad job, the capacity to ignore those things we feel we cannot change or undervalue those opportunities we know to be closed to us—what has been described in the literature as the problem of learnt or adaptive preferences.[63] Perceptions of what is desirable are formed against a backdrop of what seems possible, and choices are made from what appears to be the available range. Given these constraints, it may sometimes be outsiders rather than insiders who are better able to recognise the injustice of a particular practice or belief. Evidence of internal support cannot be taken as decisive, for it may reflect the poverty of aspirations rather than "genuine" belief.

This uncomfortable conclusion becomes still more problematic in light of arguments against treating culture as the explanation of virtually everything individuals say or do. This has to mean attaching more weight to individual autonomy and taking more seriously what people represent as their choice. In Sawitri Saharso's reading of this, we cannot rule out in principle any practice that offends against gender equality, not because of the disagreements noted above about what constitutes gender equality, but because the value attached to equality may come into conflict with the value attached to autonomy. "How," Saharso asks, "should the autonomy of women be balanced against sexual equality?"[64] What of a situation where a woman seeks to abort a female foetus because her family see

[63] Jon Elster, *Sour Grapes: Studies in the Subversion of Rationality* (Cambridge: Cambridge University Press, 1983); Cass Sunstein, "Preferences and Politics," *Philosophy and Public Affairs* 20 (1991): 3–34; Amartya Sen, "Gender Inequality and Theories of Justice," in *Women, Culture, and Development*, ed. Martha C. Nussbaum and Jonathan Glover (Oxford: Clarendon Press, 1995).

[64] Sawitri Saharso, "Feminist Ethics, Autonomy, and the Politics of Multiculturalism," *Feminist Theory* 4, no. 2 (2003): 205. See also her "Culture, Tolerance, and Gender: A Contribution from the Netherlands," *European Journal of Women's Studies* 10, no. 1 (2003): 7–27.

girls as less valuable than boys, and she knows her life will be made a misery if she has yet another girl child? What of the estimated ten to fifteen cases a month in the Netherlands, where young Turkish or Moroccan women request hymen repair surgery because they are about to get married and need to conform (or at least give the appearance of conforming) to a sexist virginity rule? Aborting a female foetus because a girl baby is of less value than a boy clearly offends against principles of gender equality, as does the requirement that young women (but not young men) be virgins on marriage. In societies that pride themselves on applying principles of gender equality, these might then seem easy cases: we should surely treat such operations as unacceptable capitulations to cultural differences and call on medical practitioners to refuse to carry them out. Does it make a difference, however, that it is women who are requesting the operations?

Saharso notes that the tension between equality and freedom is commonly resolved by presuming that women are being culturally coerced into their decisions, that no woman would voluntarily seek either sex-selective abortion or hymen repair surgery, and that when women ask for these operations, they are therefore bowing to illegitimate pressure. "But this seems very much like saying that, if a woman takes a decision that runs counter to the majority culture's sense of what is right and just, it cannot be her decision. It must be imposed by an outsider source—her husband, her culture, her religion."[65] This looks a denial of agency, for even if people have been subjected to an oppressive socialisation or have imbibed norms that consider women of lesser significance than men, this does not mean they lose all capacity for agency and choice. As a feminist, Saharso is deeply troubled by situations where the principles of women's equality and women's autonomy threaten to collide, but she insists that we cannot resolve such tensions by redescribing the situation such that the conflict disappears. We also, she argues, cannot make gender equality a nonnegotiable principle, for it will sometimes come into conflict with women's freedom of choice.

I am not in complete agreement with the way Saharso frames this issue—I believe, for example, that more than she allows depends on disagreements in the interpretation of gender equality, rather than a stand off between autonomy and equality—but the issue she identifies is central to the questions explored in this book. Arguments from women's rights and women's equality are increasingly employed to override the stated preferences of women from cultural minorities, and particularly, to override the stated preferences of young women from cultural minorities. In

[65] Saharso, "Feminist Ethics," 209.

my reading of culture, which questions the understanding of individuals as at the mercy of cultural dictates, these moves are problematic. It is important to recognise the choices people make, not read these as a reflection of their so-called culture or treat them as a false consciousness that can be set to one side in the promotion of gender equality. Yet the insight about learnt or adaptive preferences remains, as does the more standard point about many people not having much of a choice at all. We cannot assume that all is well just because people nod their heads and bear it, or that individuals have consented to the way they are being treated so long as they refuse to leave. In many cases, the issue will be how to differentiate choice from coercion. This has to be approached differently once we drop the misguided understandings of culture.

Much recent literature on multiculturalism has turned towards practices of deliberative democracy as the preferred way of addressing cultural disputes, arguing that intercultural dialogue can generate a more culturally sensitive agreement on core values, while avoiding the appeal to external principles of justice as a deus ex machina to settle the debate.[66] The points of overlap with my own approach are the recognition that principles of justice are formed in particular historical contexts, and the belief that when people are sufficiently open to debate and discussion, they often discover significant common ground. But despite an encouraging view of value resolution, the deliberative approach can still be said to exaggerate the scale of value conflict, while understating the difficulties of what to do next. My own emphasis is not so much on getting agreement across different value systems, for I do not regard this as the major issue in the multicultural societies of contemporary Europe or America, where there already is substantial agreement on fundamentals. The more pressing question is whether—and how—to intervene in practices that may or may not be consensual. To give an example used extensively in this book, there is no great value disagreement in contemporary Europe over the acceptability of forced marriage, and you would be hard-pressed to find a spokesperson for any cultural or religious group prepared to say that this practice is condoned by their culture. The question, rather, is at what point do the familial and social pressures that make arranged marriage a norm turn into coercion, and how, short of banning all arranged marriages, can public agencies act to protect young people from ones that are forced? Differentiating between choice and coercion is central to solving this problem. This means understanding cultural pressures, but not assuming that culture dictates.

[66] See, for example, Parekh, *Rethinking Multiculturalism*; Benhabib, *The Claims of Culture*; Monique Deveaux, *Cultural Pluralism and Dilemmas of Justice* (Ithaca, NY: Cornell University Press, 2000); Amy Gutmann and Dennis Thompson, *Democracy and Disagreement* (Cambridge, MA: Belknap Press, 1996).

CHAPTER TWO

Between Culture and Cosmos

SCEPTICISM ABOUT CULTURE is rife in the sociological and anthropological literatures, to the point where it has become commonplace to counterpose old and new ideas of culture, and criticise the former for treating cultures as if they were things.[1] Edward B. Tylor's 1871 definition is frequently served up as the example of the classical conception. "Culture or civilisation, taken in its wide ethnographic sense, is that complex whole which includes knowledge, belief, art, morals, law, custom, and any other capabilities and habits required by man as a member of society."[2] "Complex whole" is the key phrase here. On this reading, the various components—knowledge, belief, art, morals, law, custom, and so on—fit together in what can then be described as a single, unified culture. On this reading, there also isn't much other than culture.

In the evolutionary framework typical of the late nineteenth century, Tylor had regarded cultures as stages along a common developmental path, with primitive cultures showing the advanced ones their own prehistory, and advanced cultures showing the primitive ones where they might eventually hope to go. Later anthropologists rejected this hierarchy. They came to regard all cultures as expressing an internally coherent and legitimate way of life, and all as worthy of respect. Anthropological culturalism then became one of the main counters to biological racism, providing, as Etienne Balibar puts it, "the humanist and cosmopolitan anti-racism of the post-war period with most of its arguments."[3] Yet even in challenging the characterisation of primitive, or the notion that some cultures were more complex, developed, or refined than others, this retained many of the features of the classical conception. Cultures were still largely regarded as separate and distinct—so people were either in one culture or another. Each culture was presumed to form an internally coherent whole, regulated by a system of values, practices, and shared assumptions that outsiders might find it hard to sympathise with or understand. In this conception, cultures were bounded. They were seen as reproducing them-

---

[1] See, for example, Susan Wright, "The Politicization of 'Culture,'" *Anthropology Today* 14, no. 1 (February 1998): 7–15.

[2] E. B. Tylor, *Primitive Culture* (London: John Murray, 1871).

[3] Etienne Balibar, "Is There a Neo-Racism?" in *Race, Nation, Class*, ed. Etienne Balibar and Immanuel Wallerstein (London: Verso, 1991), 21.

selves either in isolation from other cultures or alongside them, but with little mutual exchange. The behaviour and beliefs of individuals from one cultural group were likely to be pretty mysterious to individuals from another, and though some of the mystery might dissipate after a sustained period of contact, certain fundamental differences would remain. It was assumed, moreover, that the values of the culture *were* broadly shared, and that these values explained why members of the cultural group behaved the way they do. Understanding why someone acted or thought in a particular way then became a matter of understanding the underlying principles of their culture.

Though these notions originated with anthropology, anthropologists have been criticising them for many years. A number have commented on the role their discipline played in constructing and even inventing cultures. Sometimes, this was done at the behest of colonial authorities, who needed the anthropologists to give them an angle on the societies they were seeking to control.[4] At other times, it has seemed that the only way to make sense of something is to treat it as a thing and investigate how it works.[5] The objects of the investigation have, on occasion, proved willing participants because they have come to see claims about culture or cultural authenticity as a way to tap social or political power. Terence Turner's study of the Kayapo villagers of the Brazilian Amazon is a classic example.[6] When Turner began his fieldwork in the 1960s, the villagers did not perceive themselves as having a culture—they just saw themselves as human beings—and partly under pressure from the missionaries, had started to evolve different practices, including adopting a more Brazilian style of dress (wearing shorts or trousers) when they went into town. Through contact with anthropologists keen to document the Kayapo way of life, but even more important, through coming to realise that their culture could be a resource around which to mobilise the support of environmentalists and human rights activists, the Kayapo later discarded some of their Brazilian ways, elaborated old and new rituals, and made effective use of the Western media in their struggle for survival.

In that case, making the culture more of a thing worked to broadly good effect. In other instances, the results have been less positive, for the codification of a culture sometimes means that only one of what was

[4] Talal Asad, ed., *Anthropology and the Colonial Encounter* (London: Ithaca Press, 1973).

[5] Roy Wagner, *The Invention of Culture* (Chicago: University of Chicago Press, 1981).

[6] Terence Turner, "Representing, Resisting, Rethinking: Historical Transformations of Kayapo Culture and Anthropological Consciousness," in *Colonial Situations: Essays in the Contextualization of Ethnographic Knowledge*, ed. George W. Stocking Jr. (Madison: University of Wisconsin Press, 1991).

previously a range of ways of being gets recognised as legitimate or boundaries that were previously more fluid get closed. The first has been a recurrent bone of contention for feminists, who have observed that the more hierarchical and misogynous aspects of a culture often get installed as defining components, while more egalitarian elements fall into disuse. The second has been widely argued in studies of colonial rule (especially the indirect rule variant favoured by British colonialism), where it is plausibly suggested that the administration of populations through what were considered to be their religious or tribal affiliations did much to forge the bitterly competitive identities of the postcolonial world. In this view, the tribalism now said to cause civil wars in Africa was produced by colonial rule.[7] Meanwhile, in India, "counting Hindus, Muslims, Sikhs and Untouchables became a critical political exercise."[8] Dipesh Chakrabarty argues that this had the effect of simplifying and homogenising identities that people lived daily in a far more heterogeneous way. The irony is that the obsession with differentiating and counting arose partly from reasons of fairness: trying to ensure that economic resources and positions of political representation were distributed reasonably evenly between different groups. But "the sense of multiple identities that propels people in their everydayness is too complex for the rules that govern the logic of representation in modern public life."[9] People had to place themselves in one ethno-religious-cultural group or another—with what have sometimes been disastrous results.

One problem, therefore, in earlier notions of culture is that they exaggerate lines of demarcation between different cultural groups. This has combined with an almost opposite problem—more common in popular than anthropological usage—which is the tendency to treat cultures as coterminous with countries. Akhil Gupta and James Ferguson observe that " 'society' and 'culture' are routinely simply appended to the names of nation-states, as when a tourist visits India to understand 'Indian culture' and 'Indian society.' "[10] This rough-and-ready understanding of culture leads to the oddity that people living on one side of a national frontier are taken as belonging to a different culture from cousins who live on the other. Alternatively, it may lead to gradations of authenticity, such that a Scot living just north of the English border is regarded as only faintly

[7] For a critical discussion of tribalism, see Leroy Vail, ed., *The Creation of Tribalism in Southern Africa* (Berkeley: University of California Press, 1989).

[8] Dipesh Chakrabarty, "Modernity and Ethnicity in India," in *Multicultural States: Rethinking Difference and Identity*, ed. David Bennett (London: Routledge, 1998), 98.

[9] Ibid., 101.

[10] Akhil Gupta and James Ferguson, "Beyond 'Culture': Space, Identity, and the Politics of Difference" *Cultural Anthropology* 7, no. 1 (1992): 6–7.

tinged with Scottishness, while those in the Highlands count as real Scots. Once culture becomes synonymous in this way with country, it loses much of its explanatory value. So while the "discovery" of many distinct and separate cultures can erect walls between people who previously lived together in more heterogeneous ways, marshalling everyone who lives in a particular territory under a single national culture renders the term pretty meaningless. One of the arguments employed in support of multicultural policies is that increased migration means that countries are now composed of a diversity of cultural groups, and because of this, need to modify their previously monocultural ways. But this already concedes too much, for it suggests that there was indeed a single national culture, coterminous with the borders of the nation, that previous inhabitants could be said to have shared. Even Gupta and Ferguson slip into this when they describe multiculturalism as "a feeble acknowledgement that cultures have lost their moorings in definite places."[11] "Lost their moorings" cannot be quite right, since it implies that cultures were once firmly secured within their national bounds.

The way the boundaries are drawn around each culture changes through time, as do the definitions of core practices and beliefs, with the first process often reflecting an outsider need to categorise and place people, and the second an internal struggle for power. Characterising a culture is itself a political act, and the notion of cultures as preexisting things, waiting to be explained, has become increasingly implausible. People draw on a wide range of local, national, and global resources in the ways they make and remake their culture. (So culture is not bounded.) There are always internal contestations over the values, practices, and meanings that characterise any culture. (So cultures are not homogeneous.) There is often some political agenda—reflecting power struggles within the group or the search for allies outside—when people make their claims about the authoritative interpretation of their culture. (So cultures are produced by people, rather than being things that explain why they behave the way they do.) All these developments undermine the notion of a culture as defined by core values or underlying principles that differentiate it from all others.

Against Culturalist Explanation

The further point to stress is that there has been too much attributing to culture behaviour that is readily explicable in cross-cultural terms. The explanatory weight currently attached to culture is high, superseding both

---

[11] Ibid., 7.

biological racism and a now-jettisoned Marxism that had represented culture as superstructure to the economy's base. The subsequent revival of cultural explanation has been a welcome counter to some strands of genetic or economic determinism. It has also, however, encouraged a tendency to call on culture when faced with anything we cannot otherwise understand. Commenting on the burst of cultural theorising in twentieth-century modernisation theory, Adam Kuper notes that "culture was invoked when it became necessary to explain why people were clinging to irrational goals and self-destructive strategies. . . . Culture was the fallback, to explain apparently irrational behavior."[12]

Yet in many of the contexts where culture is invoked, there turn out to be plausible noncultural accounts. Gerry Mackie gives one telling example in his account of the successful village-led campaign against female genital cutting in Senegal, carried out under the auspices of Tostan (Wolof for "breakthrough"), a nongovernmental organisation focusing on education.[13] The practice of female genital cutting looks paradigmatically cultural, involving as it does culturally specific notions of modesty and honour, and linked as it sometimes is to rites of passage to adulthood. It is paradigmatically cultural on the older materialist understanding, because it is hard to identify the economic purpose served by the practice. And it is paradigmatically cultural in Kuper's "fallback" sense, because those who do not (or no longer) practice it usually find it hard to make sense of those who continue to defend it. In Mackie's analysis, though, the persistence of genital cutting reflects the kind of collective action problem that can arise in any society, and it was overcome in the Senegalese example by the device of the collective pledge. He argues that the main reason the villagers continued with what they knew to be a dangerous and painful practice was neither ignorance of the dangers nor the overwhelming power of custom and tradition, but rather the knowledge that their own daughters would become unmarriageable if their family was the only one opting out. The women leading the Tostan initiative persuaded villagers to sign themselves up to a date when they would all simultaneously abandon the practice. Faced with a reasonably reliable guarantee that others would follow suit, it became much easier for everyone to act, and in a snowball effect from 1997 onwards, one village after another

[12] Adam Kuper, *Culture: The Anthropologists' Account.* (Cambridge, MA: Harvard University Press, 1999), 10.

[13] Gerry Mackie, "Female Genital Cutting: The Beginning of the End," in *Female "Circumcision" in Africa: Culture, Controversy, and Change*, ed. Bettina Shell-Duncan and Ylva Hernlund (New York: Lynne Rienner, 2000). See also Tostan, *Breakthrough in Senegal: The Process That Ended Female Genital Cutting in 31 Villages* (Washington, DC: U.S. Agency for International Development, 1999).

collectively abandoned the practice. In 1999, the government—which had been supportive of the initiative—enacted legislation officially prohibiting genital cutting.

What is striking about this story is how easy it proved to bring about the change. In the villages described in the reports, loyalty to the practice turned out to be paper-thin. There was, it seems, no deep cultural attachment, but more simply and practically the difficulty of breaking out unless others did so at the same time. The reasons village representatives gave for wanting to renounce the practice were much the same as parents the world over might offer (wanting to ensure their girls' health, bodily integrity, and human dignity). The reasons previously given for carrying on with the practice (not wanting to make their daughters unmarriageable) were equally lacking in mystery. This is not to say that there are no cultural differences between the Senegalese villagers and, say, villagers in rural France, or indeed between the Senegalese villagers and the Senegalese political elite; nor does it imply that we all make sense of our lives and relationships in the same way. It nevertheless suggests that there was no special need for a theory of cultural difference to make sense of either the persistence or eventual ending of genital cutting. There was no need in this case for culture as fallback or for complex cultural readings to make sense of otherwise incomprehensible acts. The behaviour proved thoroughly explicable in cross-cultural, human terms.

Didier Fassin provides another example from the field of reproductive health.[14] In the late 1980s, Ecuador had one of the highest rates of maternal mortality in Latin America. It was believed that this was substantially due to the reluctance of rural Indian women to attend the maternity clinics for prenatal consultations and medically supervised childbirth. A study commissioned by the Ministry of Public Health concluded that the problem was largely cultural; that "cultural aspects relating to their sense of modesty" inhibited the women from attending the clinics, and that there was too big a gap between their own symbolic world and the more formal cultural system of the health service.[15] While not discounting all possibility of a culturalist explanation, Fassin argues that these women's reluctance can be understood in terms of an almost "*banal universality of attitudes*"[16]: the practical difficulties they faced in travelling to the clinics, the well-grounded anticipation of being treated with disdain once they got there, and the fear (again, well-grounded, given the high reliance on cesarean sections in Ecuadoran obstetrics) that they would end up having a

---

[14] Didier Fassin, "Culturalism as Ideology," in *Cultural Perspectives on Reproductive Health*, ed. Carla Makhlout (Oxford: Oxford University Press, 2001).

[15] Cited in ibid., 303.

[16] Ibid., 304.

cesarean birth. When all this is reduced to something called culture, it turns attention away from any failings in the health care system (multiple failings, in Fassin's account) and puts the blame on the women instead.

I do not wish to present either of these counternarratives as the final word on culture. Mackie's account draws on the modes of explanation found in game theory—modes of explanation that in other contexts, I would criticise for relying on a simplistic psychology of the "rational man."[17] Fassin tends to counterpose the cultural to the social or economic, as if a belief is *either* socially founded *or* culturally determined; there are plenty of social critics who would see this as a false distinction.[18] What I take from both, however, is a scepticism about culture as fallback, a resistance to what Fassin describes as the ideological uses of culture, and a willingness to see similarities as well as differences in the ways we all organise our lives. To repeat what Lila Abu-Lughod said, when we get down to the particulars, people don't live their lives "as robots programmed with 'cultural' rules, but as people going through life agonizing over decisions, making mistakes, trying to make themselves look good, enduring tragedies and personal losses, enjoying others, and finding moments of happiness."[19]

So What's Left?

So why bother with culture? Why not abandon it as an absurd simplification or hopelessly compromised concept? In some of the sociological literature, the scepticism towards culture does come close to jettisoning it altogether. Many social theorists now stress hybridity, diaspora, border crossings, and translation, arguing that the characteristic phenomenon today is a mixture of cultural assertion and refusal, cultural borrowing and reimagining: a complex negotiation and renegotiation of identities that defies the simple categories of *original* or *traditional* culture.[20] Attrib-

---

[17] Feminists have long been sceptical of rational choice theory, for example, largely because it seems to rely on such notions. For a nuanced critique, see Elizabeth Anderson, "Should Feminists Reject Rational Choice Theory?" in *A Mind of One's Own*, ed. Louise Anthony and Charlotte Witt. 2nd ed. (Boulder, CO: Westview, 2001).

[18] For example, Judith Butler in her critique of Nancy Fraser in "Merely Cultural," *Social Text* 52–53 (1997): 265–77.

[19] Lila Abu-Lughod, "Writing against Culture," in *Recapturing Anthropology: Working in the Present*, ed. Richard G. Fox (Santa Fe, NM: School of American Research Press, 1991), 158.

[20] See, for example, Stuart Hall, "Cultural Identity and Diaspora," in *Identity: Community, Culture, Difference*, ed. Jonathan Rutherford (London: Lawrence and Wishart, 1990); Homi Bhabha, *The Location of Culture* (London: Routledge, 1994); Paul Gilroy, *The Black Atlantic: Modernity and Double Consciousness* (London: Verso, 1993); Barnor Hesse, ed.

uting differences in behaviour to differences in culture is said to conjure up a distinction between self and other that is more driven by the need to differentiate and distance oneself than by any underlying reality. The notion that there just *are* distinct cultural groups, which must be assimilated, accommodated, or allowed to secede, then appears more as a reflection of the imperial logic. It defines minority groups by reference to some presumed majority, thereby promoting the illusion that what is left when we take away the minorities is itself unriven by difference. This notion understands difference primarily in terms of what differentiates one minority group from another, and minority groups as a whole from the majority, overlooking all manner of crosscutting differences that do not fit these supposedly basic divides. It encourages an essentialist view of black identity or cultural identity that edges uncomfortably close to the racialised identities it purports to challenge. And it entirely fails to register the complex negotiations of identity through which individual members of an ethnic minority group reposition themselves and their so-called traditions.

Among anthropologists, there have been more reservations about the "new" conception of culture, and three of these are particularly pertinent to my project. The first addresses the claim about people producing their culture in response to government initiatives (the colonial counting and administration, the multicultural calculations of who gets what) or to meet the expectations of anthropologists from the West. As is often the case with such contentions, the key question is how far to go. In this instance, does the (reasonably convincing) evidence about cultures becoming more tightly codified in response to outside demands mean there was *nothing* there before? Turner, whose work on the Kayapo provides an excellent illustration of the way culture is produced, has been insistent that this does not mean the culture was all made up or is in some sense inauthentic. In fact, if you take any evidence that people have modified or manipulated their cultural traditions to achieve some political effect as proof that there was no culture before, you are either buying into a purist idea of culture or reading things too much from the perspective of the West.[21]

The deconstruction or de-essentialising of culture looks the more radical position because it rejects fixed notions of culture and refuses to see the other as profoundly different from oneself. But it can also be seen as worryingly ethnocentric because of the extraordinary potency it attrib-

---

Un/settled Multiculturalisms: Diasporas, Entanglements, Disruptions (London: Zed Books, 2000).

[21] Terence Turner, "Defiant Images: The Kayapo Appropriation of Video," *Anthropology Today* 8, no. 6 (December 1992): 5–15; see also David Scott, "Criticism and Culture: Theory and Post-colonial Claims on Anthropological Disciplinarity," *Critique of Anthropology* 12, no. 4 (1992): 391–94.

utes to Western anthropology, Western human rights activists, or the Western media in producing this thing called culture. Marshall Sahlins puts it like this:

> There is a certain historiography that is quick to take the "great game" of impe-
> rialism as the only game in town. It is prepared to assume that history is made
> by the colonial masters, and that all that needs to be known about the people's
> own social dispositions, or even their "subjectivity," is the external disciplines
> imposed upon them: the colonial policies of classification, enumeration, taxa-
> tion, education, and sanitation. The main historical activity remaining to the
> underlying people is to misconstrue the effects of such imperialism in their own
> cultural traditions. . . . In the name of ancestral practice, the people construct
> an essentialized culture: a supposedly unchanging inheritance, sheltered from
> the contestation of a true social existence. Thus they repeat as tragedy the farci-
> cal errors about the coherence of a symbolic system supposed to have been
> committed by an earlier and more naïve generation of anthropologists.[22]

The implication, I take it, is not that colonial—or other—authorities should be absolved from all responsibility for their role in formalising practices that were previously more fluid or heightening a sense of differ-ence between peoples who had previously lived side by side. The error is when this critique is pushed too far, to the point where culture becomes an entirely external creation.

This relates to the second reservation, which revolves around just how different people from different cultures are. I've suggested that popular culture talk as well as much of the earlier literature in anthropology has made cultures seem more separate and distinct than is necessarily the case. Evidence about cultural borrowing undermines this more pristine notion of culture. So, too, does the kind of argument Mackie makes about the persistence of female genital cutting owing more to a problem of collective action than the mysteries of cultural signification, or the one Gananath Obeyesekere makes about the 1779 killing of Captain Cook in Hawaii reflecting the Polynesians' "practical rationality" rather than the power of their myths.[23] (This last produced one of the more tetchy debates in recent anthropology: Sahlins had interpreted the events in Hawaii, where Cook was first welcomed and later killed, in mythological terms; Obeye-sekere countered that the killing was entirely understandable as a re-sponse to the violence of Cook's party and its desecration of sacred sites.) It is part of the central claim of this book that we need to challenge the

---

[22] Marshall Sahlins, "Goodbye to Tristes Tropes: Ethnography in the Context of Modern World History," *Journal of Modern History* 65 (March 1993): 6.

[23] Gananath Obeyesekere, *The Apotheosis of Captain Cook: European Mythmaking in the Pacific* (Princeton, NJ: Princeton University Press, 1992).

exoticisation of other cultures, the tendency to exaggerate differences between one culture and another, and to represent the other as driven by impulses that are mysteriously different from one's own. My suspicions on this score tempt me towards a simpler humanism that stresses the basic similarities in the ways people behave. But I am also struck by what Clifford Geertz once said: that there has to be some middle ground between "telling stories about people only a professor can believe" and "reducing people to ordinary chaps out, like the rest of us, for money, sex, status, and power," some middle way between imagining ourselves as surrounded by martians and thinking of everyone else as just "less well-got-up versions of ourselves."[24]

The third point that surfaces in the anthropological literature is that even if the critique of cultural essentialism is well-grounded, this doesn't mean we can simply abandon essentialised notions of culture as wrong. As noted earlier, Gerd Baumann has been highly critical of an ethnic reductionism that denies human agency and represents culture as "an imprisoning cocoon or a determining force."[25] But while he wants to challenge the reification (and equation) of culture, ethnicity, and community—and finds plenty of evidence from his fieldwork in Southall, London, that people don't see every community as having a culture or every culture as being a community—he also discovers that reified notions of culture are widely employed by Southallians themselves. "In tune with the dominant discourse, Southallians find it useful and plausible, in some contexts, to reify culture at the same time as making, remaking and thus changing it."[26] In the language of conventional multiculturalism, the Southall population is described as made up of Sikhs, Hindus, Muslims, African Caribbeans, and whites (the last category including the Irish). The people that Baumann interviewed often challenged these standard divides. For some, for example, it was more important to know whether people were Punjabi, Gujarati, or Bengali, while for many of the young people, a new Asian identity was emerging that cut across distinctions between Sikh, Hindu, and Muslim. This suggests a contextual understanding of culture, and one in which the boundaries defining and differentiating each culture are continually up for question. But people were also happy enough to reproduce the standard five-way divide and had no particular problems with talking about their culture as though it were a clearly defined thing. Baumann concludes that there is no point rubbishing culture

---

[24] Clifford Geertz, *Local Knowledge: Further Essays in Interpretive Anthropology* (1983; repr., London: Fontana Press, 1993), 16.

[25] Gerd Baumann, *Contesting Culture: Discourses of Identity in Multi-Ethnic London* (Cambridge: Cambridge University Press, 1996), 1.

[26] Ibid., 13.

as reified essence as something that is analytically wrong, for once people are living their identities through "folk reifications," these become a real factor in social life.[27]

When I say I want a multiculturalism without culture, I mean I want a multiculturalism without particular *notions* of culture I have found unhelpful. But while I think that cultures have been reified and cultural conflict exaggerated, it is no part of my argument to deny that people are cultural beings. Culture matters to people in many different ways. Some people actively endorse the cultural norms that have helped form them, believing that these represent a good way of living, and some may be quite strident about this, believing that their ways are not just good but the best. Others live their norms without thinking much about them, hardly even noticing that there are people who operate in a different way. Some will reject with indignation the suggestion that what they are doing is culturally inspired, insisting that this is not a matter of culture but religion, or not of culture but their well-grounded political beliefs. To say something is cultural makes it seem unthinking or unchosen, imbibed from the atmosphere rather than a position we can actively defend. But even when people have the most acute sense of themselves as autonomous, transcendent, self-propelled individuals, their beliefs, values, and choices will be pervaded by cultural assumptions and norms. Everyone is shaped, in some ways that we recognise and others of which we remain largely unconscious, by the norms and practices through which we have become the people we currently are. People are cultural beings.

Saying that people are cultural beings, however, carries a different resonance from saying they are from a particular culture. Talk of "a culture" summons up a unity of beliefs, practices, and ways of understanding the world that in most cases do not go together, while talk of people as cultural beings simply draws attention to the mediation of everyone's relationship to their social world. People live their lives through social norms that derive (as the term suggests) from what they have come to regard as normal, and this implies both that there will be considerable diversity between groups and over time, and that people will be strongly attached to their own values and norms. This affects behaviour. How else can one explain why, barely a generation ago, some parents in Ireland could be so horrified by a daughter getting pregnant outside of marriage that they would agree to her incarceration in a house of correction, while nowadays this would be regarded as brutal treatment? Both then and now, there has been enormous individual variation: some parents much more horrified

---

[27] Gerd Baumann and Thijl Sunier, "De-essentialising Ethnicity," in *Post-Migration Ethnicity: Cohesion, Commitments, Comparison*, ed. Gerd Baumann and Thijl Sunier (Amsterdam: Het Spinhuis, 1995).

than others, some horrified but nonetheless supporting their daughters, and some relatively untroubled by what others regard as transgression. What each individual does will not lend itself neatly to cultural explanation—or perhaps only lends itself to a more microlevel cultural explanation than is currently offered. But when we observe shifts like that over the course of a generation, it is clear that something is happening at the level of social norms, and the shorthand for this is to say that something has changed in the culture. I want to challenge that shorthand because it suggests, first, that there is *the* culture (singular, unified, and bounded), and second, that changes in this culture provide the exclusive explanation for what a myriad of individuals do. In contesting these understandings of culture, I do not deny either the diversity or power of cultural norms.

Culture, Ethnicity, Religion, and Race

My main interest in this book is on the way notions of culture are mobilised in the broadly liberal and roughly democratic societies that are my focus—societies where citizens are ethnically, culturally, and religiously diverse, and where the pros and cons of multicultural policy are most hotly debated. Bounded notions of culture are undoubtedly in evidence here, as is the tendency to attribute differences in behaviour to differences in culture. There are two further aspects that particularly merit discussion: the slippage between culture, ethnicity, religion, and race; and the tendency to equate culture with non-Western or minority groups.

Culture is now widely employed in North America and Europe as the acceptable way of referring to race, such that people describe a society as multicultural when previously they would have said multiracial or talk about there being many cultural minorities when really they mean many people who are black.[28] Some of this is camouflage, with people concealing their racism behind a language of culture. But much of it reflects an uncertainty about the term *race*, and a perception that any use of it could be seen as racist. This can lead to an exaggeration of cultural difference in contexts where cultural classification is not really the point. Social workers in Britain, for example, now routinely employ the term *dual heritage* to refer to clients they might previously have described as *mixed race*, the argument being that categorising people according to race gives a false credibility to the belief that there *are* distinct races. This is an entirely legitimate concern, but it can lead to muddled thinking—for instance, in

[28] David Hollinger notes that " 'culture' has often turned out to be a euphemism for 'ethnicity' or 'race' "; *Postethnic America: Beyond Multiculturalism* (New York: Basic Books, 1995), 13.

adoption placements, where social workers may represent themselves as searching for adoptive parents who match a child's cultural or religious heritage when in practice they are most concerned with finding people who share the child's racial identity. (White converts to Islam are not likely to be seen as a particularly good match for a baby whose birth mother is from Pakistan.) In the United States, multiculturalism became a way of talking—but not really talking—about racial disadvantage and inequality, which then got refracted through the prism of cultural difference, even where the cultural differences between white and black Americans were slight.[29] When culture is employed as a euphemism for either race or ethnicity (and ethnicity, being thought to be more cultural, is itself commonly employed as a euphemism for race), this can encourage policymakers to propose cultural solutions to problems that are better understood as social or economic.

For many on the Left, this is what brings multicultural policies into disrepute. The pursuit of multiculturalism has been described as "a handy and inexpensive solution to the problem of ethnic politics,"[30] or as diverting attention from structural and class domination, fragmenting what might otherwise be class-based oppositional movements. For me, this evokes memories of socialist critics of feminism who used to allege that women's self-organisation was undermining class unity, and my instinctive response is to say that this take on multiculturalism ignores the real harm that can be done to people when their cultural identities are trivialised and ignored. But it would be an appropriate criticism if something that has little or nothing to do with culture is misrepresented in exclusively cultural terms. This is precisely what many have claimed to be the case in relation to African Americans.

Richard Ford, for example, has argued that affirmative action programmes in the United States are now authorised by reference to cultural rather than racial difference, with potentially disturbing effects. In the landmark case *University of California Regents v. Bakke* (1978), the U.S. Supreme Court ruled unconstitutional a medical school admissions policy that had accepted applicants from racial minorities with lower grades and test scores. It argued that racial classification would only be permissible if it could be shown to serve a compelling governmental interest in rectifying

---

[29] In *We Are All Multiculturalists Now* (Cambridge, MA: Harvard University Press, 1997), Nathan Glazer argues that the real issue of multiculturalism in the United States is the segregation and inequalities of the black/white divide, and that most of the other groups cited in discussions of multiculturalism (women, Spanish-speaking Americans, and a range of other minorities) neither need nor, mostly, want it.

[30] Stephen Castles, Mary Kalantzis, Bill Cope, and Michael Morrissey, *Mistaken Identity: Multiculturalism and the Demise of Nationalism in Australia* (Sydney: Pluto Press, 1988), 122.

specific instances of discrimination, and concluded that this did not apply to the university's admissions policy. But the Court left open the possibility that universities could continue to utilize affirmative action programmes so long as these avoided numerical quotas and had the object of promoting cultural and ethnic diversity. This possibility was confirmed in the later case *Grutter v. Bollinger* (2003), which upheld the race-conscious admissions policy of the University of Michigan Law School because its declared object was to promote diversity in the student body.[31] Training more African American doctors and lawyers would not be regarded as a legitimate policy objective, nor would compensating people for some generalised history of educational disadvantage, but increasing the cultural diversity of the student population was seen as fair enough. Welcome as this judgment was in upholding the admissions policy, it means that the only way to continue to promote affirmative action policies is to represent the potential beneficiaries as *different*, and perhaps in the process to represent them as more culturally distinct than they either are or wish to be. Indeed, Ford maintains that "the post-*Bakke* universities and their minority applicants needed not only to assert that racial minorities would bring distinctive ideas and perspectives to the seminar table, they also needed at least a sketchy working account of the distinctive perspectives that racial minorities would bring."[32] It is a small step from this to the kind of racial and cultural stereotyping that multiculturalism ought to be challenging.

The emphasis on *cultural* identity and distinctiveness (rather than, say, a history of racism) also obscures important distinctions between those who have experiences of racial disadvantage and abuse and those who can more readily luxuriate in their ethnocultural difference. In her study of white ethnic groups (mainly Irish, Italian, and Polish) in the United States, Mary Waters has documented the delight many take in their identities—their pleasure in celebrating holidays in distinctively ethnic ways, cooking ethnic meals, remembering fragments of a foreign language—and the tenaciousness with which they hold on to their ethnic labels. People attach enormous importance to what they perceive as their ethnic identity, and yet in most cases, the identity comes with minimal costs attached. "It does not, for the most part, limit choice of marriage partner (except in almost all cases to exclude non-whites). It does not determine where you will live, who your friends will be, what job you will have, or whether you will be subject to discrimination."[33] Ethnicity was, of course, more

[31] Richard T. Ford, *Racial Culture: A Critique* (Princeton, NJ: Princeton University Press, 2005), 44–57.

[32] Ibid., 46.

[33] Mary C. Waters, *Ethnic Options: Choosing Identities in America* (Berkeley: University of California Press, 1990), 147.

costly in an earlier period, when Irish, Italian, or Polish Americans could be readily identified by their language or accent, and experienced considerable discrimination. But by the time of Waters's study, these identities had become a matter of personal choice and an almost unadulterated pleasure. She argues that this contributed to an impatience with racial minorities and a backlash against affirmative action: since Polish, Irish, or Italian Americans neither needed nor expected favourable treatment on the grounds of their ethnicity, why should African Americans benefit from affirmative action?

Turning racial difference into cultural difference is, then, problematic. It can mean buying into racial stereotypes we would do better to challenge, substituting bland talk of cultural diversity for a more pointed analysis of racism, and obscuring what may be significant distinctions between those who live a chosen identity that enlarges and enhances their life and those who are discriminated against on the basis of their presumed identity. And while talking of cultural rather than racial difference avoids assumptions about biological determination and conveys no obvious implication about some cultures being better than others, it does not thereby avoid all hint of racism. Indeed, it will often reproduce the fixity that has been the marker of more classical racism. When culture is treated (as in much popular usage) as something from which we can predict a whole swath of human behaviour, this edges disturbingly close to the racist treatment of skin colour or physiognomy as predictors of human behaviour. When people speak of the dangers of their culture being swamped by the migration of too many people from another, or it being better to keep some distance between cultures because of a natural human preference for living with one's own, this is not so different from the fear of miscegenation. In what Balibar terms a "racism without races," the dominant theme is "not biological heredity but the insurmountability of cultural differences," not "the superiority of certain groups or people in relation to others but 'only' the harmfulness of abolishing frontiers, the incompatibility of life-styles and traditions."[34] That the discourse employs the language of culture rather than race does not ensure its innocence.

Yet reducing culture to race is also problematic. This has been especially pertinent in Britain, where it became normal practice for a period to refer to all minority ethnic groups as black, thus dividing the population into two racial categories—black or white—with no further differentiation between African, Caribbean, Indian, Pakistani, Bangladeshi, Chinese, and so on. When the chair of the Commission for Racial Equality

---

[34] Balibar, "Is There a Neo-Racism?" 21. See also Verena Stolcke, "Talking Culture: New Boundaries, New Rhetorics of Exclusion in Europe," *Current Anthropology* 36, no. 1 (1995).

advised politicians on appropriate terminology in 1982 (a few years before, the government had been talking of "black and brown"), he acknowledged that the majority of British Asians, themselves the majority of nonwhite British, would not describe themselves as black, but still recommended it as the best term for those who suffer "the particular disadvantage related to colour."[35] With hindsight, it is extraordinary that academics, policymakers, and politicians could have converged on a term not employed by the majority of those it was supposed to represent. Adopting black as the preferred terminology for discussions of racial disadvantage and inequality contributed to a popular perception that African Caribbeans were the main victims of racism (perhaps, indeed, the main nonwhite group), and even the policymakers were surprised when disaggregated studies revealed that it was South Asian Muslims of Bangladeshi and Pakistani origin who constituted the most disadvantaged ethnic groups in the country.[36] The same studies showed that South Asian Muslims felt themselves more vilified because they were Muslim than because they were Asian.[37]

Tariq Modood, one of the leading critics of racial dualism, argues that cultural racism can exist independently of colour racism, and vice versa, and that it is analytically important to distinguish the two.[38] Part of his object is to draw attention to the different kinds of racism experienced by different groups: thus, in the British context, he contrasts the role played by imputed physical characteristics in racism against those of African or Caribbean origin with the role played by imputed cultural defects in racism against those of South Asian origin. But Modood also queries what he sees as a tendency to think of culture racism only as a proxy for "real" racism (standard colour racism cloaked in culturalist language), and he explores the possibility that cultural racism could at some point become entirely detached from colour racism, with certain groups continuing to experience the vilification of their culture even as colour racism against them declines. We might, for example, say this was happening if culturally assimilated individuals from a vilified cultural group found they thereby escaped all experiences of racism or exclusion.

Modood's exploration of these themes starts from what, in my view, is a somewhat narrow definition of colour racism, which he takes as the

[35] Cited in Tariq Modood, *Multicultural Politics: Racism, Ethnicity, and Muslims in Britain* (Edinburgh: Edinburgh University Press, 2005), 47.

[36] Ibid., 153.

[37] Tariq Modood, Richard Berthoud, Jane Lakey, James Nazroo, Patten Smith, Satnam Virdee, and Sharon Beishon. *Ethnic Minorities in Britain* (London: Policy Studies Institute, 1997).

[38] Modood, *Multicultural Politics*, esp. introduction, chap. 1, and chap. 2.

unfavourable treatment of groups on the grounds of colour. On this understanding, cultural racism must by definition be distinct. My own preference is for Balibar's more inclusive definition, which does not delineate what counts as racial, ethnic, cultural, or religious but instead stresses the underlying pathologies that link all these and the connections between different fantasies of segregation. As Balibar puts it, racism inscribes itself in "practices (forms of violence, contempt, intolerance, humiliation, and exploitation), in discourses and representations which are so many intellectual elaborations of the phantom of prophylaxis or segregation (the need to purify the social body, to preserve 'one's own' or 'our' identity from all forms of mixing, interbreeding or invasion) and which are articulated around stigmata of otherness (name, skin colour, religious practices)."[39] This highlights what both Modood and Balibar have drawn our attention to: the way that racism today becomes bound up with the search for cultural and religious stigmata, and the large part a supposed incompatibility of cultures now performs in its intellectual elaborations.

It is not my object (nor Modood's or Balibar's) to suggest that any form of cultural stereotyping is racist. As I have argued in chapter 1, any analysis that divides up the world through categories like sex, gender, culture, sexuality, ethnicity, or religion will invoke stereotypes—stylised representations that deal in probabilities and typical features, and flatten out much difference. These stereotypes are problematic and need continual interrogation, but they are not things we can readily avoid. The point is not that cultural stereotypes always mean cultural prejudice or that cultural prejudice always involves racism. The more historically specific point is that ideas of what is deemed unacceptable or inferior increasingly revolve around characteristics of culture, and also increasingly, around components of religious belief. This last is especially striking, given that liberal societies have so long prided themselves on their toleration of religious differences, and that manifestations of religion have usually been accorded greater protection under human rights regimes than manifestations of culture.

The shift from race to ethnicity to culture, and more recently, to religion is bound up in wider social, economic, and political developments that I do not pretend to examine here. But the legal and policy framework of each country plays some part in it, for it affects the way racial, ethnic, cultural, and religious differences come to be understood or defined. Countries that would place themselves in similar positions on a liberal democratic spectrum vary considerably in the legal protections they offer their citizens regarding race, ethnicity, culture, and religion, and the policy

---

[39] Balibar, "Is There a Neo-Racism?" 17–18.

framework that evolves in each then plays a part in deciding which aspects will come to the fore. In some countries, legislation provides particularly strong protection against discrimination on the grounds of ethnicity and race. In these circumstances, individuals and groups seeking redress will need to establish that they do indeed constitute a distinct ethnic or racial group, even if, in other circumstances, they might not have thought this important. The classic case from Britain is *Mandla v. Dowell Lee*, where Sikhs had to prove they counted as an ethnic group in order to qualify for redress under the 1976 Race Relations Act. In the United States, legal judgments on the acceptability of affirmative action can be said to have promoted a brand of culturalism that represents racialised groupings in terms of their supposedly distinctive perspectives and characteristics. In the United Kingdom, the preference of the race relations industry for a particular terminology of black and white can be said to have subsumed, for a period, critical differences of culture or religion, while the categories now employed by personnel departments to monitor the progress of their equal opportunities' policies typically take a combination of skin colour and country of origin (white, Indian, Pakistani, Bangladeshi, black African, and so on) to define who we are. In most countries, legislation provides for the freedom of religion, including the freedom to manifest one's religion or beliefs, and this widespread protection on the grounds of religion could be said to act as an incentive to groups to redefine what had previously been considered a more optional cultural practice as a religious requirement—perhaps in the process making it a more rigid and less negotiable part of one's identity.

One recent UK judgment—since overturned—held that a young girl excluded from school for insisting on wearing a jilbab (a gown covering arms to the wrist and legs to the ankle) had been unlawfully denied the right to manifest her religion. The school, a coeducational state school where 79 percent of the pupils were Muslim, had adopted a uniform requiring girls to wear either a skirt, trousers, or shalwar kameez (tunic and trousers) in the school colours. From 1993, it had also permitted girls to wear headscarves. The head teacher (herself Muslim) had worked out the uniform policy in consultation with parents, students, staff, and imams from three local mosques, and it seems that the school had gone to some lengths to ensure that religious concerns regarding modest dress were adequately addressed. The claimant in the case, however, had come to believe that girls over the age of thirteen should cover their bodies completely, and in 2002, attended school wearing a jilbab. She was to told to change back into school uniform, or failing that, transfer to other schools in the area that permitted this form of dress. In the event, she continued to press her rights to attend the original school and lost nearly two years' schooling.

In the first of three cases dealing with this, the judge decided that Sha-bina Begum's rights to manifest her religion, as protected under Article 9 of the *European Convention for the Protection of Human Rights*, had *not* been infringed.[40] This was reversed by the Court of Appeal in 2005, though mainly on the procedural ground that the school had not recog-nized her right to manifest her religion, and not therefore offered any *justification* for the restriction its uniform policy imposed on this right. The judges did not conclude it would be impossible to justify the policy (this was a technical rather than substantive judgment), and indicated considerable sympathy for the school's stance. The point they stressed was that sincerely held religious beliefs cannot be dismissed without con-sideration, even if they represent the views of a small minority—in this instance, the minority of what they described as "very strict" Muslims. As one of the three judges put it, "It is not for the school authorities to pick and choose between religious beliefs or shades of religious belief."

The case subsequently went to the House of Lords, which concluded that there had been no interference with the claimant's rights to manifest her beliefs, because there was nothing to stop her going to an alternative school, and in a minority opinion, that there *had* been interference with her rights but that this was objectively justified. This final judgment was informed by the care the school had taken in devising its uniform policy, and the reluctance of the court to override the considered opinion of those best informed about local circumstances, but it is evident from the text—and of course, from the previous Court of Appeal judgment—that the right to manifest one's religion is accorded a special centrality in the judi-cial decisions of liberal democracies. Certainly, it is hard to imagine that the case would have gone as far as it did had Begum simply claimed that wearing a gown that fully covered her arms and legs was an im-portant part of her cultural identity. Had she chosen culture, rather than religion, as the basis for her claim, it is more likely she would have fared like Renee Rogers, who failed in her 1981 bid for damages against her employer, American Airlines, because she did not manage to convince the court that wearing her hair in cornrow braids was a crucial part of "the cultural and historical essence" of a black American woman. (I discuss this case in more detail in chapter 4.) On the whole, claims regarding

---

[40] In June 2004, Judge J. Bennet dismissed an application for judicial review of the school's decision. [2004] EWHC 1389 (Admin). In 2005, the Court of Appeal reversed this, deciding that Begum, the claimant, had been unlawfully denied the right to manifest her religion. *R (on the application of B) v. Governors of Denbigh High School* [2005] 1 FCR 530. In 2006, this went to the supreme court of appeal, the House of Lords, which con-cluded that her rights had not been unlawfully denied. *R (on the application of Begum) v. Head Teacher and Governors of Denbigh High School)* [2006] UKHL 15.

cultural discrimination have found a less ready audience than those concerning religion or race. When members of minority groups argue that they have been put at a disadvantage because of their skin colour, the discrimination they suffer is widely acknowledged as such. When they represent the disadvantage as connected with their religious beliefs, there is also a strong presumption of discrimination. But when members of minority groups say they are being discriminated against on the basis of culture—being unfairly coerced into adopting the norms of a dominant culture or disparaged for cultural practices that differ from the majority norm—there is much less agreement as to whether these count as legitimate complaints. When culture is employed as part of a political claim, its best chances of success lie in allying itself with either ethnicity, on the one side, or religion, on the other. On a practical level, this is one of the reasons for the persistent slippage between race, ethnicity, culture, and religion. It is hard to make political or legal headway on a charge of cultural discrimination alone.

It would be nice to resolve these slippages by a definitional fiat that sorted out once and for all what belongs in each box, but part of the point about culture is that this is not something we can readily do. We cannot point to some preexisting entity that constitutes the race, the ethnos, the culture, or the religion, for these entities are themselves defined and shaped in response to the wider political environment. It is clear, moreover, that contestations over what goes where are extremely important. For an organisation like Women Living Under Muslim Laws, for example, the question of what is cultural versus what is religious is of vital significance, for if it can be demonstrated that legal procedures that treat the allegations of a single man as of equal weight to the testimony of four women, or punitive legislation that prevents women from driving cars, are *not* required by Islam, this opens up space for a progressive, yet still religious, politics. In Britain, there seems to be a generational difference developing between younger and older Muslims, with young Muslims more insistent on separating religious from cultural or ethnic considerations, and their parents (in their eyes) muddling the three. In a study of attitudes towards marriage, for instance, younger Pakistanis or Bangladeshis were more willing than their parents to consider partners from outside their families' caste groups or countries of origin, while some were willing to consider partners who were white, so as long as they were Muslim.[41] Another study indicates that young women employ their textual

---

[41] One young middle-class Bangladeshi woman said, "If the family is properly religious . . . they wouldn't care whether he was White or Black as long as he was Muslim. . . . But for some people it does matter—the cultural people. They get religion and culture mixed up"; cited in Yunas Samad and John Eade, *Community Perceptions of Forced Marriage* (London: Community Liaison Unit, Foreign and Commonwealth Office, 2002), 86.

understanding of Islam to challenge what they see as cultural restrictions imposed by their parents, to the point where one reported that "the more Islamic I become the less likely it is I will be pushed into an unwanted marriage."[42] The fact that religion, culture, and ethnicity do not map onto one another in simple ways can provide useful ammunition in contesting what people come to perceive as "merely cultural" injunctions. The presumption that they *do* map on, however, remains one of the problems in much multicultural discourse.[43]

Culture as Non-Western or Minority

The second point to stress about the way culture is mobilised in contemporary liberal democratic societies is that it tends to be equated with non-Western or minority culture. Culture is, in most people's lives, such a taken-for-granted background that we only become aware of the norms and assumptions that give meaning to our actions when confronted with cultures very different from our own. This was what Turner observed among the Kayapo, who initially regarded themselves "simply as the prototype of humanity."[44] It is also a common experience among first-time travellers, who only begin to identify their expectations or behaviour as culturally specific when they realise how differently other people behave. As Raymond Williams once remarked, culture is "ordinary," and its very ordinariness means it remains invisible up to the point where we need to define and claim it.[45] I have noticed, for instance, that I sometimes slip in my formulations from *cultural* to *social*, or write of what we do in a particular society where others might have said a particular culture. This slippage was initially unintentional, but on reflection became deliberate, for part of the distortion attached to the term culture is that it is made to do for non-Western or minority groups what society often does for the rest.

---

[42] Cited in Haleh Afshar, Rob Aitken, and Myfanwy Franks, "Feminisms, Islamophobia, and Identities," *Political Studies* 53, no. 2 (2005): 278.

[43] In an early application of anthropological understandings of culture to the political debates on multiculturalism, Turner noted the tendency to merge culture with ethnic identity, and identified pretty much all the worries subsequently voiced over this move. "It risks essentializing the idea of culture as the property of an ethnic group or race; it risks reifying cultures as separate entities by overemphasizing the internal homogeneity of cultures in terms that potentially legitimize repressive demands for cultural conformity; and by treating cultures as badges of group identity, it tends to fetishize them in ways that put them beyond the reach of critical analysis"; Terence Turner, "Anthropology and Multiculturalism: What Is Anthropology That Multiculturalists Should Be Mindful of It," reprinted in *Multiculturalism: A Critical Reader*, ed. David T. Goldberg (Cambridge, MA: Blackwell, 1994), 407.

[44] Turner, "Representing, Resisting, Rethinking," 296.

[45] Raymond Williams, *Keywords: A Vocabulary of Culture and Society* (London: Fontana/Croom Helm, 1976).

In a genuinely monocultural society (especially one where people did little travelling), we would be inclined to think that our ways of greeting, eating, and dressing, or our attitudes to sex, money, and power, were simply the way people are. This ignorance of one's cultural specificity is less likely in a society that is multicultural. But even there, culture remains relatively invisible to those in the hegemonic position, who may readily acknowledge the influence of class or gender on their attitudes and behaviour, yet rarely cite culture as explaining why they think or act the way they do. I should say that I am not convinced that culture is lived in such a different way by those who find themselves in a minority. Nevertheless, the experience of being in the minority makes people more conscious of the distinctiveness of their culture, while the sense of being pressured to conform to majority norms sometimes (though not universally) makes them more committed to sustaining that distinctiveness. Culture also operates as a resource in mobilising against majority dominance. With all this, it is hardly surprising if individuals occupying a minority position more commonly refer to their culture as a defining part of their identity and being.[46]

For those occupying a majority position, the different ways of living a hegemonic and nonhegemonic culture help sustain the view that culture (in the sense of cultural traditions, practices, or beliefs—not, god forbid, of opera, great literature, or chamber music) is primarily a feature of non-Western or minority cultural groups. In *Dislocating Cultures*, Uma Narayan conjures up an imaginary Indian journalist who is trying to write an analysis of the way "American culture" kills women—a book that will do for domestic violence in the United States what analyses of "Hindu tradition" have done for dowry murder in India. She concludes that this can only remain "an imaginary chapter in an improbable book," for "while Indian women repeatedly suffer 'death by culture' in a range of scholarly and popular works, even as the elements of 'culture' proffered do little to explain their deaths, American women seem relatively immune to such analyses of 'death or injury by culture' even as they are victimized by the fairly distinctively American phenomenon of widespread gun-related violence."[47] Americans do, in fact, have a strong sense of themselves as American, linked to particular notions of freedom, mobility, and democracy. But the language of cultural practice or cultural tradition is now mostly reserved for the practices and traditions of non-Western culture.

---

[46] There are obvious parallels in relation to national identity. The English, for example, are the hegemonic nationality within Great Britain, and it is often noted that they have a less developed sense of their national identity than the Welsh or the Scots.

[47] Uma Narayan, *Dislocating Cultures: Identities, Traditions, and Third World Women* (London: Routledge, 1997), 117.

Culture is so thoroughly equated with minority or non-Western culture that it has become virtually redundant to preface it in this way.

This is a deeply troubling equation. Because it makes the cultural specificities of people from majority groups less visible, it encourages them to treat their own local practices as if these were universal rules of conduct, spawning much indignation against newcomers, foreigners, or immigrants who fail to abide by the rules. Cultural difference then becomes loaded with moral significance; being different equates with being wrong. Moreover, in many cases the individual from the minority or non-Western culture disappears as a moral agent, so that being different comes to be viewed as a reflection of a morally distasteful culture, rather than anything to do with individual judgment and choice. The wrongness is attributed to the entire culture; in Narayan's example, it is Hindu tradition that kills women, not Hindu men. When individuals from the majority cultural group fail to abide by the rules of local conduct, they might be condemned as selfish, greedy, cruel, or immoral, with the nature of the condemnation varying in some relationship to the gravity of the act. When individuals from a minority cultural group transgress, their entire culture has to take the rap.

Supporters of multiculturalism will, of course, challenge this. But most of the arguments for multiculturalism represent culture as a major source of people's identity, and a major influence on their actions and behaviour, and this representation encourages an association between culture and non-Western or minority cultural groups. As the case for multicultural policies comes to rest, in part, on the importance people attach to their cultural identities, the hold that culture exerts over people is exaggerated, and culture is thereby exoticised. To be effective, the argument depends on culture mattering intensely to people—otherwise it becomes vulnerable to the criticism that assimilation into a dominant culture is a small price to pay for increased labour mobility, greater gender equality, or ease of access to the society's institutions. Yet few of those writing on multiculturalism really feel that culture has such a powerful grip on their own thoughts and actions. Most are themselves from the hegemonic culture, hence live their culture in a more taken-for-granted, less visible way. Many exist in an atmosphere of geographic and intellectual mobility. However strongly they defend a right to culture, they are likely to be less culturally embedded than they believe to be the case for those they write about. The greater the importance attached to cultural belonging, in other words, the more likely it is that culture will be seen as something that matters to others, not to me. This feeds, in worrying and unintended ways, into an opposition between traditional and modern.

One consequence is a tendency to overstate the degree and depth of value conflict between supposedly distinct and separate cultures. The literature on multicultural rights developed in close association with that on indigenous rights, and was strongly inflected by the Canadian experience, where the rights of the First Nations have been a particularly compelling political concern. There is a widely shared presumption (often encouraged by indigenous peoples) that the religious and value systems of indigenous peoples are radically different from those of other groups: that they represent a wholly other way of relating to one's ancestors, one's community, and the land. The early linkage between multiculturalism and indigenous rights then contributes to a strong sense of alterity. This is stronger, I suspect, than is warranted for most indigenous groups. It is certainly stronger than is warranted for those who constitute the main subject matter of multiculturalism in contemporary Europe: citizens and residents who moved to Europe at some point over the past sixty years, are ethnically differentiated from the majority, and may not adhere to the dominant Christianity.

In Europe, at any rate, deep value conflict is relatively rare, and values are often mistakenly invoked to explain tensions that have their roots elsewhere. Consider the example of forced marriage, which has emerged as a focus of public policy in a number of European countries. Forced marriage mainly occurs within communities where it has been commonplace for parents to select marriage partners for their children—that is, among communities that have a long-established practice of arranged marriage.[48] In contemporary Europe, this may include families of Indian, Pakistani, Bangladeshi, Turkish, or Moroccan origin; the practice itself is not confined to any one continent or religion. In many of these families, tensions have arisen between parents and children. The young people (mostly born and brought up in Europe) do not necessarily reject arranged marriages, and are often happy enough for their parents to search out and suggest suitable marriage partners, but they are less willing than their predecessors to accept their parents as the final arbiter, and usually prefer a spouse whose life experiences are similar to their own. In some cases, they may already have chosen a partner from a different religious or ethnic group. Meanwhile, parents are frequently shocked by what they see as their children's uncontrolled behaviour—the effects, as they perceive it, of Western influences, sex, drugs, and rock and roll—and this can make them more determined than ever to marry their children off to a hopefully uncontaminated spouse from their country of origin. (This is the story of a number of films, novels, and television dramas, but the picture is also

---

[48] For a particularly subtle discussion of arranged marriages in British Pakistani communities, and the pressures now affecting the practices, see Pnina Werbner, "Global Pathways, Working-Class Cosmopolitans, and the Creation of Transnational Ethnic Worlds," *Social Anthropology* 7, no. 1 (1999): 17–35.

confirmed in academic research.)[49] At this point, what may previously have been a consensual practice turns nasty, for parents must either accept their children's decisions—in most of the films and dramas, the young people win out—or force the children into an unwanted marriage. In some extreme cases, young people have been kidnapped, held prisoner by their families, had their passports stolen so as to make it impossible for them to return home, and threatened with physical violence in order to coerce them into marriage. In other instances, they have been subjected to weeks and months of emotional blackmail—including the threat of ostracism by their family and community—so as to enforce "agreement."

This is rightly perceived as an urgent matter for public policy, though I argue in chapter 4 that the solution most commonly proposed, setting a higher age minimum for marriages that involve a partner from overseas, is problematic. The point to note at this stage is that forced marriage is not an issue that throws up particularly vexed questions of cultural accommodation. All the major religions—Christianity, Judaism, Islam, Sikhism, and Hinduism—regard consent as a condition of a valid marriage. None of the spokespeople for Europe's ethnic minority communities claims forced (as opposed to arranged) marriage as part of their heritage. No one suggests that states should defer to some cherished minority custom of coercing young girls into marriage against their will. Within minority communities, there is certainly a tendency to deny the extent of forced marriage, to agree that any such marriage is abhorrent, but then insist that the overwhelming majority of marriages simply reflect a willingness to take advice from elders about who will make the best spouse. In their research on attitudes towards forced marriage among Bangladeshis in East London and Pakistanis in Bradford, Yunas Samad and John Eade found the older interviewees particularly likely to deny the extent of forced marriage, while the younger interviewees reported many so-called arranged marriages as in reality forced. The researchers also uncovered widespread suspicion, primarily among middle-aged and older men, that the government's preoccupation with the issue reflected a racist and Islamophobic

---

[49] Films include Ayub Khan-Din's *East Is East* (1999) and Ken Loach's *Ae Fond Kiss* (2004). Meera Syal's novel *Life Isn't All Ha Ha Hee Hee* (New York: W. W. Norton and Co., 2000) was made into a successful television drama in 2005. Udayan Prasad's *My Son the Fanatic* (1997), based on a script by Hanif Kureishi, reverses the usual pattern by showing the father as the liberal. The idea that intergenerational tensions are part of what produces forced marriage is confirmed by the experience of the United Kingdom's Forced Marriage Unit, which reports that social and sexual control are among the main reasons why parents seek to impose a marriage on an unwilling child. See also the research by Samad and Eade, *Community Perceptions of Forced Marriage*; Anne Phillips and Moira Dustin, "UK Initiatives on Forced Marriage: Regulation, Exit, and Dialogue," *Political Studies* 52 (2004): 531–51.

agenda, and was mainly aimed at restricting further immigration. As one interviewee put it, "The British immigration [service] is just fed up of granting visa to the spouse of our sons and daughters who are having arranged marriages in Bangladesh. They are trying to stop that."[50]

There is conflict, then, over who has the right to decide who is the best marriage partner and what governments are really trying to do when they set in place policies for dealing with forced marriage. But it would be misleading to represent this as a deep value conflict between different cultural and religious traditions over whether marriage should be based on consent. First, there are plenty of indications that when parents resort to coercion, they are responding to a contemporary set of circumstances, ones that should be readily recognisable outside the communities that have traditionally practiced arranged marriage. Parents thinking their children have gone astray is hardly culturally specific; nor is children thinking their parents are stuck in old ways of thinking and doing. Second, forced marriage is not condoned in any of the value systems. There *are* values at issue—the value of arranged versus love marriages, the relationship of the individual to the family, and the legitimacy of parental authority—but the positions people take on any of these are in a state of considerable flux. Third (and this becomes of particular importance in the next chapter's discussion of cultural defence), citing values as the reason why parents kidnap, imprison, and coerce their children gives the impression that believing you are right is explanation enough for your violence. The truth is that most parents, of whatever cultural background and with whatever religious or political beliefs, stop short of brutality, no matter how strong their conviction that they know best. Values alone do not explain why some parents, but not others, are willing to use force. They may help explain why some feel more intensely than others about the authority of parents or the rights of the child, but they cannot of themselves explain the move to violence.

From Culture to Cosmos?

Critics of multiculturalism mostly fall into one of two camps. Either they see cultures as discrete, distinct ways of life (those "complex wholes" covering knowledge, beliefs, art, morals, customs, and laws) and object to multiculturalism because they think it promotes ways of life that ought to be regarded as unacceptable. Or they query the continued salience of culture and object to multiculturalism as a misguided attempt to reinstate purified forms of identity that have lost their purchase in the contemporary

---

[50] Samad and Eade, *Community Perceptions of Forced Marriage*, 105.

world. I have hopefully established that I reject the first understanding of culture and do not support a multiculturalism based on a notion of cultures as discrete, distinct, bounded, static ways of life. What of the second objection, which draws on an understanding of culture closer to my own, yet concludes from it that multiculturalism is not the way forward?

In the contemporary literature, this second position is often described as cosmopolitanism, and is sometimes represented as being in direct competition with multiculturalism. This is the part it plays in the work of Jeremy Waldron, for example, who sees multiculturalism as wanting to secure for people the integrity of "their" cultures, and preserve them against internal and external change.[51] By contrast, cosmopolitanism is built on the multiplicity of allegiances that characterise any one person, the ways that "bits of culture come into our lives from different sources" with "no guarantee that they will all fit together."[52] He cites Salman Rushdie's defence of *The Satanic Verses* as an illustration: "*The Satanic Verses* celebrates hybridity, impurity, intermingling. . . . It rejoices in mongrelization and fears the absolutism of the Pure. Mélange, hotchpotch, a bit of this and a bit of that is *how newness enters the world.*"[53] Waldron rejects the notion that the world divides up into separate and distinct cultures, arguing that in this age of mass migration, formed by empire and trade, cultural influences are radically dispersed. In his reading of it, multiculturalism is overly wedded to the idea that individuals find their sense of themselves through their communities, and to a vision of these communities as sitting side by side on a flat plane, touching perhaps at the edges, but not otherwise engaged. Cosmopolitanism is the better—and in the context of the modern world, the more authentic—alternative.

So what is wrong with this? Having set out so laboriously the dangers of a bounded or totalising conception of culture, why not just give up on multiculturalism as a bad job and embrace the cosmopolitan alternative? It might be said in criticism of cosmopolitanism that it conjures up too much the world of the global elite, the cultural tourist, the frequent flier, and the securities of wealth and position from which it becomes relatively easy to dip in and out of other people's cultures. It might be said that it attaches too little weight to local attachments, the anguish of being forced to choose between one community and another, and the unhappiness that can attend that feeling of being mixed up, of not having any true home. But most of those who currently claim the name of cosmopolitan have gone to some lengths to weld it on to a thicker understanding of culture and context, as in Bruce Ackerman's notion of the rooted cosmopolitan

---

[51] Jeremy Waldron, "Minority Cultures and the Cosmopolitan Alternative," *University of Michigan Journal of Law Reform* 25 (1992): 751–93.

[52] Ibid., 788.

[53] Salman Rushdie, "In Good Faith," cited in Waldron, "Minority Cultures," 751.

or Kwame Anthony Appiah's elaboration of the cosmopolitan patriot.[54] Martha Nussbaum, whose definition of the cosmopolitan as "the person whose allegiance is to the worldwide community of human beings" suggests someone freed from all cultural baggage, combines this with statements about the importance of diversity and the significance of local sympathies and loyalties in the development of our moral sensibilities.[55] It may be that some versions of cosmopolitanism overstate the impact of global migration or understate the importance people attach to being able to stay in one place. It may be that some are elitist. But since I evidently think some versions of multiculturalism are at fault, why work on an improved version of this, rather than an improved version of the other? What is at stake between a multiculturalism that rids itself of mistaken notions of culture and a cosmopolitanism that grafts on to itself a better understanding of cultural diversity?

My reasons for coming down on the side of a revised multiculturalism are partly theoretical and partly political. For both reasons, I think the task many have set themselves—to differentiate the new discourse of cosmopolitanism from an older one of universalism—is likely to prove beyond them, and that despite all the qualifications, cosmopolitanism will revert to a rather arrogant form of cultural imperialism. Pratap Mehta has noted that contemporary cosmopolitans "distinguish themselves from old-fashioned moral universalists by claiming to be respectful of cultural diversity, interested in dialogue across cultures, and committed to forms of cultural hybridization."[56] David Hollinger's book *Postethnic America: Beyond Multiculturalism* provides a good illustration. Hollinger sees universalists as trying to locate the common ground that underpins all differences, but cosmopolitans as seeking to engage with human diversity. "For cosmopolitans, the diversity of humankind is a fact; for universalists, it is a potential problem."[57] So where the universalist might have claimed

[54] Bruce Ackerman, "Rooted Cosmopolitanism," *Ethics* 104 (1994): 516–35; Kwame Anthony Appiah, "Cosmopolitan Patriots," *Critical Inquiry* 23 (1997): 617–39.

[55] Martha C. Nussbaum, "Patriotism and Cosmopolitanism," in *For Love of Country: Debating the Limits of Patriotism. Martha C. Nussbaum with Respondents*, ed. Joshua Cohen (Boston: Beacon Press, 1996), 4.

[56] Pratap Bhanu Mehta, "Cosmopolitanism and the Circle of Reason," *Political Theory* 28, no. 5 (2000): 620. Jonathan Friedman offers a more jaundiced contrast: "The cosmopolitan of old was a modernist who identified above and beyond ethnicity and particular cultures. He was a progressive intellectual, a believer in rationality who understood cultural specificities as expressions of universal attributes. The new cosmopolitans are ecumenical collectors of culture. They represent nothing more than a gathering of differences often in their own self-identification"; "Global Crises, the Struggle for Cultural Identity, and Intellectual Porkbarrelling: Cosmopolitans versus Locals, Ethnics, and Nationals in an Era of De-hegemonisation," in *Debating Cultural Hybridity: Multi-Cultural Identities and the Politics of Anti-Racism*, ed. Pnina Werbner and Tariq Modood (London: Zed Books, 1997), 83.

[57] Hollinger, *Postethnic America*, 84.

that questions of right and wrong transcend all differences of culture (and thereby risked favouring her own culturally shaped beliefs), the cosmopolitan is more likely to argue that what is right emerges through a reflective dialogue across cultures. Where the universalist might have assumed that she has access to norms of rectitude independent of any tradition, the cosmopolitan is likely to see norms as embedded in particular and local contexts, but capable of being mobilised beyond these through a process of critical engagement. This sounds wonderfully evenhanded—but Mehta (to my mind, rightly) detects in it a tendency to reinstate a hierarchy of cultures. In particular, he sees a tendency to think that the willingness to mix cultural influences and engage with the cultural other is more a characteristic of Western than non-Western cultures. In his view, neither cosmopolitanism nor universalism is inherently ethnocentric. "But the historical practices through which both cosmopolitanism and universalism have been articulated often enact the very parochialism they decry."[58]

One of the difficulties here is that cosmopolitanism has come to be associated with an attitude, in contrast to multiculturalism, which tends to be associated with policy. It is hard to talk of an attitude without invoking a culture, and in the process suggesting that some cultures cultivate better attitudes than others. In fact it might be said—contrary to expectations—that it is harder for the cosmopolitan than the "old-fashioned moral universalist" to shake off accusations of cultural imperialism, for it is marginally more plausible to think of ideas as floating freely from their cultural origins or contexts than to imagine attitudes in this way. Yet attitudes figure large in the self-presentation of cosmopolitanism. In Hollinger, for example, cosmopolitans seek out voluntary rather than involuntary affiliations, and are "willing to put the future of every culture at risk through the sympathetic but critical scrutiny of other cultures."[59] To be cosmopolitan is generally understood as being capable of taking a critical distance from one's habits or assumptions, willing to engage positively with those who are different, and able to adopt an attitude of reflective openness that frees you from the tyranny of the pure. I have no quarrel with the attributes, which I find highly attractive, but they are almost certainly going to develop more easily in some circumstances than in others.

In fairness, Waldron has been at pains to question the association between having a cosmopolitan attitude and being a free-floating consumer of the world's cultures.[60] He tellingly contrasts those immersed in their

[58] Mehta, "Cosmopolitanism and the Circle of Reason," 633.

[59] Hollinger, *Postethnic America*, 85.

[60] Jeremy Waldron, "What Is Cosmopolitan?" *Journal of Political Philosophy* 8, no. 2 (2000): 227–43.

own culture, but precisely because of this able to give reasons for its norms and practices to the curious outsider and engage in discussions about them, and what might be thought of as the more modern aficionado of identity politics, whose self-consciousness about culture presents it as a nonnegotiable entity. ("I dress this way or I speak this language, or I follow these marriage customs *because they are the ways of my people.*")[61] I take the point—it resonates with some of my own about the misrepresentation of difference through a false binary of traditional and modern—but this redefines cosmopolitanism mainly as a willingness to give reasons for what we do. This seems to shift the terms of the debate.

People vary enormously in their capacity for reflecting on their own taken-for-granted assumptions, partly for reasons bound up in the particularities of personal history, but also because of the cultural, religious, moral, and political influences that shape their lives. Certain ways of thinking or living your life are more conducive to critical reflection than others; it would be an odd kind of cultural relativism to deny this. I see feminism, for example, as more conducive to internal criticism than Trotskyism, and as a teacher, I believe that certain ways of approaching a subject are more likely than others to engage students in a critical enquiry. But this is not to say that all feminists are open-minded or that all Trotskyists are imprisoned by their worldview, and the precise connection between teaching style and student reaction continues to elude me. Mehta says, "It has never been clear to me why the unpropitiousness of particular social systems for reflexivity should lead one to conclude that members of those cultures could not reflexively think about their social arrangements."[62] Yet if cosmopolitanism is going to be defined by reference to an attitude, it is clearly committed to the view that some attitudes are better than others, and (despite Waldron's endeavours) is likely to encourage the view that some cultures are better as well. At this point, one begins to wonder about the much-vaunted openness to difference.

Multiculturalists are always being accused of thinking that all cultures are equally deserving of respect. If any do, I think they are wrong, though in fact most explicitly reject this position. The kernel of truth in the accusation is that multiculturalism *is* an egalitarian doctrine, committed to the view that all cultural groups have a role to play in shaping the identity of the country they live in, that those who got there first or who currently constitute the numerical majority do not automatically gain the right to impose their own cultural preferences on the others, and that if the laws and institutions turn out to be biased towards majority cultural groups, there needs to be some compelling noncultural reason to justify this. Cos-

[61] Ibid., 234.
[62] Mehta, "Cosmopolitanism and the Circle of Reason," 632.

mopolitanism is also egalitarian in insisting on our equality as human beings, but it adopts no special stance as regards the relationship between majority and minority cultural groups. Though officially disclaiming cultural bias, it is therefore less perturbed by evidence of this. Or as Daniele Archibugi puts it in a comparison of multiculturalist and cosmopolitan approaches to linguistic diversity, "Multiculturalists are keen to stress that the nation-building process leads to winners and losers and that the majority language group retains all gains. Cosmopolitans are less inclined to consider the advantages and disadvantages of the various groups because they implicitly assume that establishing a common language provides advantages to all communities, and they tend to put aside the fact that some communities get a larger share of them."[63]

The other reason for working within a discourse of multiculturalism is more directly political. Multiculturalism is currently under attack, partly for good reasons (the misleading representations of culture, or the justification it can provide for sacrificing the rights and interests of the individual to the preferences of the cultural group), but partly in a coded return to narrower and more exclusionary notions of national identity. In Europe, more specifically, acts of violence committed by Islamists become the signal for a critical review of multicultural policies. Muslims are exhorted to demonstrate their allegiance to the "British," "Dutch," or "German" way of life, and earlier multicultural ideas that saw this way of life as now including Islam threaten to drop from view. It is against this backdrop that I have chosen to pursue a multiculturalism without culture in preference to a cosmopolitanism with an improved sense of cultural diversity.[64] This is not, in my view, the moment for sounding the retreat from everything that multiculturalism implies. Rather, it is a time for elaborating a version of multiculturalism that dispenses with reified notions of culture, engages more ruthlessly with cultural stereotypes, and refuses to subordinate the rights and interests of women to the supposed traditions of their culture. This is what I hope to do in the following chapters.

---

[63] Daniele Archibugi, "The Language of Democracy: Vernacular or Esperanto? A Comparison between the Multiculturalist and Cosmopolitan Perspectives," *Political Studies* 53 (2005): 543.

[64] There are a few writers who move more seamlessly between multiculturalism and cosmopolitanism, including Paul Gilroy in *Against Race: Imagining Political Culture beyond the Color Line* (Cambridge, MA: Belknap Press, 2000).

CHAPTER THREE

What's Wrong with Cultural Defence?

CRITICS OF MULTICULTURALISM commonly argue that it encourages society to turn a blind eye to abuses of women and children. Worries about cultural sensitivity, they say, paralyse social workers, police officers, and even judges, who are made to feel that holding people from one cultural group to account for behaviour considered abhorrent by people from another smacks of cultural imperialism. Asked to show respect for other people's culture but unsure of what this entails, they decide to do nothing. As a result, we are told, women and children are inadequately protected against physical or sexual abuse. Parents who beat their children get away with it because they are thought to be doing what their culture considers normal as a means of discipline. Men who have sex with underage girls escape punishment because they are said to be following what have long been the norms of their culture. Men who kill their unfaithful wives get reduced sentences because they are able to represent the infidelity as peculiarly humiliating to a male from their culture, and argue that this makes them more prone to explode into violence than other men. According to the critics, multiculturalism has promoted a cultural relativism that can no longer distinguish between right and wrong. Culture is operating as a reason for public inaction and an excuse for immoral behaviour.

Much of this is polemical diatribe, and it is easy enough to demonstrate that some of the accusations are misplaced. The complaint about cultural relativism, for example, falls considerably wide of the mark, for most of those writing in defence of multiculturalism have explicitly rejected the thesis that all cultures are of equal moral value, and there is no country in the world that comes close to operating that kind of evenhandedness in its policies. A public discourse of multiculturalism does make for greater uncertainty among police or social workers over when it is legitimate to intervene, but before this is used to discredit multicultural policies, it needs to be backed up by nonanecdotal evidence about how many then become incapable of action and how much abuse goes unchecked. It also needs to be considered alongside compelling reasons why public agencies, engaged in service provision, need to engage with citizens in their complex diversity, rather than through narrow preconceptions derived from only one of the society's constituent groups.

The case of KR, a young British Sikh abducted by her parents and taken to India for the purposes of marriage, is instructive here because it tells two different stories.[1] KR left home at sixteen to live with an elder sister because of fears that her parents were planning to force her into marriage. The parents reported her to the police as a missing person, alleging that KR had been kidnapped by her sister (who had herself already been repudiated by the family because she was living with what they regarded as an inappropriate man). The police disregarded KR's account of the risks and returned her to her father's custody, at which point she was indeed taken to the Punjab and held in custody with relatives. This looks very much like the police deferring to what they took to be the cultural norms within a Sikh family and failing to offer adequate protection to a young girl struggling against coercion. But the next stage tells a different story, for when the sister applied to have KR made a ward of the court, the judge in the case sprang into action, drew up an order for cooperation in securing her return to England, and worked with the British High Commission in Delhi to get her flown back to the United Kingdom. He then authorised the publication of his judgment (an unusual step with family court cases) so as to alert legal practitioners, educational authorities, and others to the issues involved. The case thus simultaneously confirms fears about an injunction to respect cultural diversity inhibiting police intervention *and* demonstrates a high level of intervention to protect a young person from abuse.

In *Generous Betrayal*, Unni Wikan recounts a parallel story from Norway, though this time without the second stage. "Aisha" was fourteen years old when she tried—but failed—to convince the welfare authorities that her family was planning to force her into a marriage; she subsequently disappeared, presumably to precisely this fate.[2] Wikan argues that it was the fear of being accused of racism if they removed a Muslim girl from her family that explains the social workers' inaction—a fear that "pierces the heart of the well-meaning Scandinavian whose cherished identity is that of world champion of all that is kind and good."[3] This idea that public service workers are inhibited by the fear of being called a racist is a common theme among critics of multiculturalism, and although firm evidence is still limited, there can be no doubt that this occurs. But some of the failures will reflect patterns of nonintervention that have little to do with cultural sensitivity: a tendency, for example, to favour

---

[1] *Re KR (A Child) (Abduction: Forcible Removal by Parents)* [1999] 2 FLR 542. This was a particularly important case that helped shape the UK initiatives on forced marriage.

[2] Unni Wikan, *Generous Betrayal: Politics of Culture in the New Europe* (Chicago: University of Chicago Press, 2002).

[3] Ibid., 24.

the accounts offered by the older rather than the younger generation or a general disinclination to intervene in family affairs. I am also struck by Sherene Razack's comment that when women from minority cultures fail to get the services they need (or as in Aisha's case, have explicitly requested), this may have less to do with a misguided respect for cultural diversity and more with a racist presumption that violence and coercion are normal in certain communities and groups.[4]

When we turn to the courts, we can certainly identify some dubious legal judgments where individuals from minority cultural groups have been treated with what looks like excessive leniency. Probably the two most cited cases from the United States are *People of the State of California v. Kong Pheng Moua* (Fresno County Superior Court, February 7, 1985) and *People v. Chen* (Supreme Court, New York County, December 2, 1988), both resulting in decisions that I have little hesitation in describing as wrong. In the first, Kong Pheng Moua, originally from Laos, was charged with rape and kidnapping after abducting a young Hmong woman from her workplace at Fresno City College and forcing her to have sex with him. At his trial, it was claimed that he was acting in accordance with a traditional Hmong practice of marriage by elopement, in which the man would establish his strength and virility by seizing the woman, and she would ritually protest his sexual advances in order to establish her virtue. Kong Pheng Moua was found guilty only of a lesser charge of false imprisonment. He was sentenced to 120 days in prison and a fine of $1,000, the bulk of which was to be paid to his victim in what experts considered the traditional form of reparation. In the second case, Dong-lu Chen, a Chinese immigrant to New York, battered his wife to death with a hammer some weeks after discovering she was having an affair. At his trial, an expert witness testified that in traditional Chinese culture, a woman's adultery would be conceived as an enormous stain on the man, that a man would find it difficult to remarry if he divorced his wife for adultery, and that violence against wayward spouses was commonplace in China.[5] The judge accepted that Chen was "driven to vio-

---

[4] Sherene H. Razack, "Imperilled Muslim Women, Dangerous Muslim Men, and Civilised Europeans: Legal and Social Reponses to Forced Marriages," *Feminist Legal Studies* 12 (2004): 167.

[5] For good discussions of this case, see Leti Volpp, "(M)isidentifying Culture: Asian Women and the 'Cultural Defense,'" *Harvard Women's Law Journal* 17 (1994): 57–101; Sarah Song, "Majority Norms, Multiculturalism, and Gender Equality," *American Political Science Review* 99, no. 4 (November 2005): 474–89. In Volpp's assessment, the witness was testifying more to "his own *American* fantasy" of Chinese life: divorce rates have in fact been rising sharply in China, where less that 12 percent of the population now think of divorce as disgraceful, and the expert witness admitted that he couldn't actually recall a single instance of a man killing his adulterous wife.

lence by traditional Chinese values about adultery and loss of manhood," convicted him of second-degree manslaughter, and sentenced him to five years' probation.[6] If this is what multiculturalism permits, it is hardly surprising that so many reject it.

And yet the most extensive recent survey of the "cultural defence" suggests that judges have little time for cultural evidence, mostly rule it irrelevant, or insist on all citizens, of whatever cultural background, conforming to identical rules. From her analysis of cases in the United States and elsewhere, Alison Renteln concludes that "the preponderance of the data belies the commitment of liberal democracies to the value of cultural diversity."[7] She reports that judges commonly refuse to hear expert witnesses testifying about the cultural context, declaring this irrelevant to the case at hand, and that the courts continue to deploy the test of the "reasonable person," without recognising that the characteristics of this supposedly reasonable person may reflect dominant norms. On her reading, deference to cultural diversity is paper-thin, and defendants from minority cultures are still put at a serious disadvantage. So far as the legal system is concerned, Renteln believes we need more multiculturalism, not less, and she proposes as the guiding principle that "when the cultural claims can be shown to be true, then culture should affect the disposition of the case, unless this would result in irreparable harm to others."[8] The qualification is intended to exclude cases of wife beating, murder, child abuse, or rape.

Though I focus in this chapter on culture in the legal system, rather than the practices of social workers, teachers, or police, this is more because there is better documentation on this than because of any special status attached to the cultural defence. It is not, in fact, clear that support for multiculturalism commits one to any particular position on the uses of cultural defence. Cases like *People v. Chen* are frequently cited as part of the evidence against multiculturalism (for example, in Susan Moller Okin's critique), but this sometimes looks like a case of mistaken identity. Political—as opposed to legal—theorists have had remarkably little to say either for or against the cultural defence, presumably because what judges do is not strictly a matter of public policy. But it would be disingenuous to leave it at that, for even if there is no stated policy on how multiculturalism ought to be interpreted by public officials or in the courts, a strongly multicultural public ethos is likely to have some of the suggested effects.

---

[6] Cited in Nancy S. Kim, "The Cultural Defence and the Problems of Cultural Preemption: A Framework for Analysis," *New Mexico Law Review* 27 (1997): 120.

[7] Alison Renteln, *The Cultural Defense* (New York: Oxford University Press, 2004), 186–87.

[8] Ibid., 15.

In this chapter, I therefore review the legitimacy of the cultural defence, drawing primarily on illustrations from courts in England and the United States. As will become evident, I share many reservations regarding the uses of culture in the courtroom, and agree with much of what critics of multiculturalism have said about cases where cultural tradition is inappropriately invoked to mitigate violence against women. I have no qualms about adopting strong normative positions on matters of equality or violence, and would mostly dispute suggestions that these are culturally specific or Eurocentric. I argue, however, that the abuses of the cultural defence are best understood as illustrating the too-ready acceptance of culture that is my target in this book. Assessments of multiculturalism have been hampered by a misrepresentation of culture as more encompassing, and cultures as more distinct, than is really the case. Many of the cases discussed here highlight an abuse of cultural stereotypes that a more careful multiculturalism should help us avoid.

Assessing the Cultural Defence

There are many ways a defendant from a minority cultural group might get a raw deal in a courtroom, most of which have nothing to do with moral values or cultural norms. Minority culture defendants might not be fluent in the language used in court; they might give their evidence in a way that inadvertently leads judges and juries to doubt it; or they might tell what sounds like an implausible story to those from a different cultural background. For instance, they might have been brought up to consider it rude to look directly at a person in authority, leading to a perception of them as shifty, or they might have gone to what jurors consider inordinate lengths to assist distant members of an extended family, leading to a suspicion of their motives.

It seems a basic enough requirement of a multicultural society that the courts should be alerted to this kind of diversity, and that judges should undergo training in such matters. In the United Kingdom, the Judicial Studies Board has been organising courses on diversity issues and producing an *Equal Treatment Bench Book* for magistrates and judges since the early 1990s, and you would have to be a pretty determined monoculturalist to object to its advice. The most recent *Bench Book* includes sections on appropriate terminology, background information on a number of minority faiths, reminders about not reading too much from people's body language, not asking Sikhs, Jews, or Muslims to remove their head coverings in court, and not asking people to state their Christian names. All this looks like uncontroversial good practice (though elements of the British press still managed to whip up a minor storm about political correctness from the section on terms that might be deemed offensive). The more complicated issues arise when the courts are asked to consider whether it is fair to imprison people who are behaving in ways that would be considered normal within their culture—that is, when they are asked to consider what has been called a cultural defence.

In Paul Magnarella's definition, a "cultural defense maintains that persons socialized in a minority or foreign culture, who regularly conduct themselves in accordance with their own culture's norms, should not be held fully accountable for conduct that violates official law, if that conduct conforms to the prescriptions of their own culture."[9] A classic illustration from the English courts—probably not one that would send shock waves through the reader—is the 1975 case of *R v. Adesanya*, where a Nigerian mother was prosecuted for the ceremonial scarring of the cheeks of her nine- and fourteen-year-old sons.[10] On this occasion, the fact that the scarification would have been accepted as a normal part of Yoruba custom, and that the Nigerian community in Britain was probably not aware that the practice was contrary to English law, was felt to change the status of the offence. It also helped that the children were said to be willing parties to the ceremony, that the scars were unlikely to leave permanent marks, and that the mother was deemed of excellent character. Adesanya was still convicted: under English criminal law, a minority custom cannot be a defence to a prosecution, unless this is explicitly allowed for in legislation. She was, however, given an absolute discharge.

A more troubling example—also from the English courts—is the 1969 case of *Alhaji Mohamed v. Knott*, which involved a thirteen-year-old girl who had contracted a (legal) marriage with a twenty-six-year-old man in Nigeria. The couple then moved to England for the man to pursue his studies, and the girl was committed to the care of the local authorities after a doctor alerted the police to her probable age. The care order was subsequently revoked by the Court of Appeal, which felt that what would be repugnant "to an English girl and our Western way of life" would be "entirely natural" for a Nigerian girl. "They develop sooner, and there is nothing abhorrent in their way of life for a girl of thirteen to marry a man of twenty five."[11] The judgment has been cited as a good example of cultural tolerance,[12] though to my mind it only appears so when set

---

[9] Paul J. Magnarella, "Justice in a Culturally Pluralistic Society: The Culture Defense on Trial," *Journal of Ethnic Studies* 19 (1991): 67.

[10] Unreported, but noted in [1975] 24 ICLQ 136.

[11] *Alhaji Mohamed v. Knott* [1969] 1 QB 1.

[12] Alex Samuels, "Legal Recognition and Protection of Minority Customs in a Plural Society in England," *Anglo-American Law Review* 10, no. 4 (1981): 241–56. Samuels goes on to argue that "logically the age of the child wife ought to be irrelevant, although it has been suggested, illogically, that some sort of arbitrary lower age limit should be drawn" (251).

against the cultural arrogance of the Juvenile Court, which had deemed the continuation of the couple's association as "repugnant to any decent-minded English man or woman." The first decision managed to represent the Nigerian couple as engaged in a repugnant, indecent act; the second corrected for this, but only by representing all Nigerians as the same ("they develop sooner," "their way of life") and not to be judged by the standards of "our Western way of life." Later cases involving a twelve-year-old Iranian bride and thirteen-year-old Omani bride (also living with their student husbands) provoked a tightening of immigration regulations, and by 1986, entry clearance was no longer granted to spouses if either party was under sixteen on the date of arrival.[13] It remains an open question whether that change reflects a decline in cultural relativism or the impact of feminism on attitudes about child brides. As we shall see from later chapters, the age of admission for spouses has since been raised to eighteen.

The use of the cultural defence raises four major issues. The most general is that it threatens to undermine legal universalism because it threatens to elevate cultural membership above other considerations. Ignorance of the law, for example, is not normally accepted as a legitimate defence. Why, then, should an ignorance that derives from cultural difference or (as in Adesanya's case) a relatively recent migration be acknowledged as a salient factor? What of other groups whose perception of an offence may differ from that of the wider society, but for political rather than cultural reasons? A Proudhonist who claims that property is theft is unlikely to cut much ice if he uses this to explain why, in his world, it is entirely legitimate to appropriate his landlord's property. Why should a Rastafarian then be able to argue that smoking ganja conforms to the prescriptions of his culture and should not be regarded as a criminal offence?[14] If the Rastafarian can successfully establish the practice as intrinsic to his religious beliefs, he will probably be on stronger ground, for liberal states normally recognise the right to practice one's religion according to the dictates of one's conscience and have been reluctant to ban behaviour that is clearly required by a recognised religion. Legislation in the United States permits members of the Native American Church to use a hallucinatory drug, peyote, in their religious ceremonies, though this

---

[13] HC 3069 of 85–6 See Sebastian Poulter, *Ethnicity, Law, and Human Rights: The English Experience* (Oxford: Clarendon Press, 1998), 53.

[14] As it happens, the English courts have never accepted this last argument. In his sympathetic assessment of the case for ending the legal prohibition on the use of cannabis by Rastafarians, Sebastian Poulter (*Ethnicity, Law, and Human Rights*, chap. 9) inclined to the view that the prohibition should be ended for everyone, rather than just for those who can establish some legitimate cultural or religious claim.

exemption is carefully circumscribed to include only members of the church and specific religious occasions. By contrast, Rastafarians have been less successful in persuading the courts to view their belief system as a religion, while the fact that they use marijuana on a regular basis—not for identifiable ceremonies—probably contributes to a perception of this as cultural rather than religious. Religion is widely recognised as a basis for legal exemption. Extending the same status to culture is said to veer too far in the direction of different laws for different communities.

Culture can also lend itself to opportunistic defences. As is clear from the discussion in chapter 2, claims about what is normal within a particular cultural group are highly contentious. Something may be claimed as a cultural practice when it has long been contested or abandoned by other members of the group, and individuals who have adopted the practices and conventions of the surrounding culture may rediscover an allegiance to a different culture because it now serves their interests to do so. In the civil courts, there may be strong financial incentives to associate yourself with a legal tradition that offers you a more favourable inheritance or divorce settlement, and it has been plausibly argued that this is what lies behind some of the (male) claims to have divorces regulated according to religious rather than civil law. Similar issues arise in criminal cases, where judges may have to struggle with the question of whether defendants really are, as they claim, shaped by the prescriptions of a minority culture or just using this to secure some legal advantage. One American contributor has suggested that new immigrants should only be permitted to employ a cultural defence up to the first five years of their residence in the United States, or ten years in the case of elderly migrants, who are presumed to be less open to change.[15] Others maintain that "time is not an absolute factor for acculturation," since groups experiencing discrimination and/or isolation in their new country of residence often become more closely identified with the traditions and values of their original home.[16] It is not easy to determine which cultural influences are acting on an individual. In the absence of transparent criteria, the use of a cultural defence leaves itself open to considerable manipulation.

The third and more specifically feminist contention is that cultures operate to sustain male power: Okin tersely comments that "most cultures have as one of their principal aims the control of women by men."[17] If so,

[15] Veronica Ma, "Culture Defense: Limited Admissibility for New Immigrants," *San Diego Justice Journal* 3 (1995): 462.

[16] Jeroen Van Broeck. "Cultural Defence and Culturally Motivated Crimes," *European Journal of Crime, Criminal Law, and Criminal Justice* 9, no. 1 (2001): 13.

[17] Susan Moller Okin, "Feminism and Multiculturalism: Some Tensions," *Ethics* 108 (1998), 667.

then allowing cultural tradition as a legitimate element in a criminal defence could be said to encourage and sustain patriarchal practices. *Alhaji Mohamed v. Knott* would be an obvious example here, as would a number of cases where men have been charged with sex with an underage girl and have represented this as normal within their countries of origin.[18] In those cases now described as "honour killings," defendants who have been charged with the murder of a family member have commonly referred to their cultural background to explain the disgrace brought on the family by the sexual behaviour of their victim. Culture was successfully invoked in *People v. Chen* as a defence against a murder charge, and in *People of the State of California v. Kong Pheng Moua* as a defence against a charge of rape. In an influential critique of the cultural defence (one that provided much of the ammunition for Okin's critique of multiculturalism), Doriane Lambelet Coleman argues that "the defendant's interest in using cultural evidence that incorporates discriminatory norms and behaviors must be weighed against the victims' and potential victims' interests in obtaining protection and relief through a non-discriminatory application of the criminal law," and concludes that this is an area where the interests of the victims—mostly women and children—should be paramount.[19]

The fourth concern—somewhat at a right angle to the others—is that the cultural defence lends itself to stereotypical representations of the non-Western other, and that in these representations, both women and men are diminished. Pascale Fournier talks of a "vulgar use of culture," and cites as one of her illustrations the Canadian case of *R v. Lucien*, heard in 1998.[20] Two men in their early twenties, both originally from Haiti, were convicted of sexually assaulting an eighteen-year-old girl; although the penalty for gang rape normally ranges between four and fourteen

---

[18] Two early examples from the English courts are *R v. Bailey* [1964] CLR 671, and *R v. Byfield* [1967] CLR 378. The first involved the prosecution of a twenty-five-year-old West Indian man for intercourse with two girls aged twelve and fourteen; the second involved the prosecution of a thirty-two-year-old West Indian for sex with a girl aged fourteen. The girls were described in the judgment as either "precocious" or "mature"—a worrying description that represented them as somehow responsible for the course of events—but there was no suggestion of nonconsensual sex in either case. Culture was invoked at the appeal stage to explain why the men might be unaware that their actions were either unusual or unlawful. Bailey's nine-month prison sentence was reduced to a £50 fine, while Byfield was discharged after serving three and a half months of his eighteen-month sentence.

[19] Doriane Lambelet Coleman, "Individualizing Justice through Multiculturalism: The Liberal's Dilemma," *Columbia Law Review* 96, no. 5 (June 1996): 1097. Leti Volppi criticises Coleman in "Talking 'Culture,' Gender, Race, Nation, and the Politics of Multiculturalism," *Columbia Law Review* 96, no. 6 (1996): 1573–617.

[20] Pascale Fournier, "The Ghettoisation of Differences in Canada: 'Rape by Culture' and the Danger of a 'Cultural Defence in Criminal Law Trails," *Manitoba Law Journal* 29 (2002): 88.

years, the men were sentenced to only eighteen months' curfew and community service. Noting their lack of remorse (usually a factor that would bring a more severe penalty), the judge suggested that it arose "from a particular cultural context with regard to relations with women," and described the defendants as "two young roosters craving for sexual pleasure."[21] In this case, the invocation of culture not only meant that a crime against a woman was treated with unusual leniency. It also conveyed what many saw as a racist slur on Haitian men. Complaints were filed against the judge with the Quebec Judicial Council, but the council accepted her claim that "cultural context" meant certain groups of youths—not specifically black or Haitian—and decided not to reprimand her.[22]

Though this is most evident in the point about stereotypical representations of the non-Western other, there is a sense in which all four objections recognise culture as historically changing, open to a variety of interpretations, and internally contested. Between them, they suggest that the use of a cultural defence inappropriately elevates cultural membership above other features, lends itself to opportunistic defences, sustains and legitimates patriarchal practices, and encourages stereotypical representations. Each of these implies that culture is not quite what it is being claimed to be: either that it isn't as important to people's sense of identity as is being argued in the courtroom or that the features of a culture that have been highlighted in the defence reflect not so much objective facts about the culture as some other kind of (perhaps patriarchal, perhaps racist) agenda. They all suggest, that is, a degree of scepticism about what constitutes a culture, and it is partly because of that scepticism that they query the appropriateness of a cultural defence. But where the first three points can be construed as reasons to *disregard* cultural difference (which then, by implication, is presumed to be significant), the last more seriously queries what it means to attribute cultural difference.

I do not accept the argument that employing cultural evidence undermines legal universalism, for I do not accept what seems to be its premise: that culture attaches only to members of minority groups. It would be a harsh legal regime that refused to consider evidence about a defendant's personal circumstances or social background, or declared these irrelevant to understanding intentions and determining an appropriate sentence, and I doubt if there is a legal system in the world that does so. Yet on

---

[21] Ibid., 93.

[22] A parallel case, also discussed by Fournier ("Ghettoisation," 103–8), involved a Muslim man found guilty of sexual misbehaviour—including anal intercourse—with his stepdaughter. He was treated with leniency, partly it seems because he had respected the value that Islam attaches to virginity, and had "spared his victim" from vaginal intercourse. In this case, the sentence was raised on appeal.

my understanding, this kind of evidence is cultural: it is evidence about the kinds of expectations and assumptions an individual brings to a situation, presumably arising from what is considered normal among those with whom she works and lives, and how these might have influenced her acts. Singling out something called cultural evidence as uniquely unacceptable in a courtroom then seems distinctly unfair. It has the effect of denying to minority defendants what is regarded as acceptable practice for those from majority groups, for in allowing only what it considers "decultured" evidence, it privileges those whose assumptions and expectations are so much part of the background that they are no longer perceived as cultural. This makes it easier for majority rather than minority defendants to explain to judges and juries why they behaved the way they did.

The point about opportunism is more telling, precisely because courts *are* better attuned to majority as opposed to minority norms. All defences leave themselves open to opportunism and manipulation. If you are defending yourself against a possible criminal sentence, you will presumably take what opportunities you can to present your acts in the most favourable light, and if citing some cultural practice or tradition promises to help, it's likely that you will choose to do so. But testing out defendants' claims is part of the courts' job, so there is nothing intrinsically troubling about this. The risk as regards minority cultural practices and traditions is that courts may lack the knowledge to assess the evidence and may be too ready to accept what they are told. Ignorance can lead to gullibility, and exaggerated beliefs about cultural difference can lead people to believe the strangest things about how those from other cultures behave. There is a danger, in other words, that cultural claims might not be adequately scrutinised. Though she is generally sympathetic to cultural claims, and mostly stresses the reluctance of the courts to recognise them, Renteln notes that in the *Adesanyo* case, no one took the trouble to establish whether scarification *was* still widely practised in Nigeria or whether the cuts administered to the children had followed an accepted pattern; the claim was simply accepted at face value.[23] In the more troubling *Chen* case, the analysis of contemporary Chinese norms rested on the assessment of one expert witness.

As might be anticipated, I take the third point very seriously, but don't think it can be resolved by determining in advance to favour victims over defendants or women over men. It would be misleading to suggest that the cultural defence is wielded to aid men, never women, or to mitigate male offences against women, and never the other way around. In fact,

[23] Renteln, *The Cultural Defense*, 51.

there are numerous examples of cultural context being taken as significant in interpreting the actions of female defendants, one much-cited U.S. case being that of Fumiko Kimura, a Japanese American woman who tried to drown herself, and succeeded in drowning her two children, after learning of her husband's adultery.[24] At her murder trial in 1985, it was claimed that this constituted a traditional Japanese practice of parent-child suicide (*oyaka-shinju*), that a wife shamed by her husband's adultery might choose suicide as the more honourable course of action, and that she would think it cruel to leave her children to live on without her in conditions of disgrace. The cultural evidence was not used to suggest that the practice was excusable but rather to establish Kimura's mental instability at the time of the offence. She was convicted of voluntary manslaughter, sentenced to one year's imprisonment and five years' probation, and instructed to undergo counselling.[25] Interestingly, in a later case involving a man who killed his three children and tried but failed to kill himself in desperation about his wife's affair (on the face of it, a similar set of circumstances), the cultural evidence held no sway with the court.[26] Unlike Kimura, Quang Ngoc Bui was convicted of murder, and his death sentence was later upheld on appeal. An otherwise-good mother who kills her children in pitiable circumstances can be viewed as mentally unstable and a deserving object of compassion. A man who kills his children is likely to be seen as pitiless and cruel.[27]

In these examples, the question of stereotypes looms large: the stereotyping of culture as a purely minority phenomenon, the stereotyping of what are taken to be the practices of specific cultural groups, and within that, the stereotyping of male and female behaviour. This is what I focus on here, not what seems to me the simpler question about whether the courts have been too generous or resistant to the uses of a cultural defence. I take it as my starting point that any deployment of culture involves a stereotype. The question I ask is not whether it is legitimate to draw on attributes of a culture to explain or mitigate criminal behaviour. My rather irritating answer to this would be largely definitional: that there is no such thing as *a* culture, so how can *it* explain or mitigate anything?

[24] *People v. Kimura*, No A-091133 (Super Ct LA County, 24 April 1985).

[25] This brought the penalty closer to what would have happened in Japan, where attempted parent-child suicide is regarded as a crime, but is usually punished with a rather lenient sentence. See Julia P. Sams, "The Availability of the 'Cultural Defense' as an Excuse for Criminal Behavior," *Georgia Journal of International and Comparative Law* 16 (1986): 343.

[26] *Bui v. State* (Alabama Crim App 1988).

[27] Daina C. Chiu, "The Cultural Defense: Beyond Exclusion, Assimilation, and Guilty Liberalism," *California Law Review* 82, no. 4 (July 1994): 1116–119.

The more compelling question is what kinds of stereotypes get mobilised in a cultural defence?

Stereotypes of Culture: Women

Explaining behaviour through culture is always going to involve stereotypes and simplifications. Witness the enormous simplification in the *Chen* case of "traditional Chinese culture," applied to a country that contains one and a quarter billion people, and has passed through one of the most dramatic and contested political histories of the twentieth century. The important question is which of the many characteristics that lawyers or defendants might think of linking to a particular culture get picked up and mobilised in a cultural account or defence. And related to this, why are the stereotypes of culture being cited, rather than those of gender or class? It is common enough in any courtroom for individuals to be represented by their defence lawyers as weak willed, led astray, or overinfluenced by their peers, and stereotypes already play a large role in this, for it is mostly young people, women, or those with fewer educational qualifications who are described in this way. But it is mainly when people can also be identified as coming from a minority culture that culture is offered as an additional explanation. Individuals from minority groups are regularly presented as defined by and definitive of their culture, to the point where even the most aberrant can serve as typical products of their culture's norms. In his judgment in the *Chen* case, Judge Pincus described Chen as "the product of his culture."[28] The individual was read from the culture, and the culture from the individual in turn.

Men and women fare rather differently in this. Culture tends to be invoked for men to explain a heightened sense of sexual outrage, a heightened sense of having been betrayed by a woman (who might be a sister, wife, daughter, or cousin) whose illicit sexual behaviour is said to have brought disgrace on the family name. Culture tends to be invoked for women to explain an unusual level of passivity, a submissiveness to male dictates, family or community expectations, or simply what is perceived as fate. In what has been described as one of the best illustrations from the English courts of a successful cultural defence, Bashir Begum Bibi had a three-year prison sentence reduced to six months because of her presumed submissiveness.[29] Bibi was a widow, living with her brother-in-law, and had been sentenced along with him for her role in importing cannabis

[28] Cited in Chiu, "The Cultural Defense," 1053.
[29] Sebastian Poulter, "The Significance of Ethnic Minority Customs and Traditions in English Criminal Law," *New Community* 16, no. 1 (1989): 122.

from Kenya. She was initially sentenced to three years' imprisonment, and her brother-in-law was sentenced to three and a half. Reviewing the similarity in the sentences in 1980, the Court of Appeal noted that the social enquiry report on Bibi had described her as totally dependent on her brother-in-law for support and socially isolated by her poor English. It suggested, moreover, that she was so thoroughly socialised into subservience that it was hard to consider her as an autonomous actor. "It is apparent that she is well socialised into the Muslim traditions and as such has a role subservient to any male figures around her. . . . Because she has assumed the traditional role of her culture any involvement in these offences is likely to be the result of being told what to do and the learned need to comply. . . . In the light of that history, it would not be safe to credit her with the same independence of mind and action as most women today enjoy."[30] The Court of Appeal reduced her sentence to six months.

The suggestion that Bibi could not be credited with "the same independence of mind and action as most women today enjoy" goes considerably beyond her level of complicity in the drugs offence towards a general denial of her status as an autonomous agent. However appropriate the judgment (correct, in my view), it still gives cause for concern that it drew on stereotypical notions of "the Muslim traditions" and "the traditional role of her culture." It also gives cause for concern that this kind of defence can differentiate so sharply between women who conform to prevailing images of female subservience and those who in some way deviate from this norm.

The case of Kiranjit Ahluwalia is particularly revealing here because it illustrates both sides of this divide. Kiranjit Ahluwalia had been persuaded by her brothers into an arranged marriage, which turned into a nightmare of violence, social control, and sexual abuse within days of the wedding. Two court injunctions failed to stop her husband's attacks on her, her family was unwilling to support her in leaving him, and after ten years of abuse and two attempts at suicide, she set fire to her husband's bed while he was sleeping in it. He died ten days later of the injuries. In the initial trial (where Ahluwalia decided not to give evidence in person), the judge's directions to the jury tended to minimise any cultural considerations. He reminded the jury that the marriage had been an arranged one, but noted that this "may have been the custom"; he observed that Ahluwalia's mother-in-law had advised her to separate from her husband if she did not like him, and commented that "if it was really as bad as all that, it may have been the best thing to do."[31] There was little acknowledg-

---

[30] *R v. Bibi* [1980] 1 WLR 1193.

[31] *R v. Kiranjit Ahluwalia*, unreported case (Lewes Crown Court, December 1989) (transcript: Hibbit and Sanders).

ment in this of the difficulties many Asian women have spoken of in exiting from an arranged marriage into a community or extended family that regards women as responsible for the family honour. In one revealing comment, the judge advised the jury that "the only characteristic of the defendant about which you know specifically that might be relevant are that she is an Asian woman, married, incidentally to an Asian man, the deceased living in this country. You may think she is an educated woman, she has a university degree. If you find these characteristics relevant to your considerations, of course you will bear that in mind." The only meaning I can give to this is that the jury might think she was more trapped in her marriage and less responsible for her actions because she was an Asian woman, but might (and perhaps should) see this as cancelled out by the fact that she had a university degree.

Ahluwalia's case became a cause célèbre in Britain, taken up by groups such as Southall Black Sisters and Justice for Women, and widely cited as a miscarriage of justice. Three years later, an appeal court overturned the murder conviction, largely on the grounds that the original directions to the jury had ignored medical evidence that indicated that the defendant was suffering from a major depressive disorder. At the retrial, Kiranjit Ahluwalia was found guilty of manslaughter due to diminished responsibility; having by then served the reduced sentence, she was released from prison. This time around, the judgment stressed her vulnerability, describing her as physically slight, as having suffered many years of abuse from the onset of her marriage, and trying to hold her marriage together because of her (by implication, culturally specific) "sense of duty as a wife."[32] It represented her, in other words, more as a passive victim of events, a Bibi-like figure who could not be regarded as fully responsible for her acts.[33] This contrasts with the message implied in the original direction: that were Kiranjit Alhuwalia the typical victim of an abusive arranged marriage, the jury might be inclined to see her as someone driven to desperate measures, but since she was an educated woman, they probably shouldn't give this much weight. It seems that culture becomes available to female defendants when they can be shown to conform to images of the subservient non-Western wife. When they deviate in some way from that stereotype, they cannot so easily figure as emblems of culture.

This last has been tellingly demonstrated in the case of Zoora Shah, who was convicted in 1992 of the murder of Mohammed Azam and sen-

---

[32] *R v. Ahluwalia* [1992] 4 All ER 889.

[33] Drawing on the appeal case rather than the initial trial, Matthew Rowlinson stresses how Ahluwalia's intentionality was effaced; "Re-Reading Criminal Law: Gendering the Mental Element," in *Feminist Perspectives on Criminal Law*, ed. Donald Nicolson and Lois Bibbings (London: Cavendish, 2000), 114–16.

tenced to serve twenty years. (This is an unusually long sentence for the English courts.) At the initial trial, the prosecution had presented Shah as voluntarily involved in sexual relationships with at least two married men, seeking to secure from the first of these, Azam, the title deeds of the house she lived in (bought in his name, but in fact paid for with her money), conspiring with a second lover to forge Azam's name to a transfer of ownership, paying a hit man to kill Azam, and when this came to nothing, poisoning him with arsenic. Shah gave no evidence in court, but denied the charges against her. Her case, too, was taken up by Southall Black Sisters, which drew up a statement based on months of interviews in which Shah told of being abandoned by an abusive husband, befriended by Azam, a heroin dealer, who had beaten and raped her and forced her into prostitution, and finally putting a powder in his food when he began to take a sexual interest in her twelve-year-old daughter. The Court of Appeal reviewed the case in 1998, but the judges refused to order a retrial.[34] They argued that the fresh evidence was inadmissible because Shah had provided no reasonable explanation as to why she had not told this story before, or why she had confided in no one through what she now claimed to be years of physical and sexual abuse. Shah, like Bibi, spoke little English. Like Bibi, she had been "socialised into Muslim traditions." But the cultural stereotypes were not available to her, presumably because of her failure to conform to the images of the submissive South Asian woman—her failure, as Anne Carline puts it, to conform to the recognised gender and racial scripts.[35]

In considering whether to admit the new evidence, the judges accepted "up to a point," "the importance of honour in the society from which the defendant springs," and the particular difficulties a woman like Zoora Shah might have faced in making public a history of sexual abuse—but only up to a point, "because the appellant, as it seems to us, is an unusual woman. Her way of life had been such that there might not have been much left of her honour to salvage, and she was certainly capable of striking out on her own when she thought it advisable to do so, even if it might be thought to bring shame on her or to expose her to risk of retaliation." Honour, by implication, attaches to the sexually chaste or the dutiful wife, while those exhibiting a capacity for action cannot hope to be believed when they say they were constrained by shame or fear. The fact that one of her daughters described her as a "strong-willed woman" also seems to have told against her. A woman cannot, it seems, be both strong willed and abused by others; she has to be either the helpless victim wronged by

---

[34] *R v. Zoora Ghulam Shah* (Court of Appeal, April 1998) (transcript: Smith Bernal).

[35] Anne Carline, "Zoora Shah: 'An Unusual Woman,'" *Social and Legal Studies* 14, no. 2 (2005): 215–38.

others or capable of wrongdoing herself. Cultural issues were therefore raised in the case of Shah but not seriously addressed, and one is left, again, with a sense that culture can only be recognised as relevant when women conform to particular stereotypes. A woman portrayed as entirely under the control of male family members may draw on beliefs about non-Western cultures to make a claim for diminished responsibility, but if she is sullied by past sexual encounters or overqualified by virtue of a degree, she no longer fits the prevailing image. There is little room here for the complexity of most individuals' lives.

Renteln provides a further example from the U.S. courts, *US v. Ezeiruaku and Akiagba* (1995). This case involved a woman convicted for her role in a heroin operation who later sought a reduced sentence, claiming that she had been subject to physical and psychological abuse by her husband. The case therefore had many similarities with *R v. Bibi*, with a cultural expert testifying that in Igbo culture, the man is likely to play the dominant role, but the judgment was closer to that in *R v. Shah*. The court rejected the appeal, noting that "by the age of twenty-five, she had defied both her father and her cultural upbringing by becoming pregnant out of wedlock, had moved to a foreign country with her first husband, defied that husband and moved out on her own, obtained a job, and then remarried, and defied that husband by having an affair. These are hardly the earmarks of a dependent and easily manipulated woman."[36] It is, of course, the job of the courts to test out defendants' claims, and I am not in a position to say whether their assessment in this instance was correct. But what stands out is the inability to consider someone in cultural terms once she has broken with what are assumed to be core conventions of her culture. In this case, a pregnancy out of wedlock is taken as evidence that she has "defied her cultural upbringing." From that point onwards, it becomes less possible for the courts to think of her as subject to cultural influences, and less possible for her to play the culture card.

Stereotypes of Culture: Men

The cases discussed above do not add up to an exhaustive study, yet they suggest that culture is allowed or disallowed for women depending on their conformity to cultural stereotypes, leading not only to an inconsistency of treatment between different cases but to a perpetuation of these stereotypes. The pattern for men is rather different. When culture is invoked for male defendants, it is often in relation to crimes of violence against women: to explain a particularly violent reaction to the discovery

[36] Renteln, *The Cultural Defense*, 89.

of marital infidelity, an especially violent reaction to a daughter choosing her own boyfriend, or an intense perception of the disgrace brought on the family name by the sexual behaviour of a female family member. The cultural stereotype here is of a man driven by an unusually strong conviction that women who have extramarital or premarital sex have disgraced the honour of their family. The conviction itself is a common enough one across many societies, so culture figures here mainly as a way of accounting for extreme versions. In terms of honour killings, it is also employed to explain why a man might kill not just a girlfriend or wife (again, regarded as a common enough phenomenon, not needing the explanatory addition of culture) but a daughter, cousin, or sister.

The most notable example from the English courts is the case of Shabir Hussain, who was convicted in 1995 of murdering his sister-in-law, Tasleem Begum, after driving into her while she waited on the pavement for her lover and then reversing the car over her body. At the initial trial, Hussain denied his involvement, so there was no question of him submitting a plea of provocation based on either culture or religion. He was convicted of murder and sentenced to life imprisonment. Hussain successfully appealed against this conviction on the grounds of false identification,[37] and at his retrial in 1998, introduced a plea of guilty to manslaughter by reason of provocation. The provocation was hardly one that would have stood up were it not for cultural factors: all that Begum had done was to default on a marriage arranged for her in Pakistan when she was sixteen, refuse to sign the documents that would have enabled her husband to get a UK entry visa, and later embark on an affair with a married man. In his judgment, however, the judge acknowledged that her illicit affair "would be deeply offensive to someone with your background and your religious beliefs," and sentenced Hussain "on the basis that something blew up in your head that caused you a complete and sudden loss of self-control."[38] Hussain's original life sentence was cut to six and a half years.

The case clearly raises the spectre of culture being invoked to explain and minimise violent crimes against women. It also returns us to one of the earlier questions, about whether intensely held religious convictions should be treated differently from intensely held political convictions, or whether culture should be elevated above other concerns. One might imagine a parallel case in which a member of a white racist organisation claimed that he found it deeply offensive to see his sister with a black lover, and that something blew up in his head that caused a complete and

---

[37] *R v. Shabir Hussain* [1997] EWCA Crim 2876.

[38] *R v. Shabir Hussain* (Newcastle Crown Court, 28 July 1998) (transcript: J. L.Harpham Ltd.).

sudden loss of self-control. There have been occasions in the not-too-distant past when that would have been regarded as a legitimate enough claim—but it is hard to imagine any court today accepting this as provocation. One reason for the difference is that there is legislation against racism, but no law (of course, rightly so) against thinking premarital sex a sin. Critics of multiculturalism might also say it is because a public discourse of cultural pluralism gives credence to claims about culture or religion in a way that no longer holds for race.

My own reading of the *Hussain* case is that it was exceptional, in part reflecting the prosecution's anxiety about securing any conviction after the initial murder conviction had been overturned on appeal. Once the prosecution had accepted the plea of guilty to manslaughter (that is, decided not to continue trying to establish the case for murder but to settle for the lesser charge), the final sentence was more or less predictable. Six and a half years is not much out of line with the normal punishment for manslaughter of seven to eight years; the judge explicitly stated that he saw the case as falling towards the top end of the sentencing bracket, and the minor mitigation was mainly because the defendant had (eventually) pleaded guilty. The case remains a troubling illustration of the dangers of a cultural defence, but later courts have not been particularly receptive to provocation pleas based on intensely held religious beliefs about premarital and adulterous sex, or cultural understandings of honour and shame. To my knowledge, there has been no subsequent case in the English, Welsh, or Scottish courts where a man killing a woman has successfully invoked culture to get a murder charge reduced to the lesser one of manslaughter. Research across the rest of Europe suggests that there, too, the courts have retained a robust sense of the dangers of cultural defence. This seems further confirmed in Renteln's survey of U.S. practice.

I do not, in other words, see much evidence that something called multiculturalism is encouraging the courts to let men from minority cultural groups off the hook for acts of violence against women. Yet I do think, along with many feminists, that the courts have been too ready to regard violence (in both majority and minority cultural groups) as an understandable male response to women who sleep with other men, sleep with other women, or just refuse to continue their relationship with the defendant. In my reading, the issue for the coming years will not be the mitigating use of culture (leading to reduced sentences) but its explanatory role. Courts will, on the whole, reject what they see as the illegitimate use of culture to justify a more lenient treatment of defendants from minority ethnocultural groups in cases involving violence against the person. They may nonetheless accept and reproduce the idea that these defendants were driven by their culture. In doing so, they will represent minority and non-Western cultures as condoning extreme levels of violence against women, and represent members of minority and/or non-Western cultures as less than autonomous beings.

The stereotyping—rather than the legal outcomes—then becomes the more pressing concern. Consider two further cases from the English courts. In a case tried in Manchester in 2002, Faqir Mohammed was charged with the murder of his twenty-four-year-old daughter, who he had stabbed to death after discovering her (fully clothed) boyfriend in her bedroom. As part of a provocation plea, the defence counsel invoked Mohammed's strongly held beliefs that a daughter should not have a boyfriend without her father's consent and that sex outside of marriage was a sin—argued, that is, that this was a man driven by cultural norms and expectations. It became clear, however, that he was also a man with a long history of physical violence against his wife and children, and six of his remaining children testified to this effect. In summing up, the judge instructed jury members to take Mohammed's "strongly held religious and cultural beliefs" into account, along with evidence of depression after his wife's death. But he also warned jury members that a man "may not rely on his own violent disposition, by way of excuse," instructing them to weigh the depression and religious beliefs against the evidence of this disposition. The jury rapidly came to the conclusion that Mohammed was guilty of murder, and he was sentenced to life imprisonment.[39]

In a similar case heard in London in 2003, Abdullah Yones killed his sixteen-year-old daughter, who had begun a relationship with a Lebanese Christian (Yones was an Iraqi Kurd) and was planning to leave home. In this case, the father pleaded guilty to murder, so there was no question of invoking culture or religion to mitigate his behaviour. In sentencing him to life imprisonment, however, the judge described it as a tragic case of the "irreconcilable cultural difficulties between traditional Kurdish values and the values of Western society."[40] Yet here, too, there was evidence that the father had been physically violent to his daughter over a long period. In this case, moreover, the defendant's identity was more tightly bound up with his political beliefs (he was a communist and a political refugee) than his rather understated religion or culture. It was misleading under such circumstances to cite "traditional Kurdish values" as leading the father to kill his daughter. Like the earlier case, this involved a man with a greater-than-normal disposition to violence—more possibly linked to the horrors of his political experiences rather than anything specifically religious or cultural.

[39] *R v. Faqir Mohammed* (Manchester Crown Court, 18 Feb 2002) (transcript: Cater Walsh and Co.).

[40] *R v. Abdulla M. Yones* (Central Criminal Court, 27 September 2003) (transcript: Smith Bernal).

That cultural norms vary goes without saying, as does the fact that these variations will often involve different attitudes towards sex, marriage, family, or honour. But the move from disapproval to violence is *not* dictated by culture, and explaining why some people—but not others— make this move typically involves a more particularised account of the individuals concerned. On the whole, the courts have proved relatively adept in making this distinction. But a multiculturalism that encourages us to regard extreme acts of violence against women as cultural phenomena can promote the belief that it is normal in certain non-Western cultures to kill young women for engaging in premarital sex. It may also promote the (mainly false) belief that non-Western jurisdictions officially sanction such murders.[41] The question here is why culture? Why are certain kinds of phenomena regarded as cultural but not others? What is the basis for the distinction between cultural and noncultural cases? Under what circumstances do people describe a defence as a cultural defence?

Why Culture?

This question underpins much of Leti Volpp's work. Commenting on U.S. cases involving underage sex or underage marriage, Volpp notes that culture is invoked in a highly selective way, such that virtually identical misdemeanours by white North Americans and nonwhite immigrants get attributed to culture only when the defendants come from a racialised minority group.[42] In one of her examples, Texan police and child welfare officials launched a massive search for a pregnant runaway—believed at that point to be only ten years old—and her boyfriend. When the couple was located, the girl was placed in a foster home and her twenty-two-year-old boyfriend was sent to a maximum-security facility, charged with the aggravated sexual assault of a child. The charges were dropped when it emerged that the girl was fourteen, above the age of consent for sexual intercourse under Texan law, and a family court judge ruled that the couple had a valid common-law marriage. In this case, both parties were of Mexican origin, and the events were widely discussed in the press as an illustration of the collision of cultures (the same trope that appeared above in the *Yones* case). It was assumed in these discussions, and indeed argued in the courts, that marriage between an adolescent girl and older

---

[41] For an excellent discussion of the way various legal systems address "crimes of honour," see Lynn Welchman and Sara Hossain, *"Honour": Crimes, Paradigms, and Violence against Women* (London: Zed Books, 2005).

[42] Leti Volpp, "Blaming Culture for Bad Behavior," *Yale Journal of Law and the Humanities* 12 (2000): 89–116.

man was a reflection of Mexican culture. Yet in a similar case in Maryland, where a thirteen-year-old white girl married a twenty-nine-year-old white man, none of the media debate and public outcry made any reference to the marriage as a cultural phenomenon. There was no suggestion that the one should be condoned because of culture and the other criticised; the examples raise no particular issue in that respect. The point is that what was attributed to an entire culture in the first case was treated as an individual aberration in the second. Volpp concludes that "behavior that causes discomfort—that we consider "bad"—is conceptualized only as culturally canonical for cultures assumed to lag behind the United States."[43] This conceptualisation clearly lends itself to abuse by expert witnesses who might then employ it to justify the ill-treatment of women. But almost equally damaging is the way it represents individuals from the lagging cultural groups, *mis*representing their cultures and *mis*representing the individuals as less than autonomous beings.

In a recent policing initiative, the London Metropolitan Police has tried to differentiate "honour-based violence" from other forms of familial or domestic violence, arguing that the former is tacitly condoned by the communities to which both the victims and perpetrators belong, and unlike "crimes of passion," usually involves a planned restoration of honour. The categorisation does not, however, fit all the cases that have come to court in the United Kingdom, where there is often little evidence of premeditation, and where neighbours and other family members typically express horror at the violence.[44] There *are* cases where "bounty–hunters"—people employed by the family to track down and kill someone thought to have disgraced the family—are known or believed to be involved. The best-known case is that of "Jack and Zena Briggs," who went into hiding in the early 1990s to escape bounty hunters employed by Zena's family after she fled an arranged marriage to be with her white boyfriend. The two were still concealing their identities twelve years later in order to protect their lives. This case clearly fits the profile suggested by the London Metropolitan Police.[45] The (also famous) case of Rukhsana Naz, killed by her brother and mother after leaving an arranged marriage

---

[43] Ibid., 96.

[44] Purna Sen argues that the statistics may be misleading, for a premeditated killing may be represented by the defence team as committed in a fit of fury because this provides a partial defence. See Purna Sen, "'Crimes of Honour': Value and Meaning," in *"Honour": Crimes, Paradigms, and Violence against Women*, ed. Lynn Welchman and Sara Hossain (London: Zed Books, 2005), 51.

[45] Speaking at the Honour-Based Violence conference organized by the London Metropolitan Police, the New Scotland Yard, and the Home Office Police Standards Unit in March 2005, Jack stressed the importance of understanding the mind-set of their pursuers: "They think that they are justified and are correcting a wrong."

and becoming pregnant by another man, could be described as a planned restoration of honour—although there is no evidence that this particularly horrific killing was condoned by anyone other than the perpetrators. Other cases show little evidence of premeditation; there was no indication of this, for example, when Hussain drove his car at his sister-in-law, or when Mohammed and Yones killed their daughters. The really distinctive characteristic of the cases described as honour killings is not that they are premeditated or condoned by a minority cultural community but that men kill what they view as sexually wayward sisters, cousins, or daughters. In the noncultural (normal?) cases, the more typical pattern is a man killing his ex-lover or wife.[46]

The belief that the class of legitimately incensed males extends beyond that of lovers or spouse constitutes an important—and cultural—difference, but is dwarfed by the common pattern of violence towards women suspected of some sexual misdemeanour or threatening to leave. Male violence towards women is not a minority practice. Or rather, it is, in that most men do not kill the women they feel have betrayed or let them down, but it is in no way confined to minority ethnic groups. In the United Kingdom, an average of two women are killed each week by current or ex-boyfriends, partners, or spouses, often because of some suspected sexual misdemeanour or because they have chosen to end the relationship. Statistics from other countries tell a similar tale. The majority of these killings are carried out by men from majority cultural groups, some of whom will invoke the provocation of an unfaithful or nagging wife to secure the lesser conviction of manslaughter.[47] These cases involve shared cultural assumptions about normal wifely behaviour, but do not present these in explicitly cultural terms.[48]

The crimes are not peculiar to cultural minorities, and there is an important sense in which this is also true of the defences employed in the

[46] Lama Abu-Odeh makes a similar point in "Comparatively Speaking: The 'Honour' of the East and the 'Passion' of the West," *Utah Law Review* (1997): 287–307. "In the Arab world, unlike in the United States, it is mostly 'daughters' and 'sisters' that are getting killed" (291).

[47] Recent examples, taken from the Web site (http://www.jfw.org.uk/) of Justice for Women, a London-based group campaigning against discrimination in the legal system, include Joseph Swinburne, who killed his wife in 1997 by stabbing her eleven times when she told him she was leaving him for another man. He was convicted of manslaughter and sentenced to two hundred hours of community service. In 2001, John Betambeau was placed on probation after killing his wife. When she criticised the way he carved the Sunday joint of beef, it was just too much and he "snapped." In 2002, David Cummergen strangled his wife during a fight about cancelling a holiday and tried to conceal the murder by telling police that she had drowned herself in a bowl of water. He was convicted of manslaughter by reason of provocation and given a two-year prison sentence, suspended for two years.

[48] Aileen McColgan, "General Defences," in *Feminist Perspectives on Criminal Law*, ed. Donald Nicolson and Lois Bibbings (London: Cavendish, 2000).

courtroom. When the so-called cultural defence works (as noted above, not that often), it does so because it draws on attitudes that are widely assumed in cases involving individuals from the majority or hegemonic culture. Commenting on cases in the United States, Daina Chiu suggests that the U.S. courts only recognise cultural factors when these resonate with mainstream American norms.[49] So Chen got off lightly for killing an adulterous wife, but perhaps less because the court wanted to demonstrate its sensitivity to Chinese culture and more because the anger of a wronged husband—the idea that it is natural for a man to explode into uncontrollable anger when he hears that his wife has betrayed him—is standard fare in the U.S. courts. When Moua expressed his surprise that the woman who resisted his sexual advances really meant it, his incomprehension resonated with widely shared beliefs in American culture about women saying no when they really mean yes. The public sympathy for Kimura perhaps depended less on her Japanese background and more on a widespread American perception that to live with the knowledge that you have killed your children is the worst punishment any woman can face.

The suggestion here is that cultural evidence works best when it enables judges and juries to fit the defendant's actions into a pattern already familiar through mainstream culture; that in the end, it is the sameness not the difference that matters. Invocations of culture are themselves pretty clearly gendered. They convey for women a particular stereotype of passivity and for men a meaningful context for violent actions, and are then likely to figure for men in diminishing the severity of their actions and for women in diminishing who they are. This gendering of cultural expectations resonates with a wider gendering of criminal responsibility that can leave women defendants with no option but to establish their mental impairment, while allowing men the additional recourse to provocation or self-defence. The content of the defences also draws on established norms of gendered behaviour: in Moua's case, the belief that many women make a play of resisting men's sexual advances; and in Chen's, that violence is a normal male reaction when faced with an unfaithful wife. As Sarah Song argues, cultural defence arguments are given credibility not because they are foreign but because they are familiar to the majority culture.[50] It is when culture echoes gender norms in the wider society

[49] Chiu, "The Cultural Defense."

[50] Song, "Majority Norms, Multiculturalism, and Gender Equality." In her analysis of the *Moua* and *Chen* cases, for example, she notes that most U.S. states still admit a "mistake of fact" defence in rape cases, allowing men to claim that they "reasonably" mistook their victim's resistance as consent, and that courts consistently accept provocation claims in murder cases, allowing men to present not only adultery but even filing a restraining order or just threatening to leave the relationship as a provocative act of betrayal.

or gendered practices in the law as a whole that it is most likely to be recognised as an excuse.

Culture operates on a terrain already defined by mainstream assumptions: the idea that women are not really responsible for actions undertaken under the direction of male family members, or that men explode into rage when they discover their women involved in illicit affairs. References to the defendant's cultural background serve mainly to ratchet up the characteristic in question. Thus, Bibi was credited with little independence of mind and action, and was said to be different from the average woman in this; Hussain killed under circumstances that might cause other men to shout and swear. But Bibi's subservience only made sense because it resonated with what has been perceived as a general female characteristic, while Hussain's violence towards his sister-in-law fell within a recognisable spectrum of male behaviour. By contrast, neither Shah nor (in her first trial) Ahluwalia fitted the prevailing images of the vulnerable woman—the first because she was strong willed and had lived too long in a criminal subculture, and the second because she was overqualified. In some ways, it seems a misrepresentation to treat any of these as cultural cases. What we see are pretty standard conventions of gender difference, given an added twist or intensity through what are perceived as cultural codes.

This suggests that the difficulties that arise in the use of cultural evidence are best understood as part of a wider pattern. It is largely when mainstream culture itself promotes a gendered understanding of agency and responsibility—as when it perceives men as understandably incensed by the sexual waywardness of their women or women as less responsible for their actions because of the influence of men—that references to cultural context have proved effective. If so, then it is not the use of cultural evidence per se that is peculiarly gendered. It is not that this has unusually dire consequences for women and ought on that basis to be curtailed. Such a position would imply that gender inequities enter only at the moment when a minority cultural context is invoked, that the default position already secures the equal treatment of women, and that this is only threatened when culture is allowed to intrude. Pleasing as this might be, it hardly fits with a large body of literature in feminist legal theory, and is certainly at odds with (government as well as academic) concerns about the legal treatment of rape and male violence against women.

Cultural arguments work when they enable judges and juries to fit what might otherwise be deemed extreme or incomprehensible behaviour into familiar patterns. Chiu puts it thus: "The jury will process evidence about another seemingly foreign and different culture only to the extent that the jury can relate to it and understand it. Thus, where the jury finds common ground with the defendant, its deliberation and verdict become an exercise in recognizing cultural sameness, not difference."[51] She takes this as a criticism—that what looks like an accommodation of difference is in truth a reimposition of sameness—but I am inclined to think this is the best one can hope for in the context of a court. The implication, however, is that when the outcome of the process is judgments that favour men over women or defendants over victims, the reasons will lie in the dominant rather than minority culture. It is not the introduction of cultural evidence per se that generates problems in the equitable treatment of women, for such evidence only has the desired effect when it resonates with mainstream conventions. Some of these will be mainstream understandings of non-Western culture, as exemplified in the perception of Asian women as passive and subservient to men. Others will be mainstream conventions about masculine behaviour, as in the readiness to accept that men are provoked beyond reason by a woman's sexual betrayal. In either case, the problem lies as much with the gendered conventions of the dominant culture as with the introduction of a cultural defence.

This cannot be resolved by eliminating culture (which in this context is always understood as minority culture) from the courtroom, for this would unfairly discriminate between defendants from majority and minority cultures, permitting only the first to give full details of their individual circumstances and background. Moreover, it would promote the misleading notion that patriarchal norms characterise only minority cultures and thereby encourage a false complacency about majority gender norms. The more helpful move is to recognise that culture is a stereotype, just like gender or class, a rough generalisation that can be a useful way of condensing information, but should never be mistaken for the truth. Understanding a defendant's cultural and class background, and the gendered roles and expectations associated with these, will continue to be relevant to many legal cases, and only a thoroughly difference-blind system of justice would refuse to consider information on these. But no one these days would think much information was being provided by the observation that the defendant is a woman or that she is working class; most would expect a more nuanced story that blended specific experiences of gender and class to make sense of an individual history.

I cannot imagine a legal system that dispenses with stereotypes, but I can imagine one that recognises the pitfalls of its own generalisations, and employs them with the necessary care. Though the process is far from complete, many legal systems are already moving in this direction in regard to stereotypes of gender and class—that is, they are able to see class and gender as relevant without in the process assuming that all women

---

[51] Chiu, "The Cultural Defense," 1114.

are subject to identical influences and pressures, or that much can be concluded from the large generalisations of middle or working class. With culture, by contrast, there is still a willingness to accept all-encompassing notions—as when a judge describes the murder of Heshu Yones as a tragic case of the "irreconcilable cultural difficulties between traditional Kurdish values and the values of Western society," or when people feel they have explained some otherwise-mysterious behaviour by the fact that the person involved is Moroccan, Muslim, or Chinese. Culture talk today—far more so than gender or class talk—still suffers from the kind of fixity now routinely criticised by anthropologists. It is this, in my view, that is becoming the main problem with the cultural defence, rather than the fact that cultural background has come to be regarded as a relevant consideration in judging how responsible defendants are for their actions, or even that men are getting away with murder. Some are, but not as many as had been feared, and certainly not as many as already get away with murder by reference to mainstream gender norms. The difficulty with a cultural defence is that it mobilises culture in ways that encourage absurdly large generalisations about people from particular cultural groups. If it could be mobilised in the more nuanced way that has come to be available in relation to gender or class, this would be a major advance.

CHAPTER FOUR

Autonomy, Coercion, and Constraint

THE LITERATURE ON CULTURAL DEFENCE refers primarily to criminal cases, the central question being whether multiculturalism requires courts to assess defendants' actions differently depending on their cultural background. Though the immediate issue is whether culture becomes an excuse for violence against women, I have argued that there are equally pressing concerns around the use of cultural stereotypes and the tendency to misrepresent minority defendants as less than autonomous beings. I turn here to what could be described as the civil counterpart. Arguments both for and against policies of multicultural accommodation often turn out to depend on representing individuals from minority cultural groups as lacking in autonomy, or at least as lacking in the kind of autonomy that has come to be regarded as normal among individuals from majority cultural groups. For example, one common argument for multicultural accommodation rests on the notion that membership in a cultural or religious group is involuntary, and yet significantly curtails an individual's room to manoeuvre. This being so, it is claimed, it is discriminatory to require members of minority groups to abide by rules and regulations that were dreamt up with members of the majority group in mind: to require Sikhs as well as non-Sikhs to wear crash helmets when riding a bike; to tell Sikhs, Jews, and Muslims (as well as Christians, agnostics, and atheists) that they must remove their head coverings in a courtroom; or to tell Muslim schoolgirls that it is not school practice to wear a headscarf in class. These arguments generally turn on people being less able to comply because of their membership in a particular cultural or religious group. They therefore turn on people being constrained by their culture.

A similar presumption often appears in arguments *against* multicultural accommodation. For example, when politicians announce that banning the hijab in schools will help Muslim schoolgirls because it will protect them from the undue pressures of their religion and culture, they also treat culture as something that incapacitates people, something that makes it difficult, even impossible, for individuals to act in a different way. This approach to culture encourages one particularly pernicious policy development: the imposition of *blanket prohibitions* on practices like covering one's head in school or marrying an overseas spouse. It is sometimes offered as a partial justification of these prohibitions that the bans will protect young women from cultural pressures that force them to wear the hijab or coerce them into unwanted marriages. The implication is that none of the young women in question would have freely chosen to behave in this way, that they are all being coerced by their community or prevented by their culture from operating as autonomous beings. Banning headscarves in schools or imposing age limits for living with an overseas spouse can be regarded almost as the antithesis of multiculturalism; certainly, these are not policies that offer much in the way of accommodation. This makes it even more striking that they share with some of the arguments *for* multiculturalism the notion that cultures operate as constraints.

I argue here against a determinist understanding of culture that represents individuals from minority or non-Western cultural groups as controlled by cultural rules, and suggest that some of the problems that currently arise around autonomy would be less pressing if we could think of the influences of culture more in the ways that people have come to think of the influences of gender or class. In the process, I offer a partial answer to the question of what changes in multiculturalism when we dispense with strong notions of culture. The biggest difference, I suggest, comes with those issues where the accommodation of cultural and/or religious difference seems to be at odds with gender equality, and the especially challenging subset of these where it is the women themselves who are claiming the accommodation. I argue that refusing the determinist understanding of culture—recognising women as agents—will sometimes commit us to policies that are more multicultural rather than less.

Autonomy

Before embarking on the ways in which autonomy figures in the literature on multiculturalism, let me start by saying something about how I am using the term. I take autonomy as the capacity to reflect on and, within the limits of our circumstances, either endorse or change the way we act or live—thus, in some significant sense, to make our actions and choices our *own*. That is, I follow Marilyn Friedman's formulation: "Autonomy involves choosing and living according to standards or values that are, in some plausible sense, one's 'own.'"[1] This is a modest formulation in two respects. First, it only claims that in "some significant" or "some plausible" sense we make the decision our own. None of our choices can be said to come untouched out of some inner essence that is our self, for who

---

[1] Marilyn Friedman, "Autonomy, Social Disruption, and Women," in *Relational Autonomy: Feminist Perspectives on Autonomy, Agency, and the Social Self*, ed. Catriona MacKenzie and Natalie Stoljar (New York: Oxford University Press, 2000), 37.

we are is formed out of a complex of relationships, and what we know (the basis on which we make our choices and judgments) derives from what others can tell us as well as what we have experienced ourselves. Everyone is influenced by those around them, and the line between passive acceptance of what one has learnt to be the norm and making a choice of one's own is inevitably cloudy.

The other way in which this is a modest definition is that it is deliberately content neutral, saying nothing about the nature of the choices, only that they must in some plausible sense be one's own. Mary might choose to cut herself off from her family because she feels they stop her from doing what she wants and keep imposing their ideas of who she is and what she should ought to become. Jimmy might make the opposite set of choices, deciding to give up on his separate life ambitions and dedicate himself to making his parents happy. (An unlikely gender transposition.) In terms of the definition, both these rather extreme choices would qualify as autonomous—though both look risky in terms of psychological health—for even a choice that involves relinquishing future opportunities should still count as a choice. As Diana Tietjens Meyers puts it, "Autonomy must dwell in the process of deciding, not in the nature of the action decided upon."[2] Some have found this unsatisfactory, and there is a specifically feminist argument that sees the content-neutral approach as failing to address the impact of oppressive norms of femininity and the adaptive preferences generated by these.[3] The worry about this is that it is open to cultural distortion, for what each of us defines as an oppressive norm will almost certainly reflect our cultural context.

In the multicultural literature, autonomy has figured in a perplexing variety of ways. One way it enters debate is when people argue that the importance commonly attached to individuals being able to act autonomously reflects a specific set of (usually Western) values. They then criticise liberal societies for seeking to impose one version of the good life as the norm. Spokesmen for minority communities sometimes make a case along these lines, particularly when taking issue with what they regard as an excessive focus on individual rights and freedoms, and a correspondingly inadequate concern with the group. The idea that the autonomous self might be specific to Western ways of thinking also gets some support in the academic literature. In a 1974 essay, Clifford Geertz described as "Western" the conception of the person "as a bounded, unique, more or

---

[2] Diana Tietjens Meyers, "Feminism and Women's Autonomy: The Challenge of Female Genital Cutting," *Metaphilosophy* 31, no. 5 (2000): 470.

[3] Natalie Stoljar, "Autonomy and the Feminist Intuition," in *Relational Autonomy: Feminist Perspectives on Autonomy, Agency, and the Social Self*, ed. Catriona MacKenzie and Natalie Stoljar (New York: Oxford University Press, 2000).

less integrated motivational and cognitive universe, a dynamic center of awareness, emotion, judgment, and action," and suggested that this was "a rather peculiar idea within the context of the world's cultures."[4] Following Louis Dumont's work on the caste system in India, numerous anthropologists have drawn a contrast between the "egocentric" Western self—supposedly characterised by a clear differentiation between self and other, a capacity to reflect critically on values and projects, and a strong sense of independence and autonomy—and the "sociocentric" non-Western self—which sets little store by notions of autonomy and independence, and finds it hard to think of the individual except within the context of his or her social role.[5]

Bearing in mind the reservations voiced earlier about not reducing everyone to "ordinary chaps out, like the rest of us, for money, sex, status, and power" (also, mind you, a quote from Geertz), I agree that it is important not to dissolve all cultural differences into universalistic statements like that of rational utility-seeking man. But the usual characterisations of the Western self have been subjected to scathing feminist critique as not applying even in the West.[6] Even without this, the idea that conceptions of the self divide in a binary way between West and non-West looks implausible. Societies differ (but are also often in internal disagreement) over the value they attach to individualism, and they vary (again, with

---

[4] The full quote is as follows:

The Western conception of the person as a bounded, unique, more or less integrated motivational and cognitive universe, a dynamic center of awareness, emotion, judgment, and action organized into a distinctive whole and set contrastively against other such wholes and against its social and natural background is, however incorrigible it may seem to us, a rather peculiar idea within the context of the world's cultures.

Clifford Geertz, " 'From the Native's Point of View': On the Nature of Anthropological Understanding," in *Culture Theory: Essays on Mind, Self, and Emotion*, ed. Richard A. Shweder and Robert LeVine (1974; repr., Cambridge: Cambridge University Press, 1984), 126.

[5] Louis Dumont, *Homo Hierarchicus: The Caste System and Its Implications* (Chicago: University of Chicago Press, 1980). See also Richard A. Shweder and Edmund J. Bourne, "Does the Concept of the Person Vary Cross-culturally?" in *Culture Theory: Essays on Mind, Self, and Emotion*, ed. Richard A. Shweder and Robert LeVine (Cambridge: Cambridge University Press, 1984); Melford E. Spiro, "Is the Conception of the Self 'Peculiar' within the Context of the World Cultures?" *Ethos* 21, no. 2 (1993): 107–53. For radical alternatives, see Martin Sokefeld, "Debating Self, Identity, and Culture in Anthropology," *Current Anthropology* 40, no. 4 (1999): 417–47; Anthony P. Cohen, *Self-Consciousness: An Alternative Anthropology of Identity* (London: Routledge, 1994). See also Sawitri Saharso, "Is the Freedom of the Will but a Western Illusion? Individual Autonomy, Gender, and Multicultural Judgment," in *Sexual/Cultural Justice*, ed. Barbara Arneil, Monique Deveaux, Rita Dhamoon, and Avigail Eisenberg (London: Routledge, 2006).

[6] For a good summary, see Marilyn Friedman, *Autonomy, Gender, Politics* (Oxford: Oxford University Press, 2003).

considerable internal differentiation) in how tightly they regulate and prescribe individual behaviour. This certainly means that there will be differences in the degrees of agency, autonomy, and independence available to and/or desired by people: you would have to be very Pollyannaish about the state of the world to deny this. But in most social settings, the relationship between self-denial and self-affirmation remains complex. Some people find it hard to distinguish their own needs or values from the needs and values of those they live with. Others so much want to be different that they end up doing something simply because it looks the less conventional choice. Still others have a clear sense of what they need or value, but are unable to act on it because of overwhelming social restrictions.[7] People do not value autonomy to the same extent, but here there are both cultural differences and many differences between people brought up in what looks like the same culture. (Even within a single family, there will be differences in the value that members attach to autonomy.) The more useful presumption, in my view, is the one proposed by Meyers: that while cultures vary in the ways they may nurture or stifle the skills and capacities for autonomy, *no one* is without autonomy.[8] Autonomy is not an all-or-nothing concept but more a matter of degree.

In the political theory literature, the sharpest attack on the idea of autonomy comes in the work of Chandran Kukathas, who argues that the notion that the good life is the chosen life is both mistaken and destructive.[9] Assuming that people's most basic interest lies in being able to critically assess and then revise their ends can lead to frustration and bitterness, for it may just make us dissatisfied with circumstances we are not able to change. Making autonomy the centrepiece of human existence also diverts attention from what really does matter to people. In Kukathas's view, living an unexamined life is by no means the worst fate that can befall us. The worst is being prevented from doing what we think—in however unthinking or uncritical a way—to be right. Autonomy is not, he maintains, the highest good. What really matters is being able to live as our conscience dictates. This must include being able to live a life that is not autonomous, if that is what we consider right.

On this reading, multiculturalism would mean downgrading autonomy from the exaggerated centrality attributed to it in Western thought. Yet

---

[7] Sumi Madhok argues that we should move away from action as the measure of autonomy to consider how people express themselves in speech; "Autonomy, Subordination, and the 'Social Woman': Examining Rights Narratives of Rural Rajasthani Women" (PhD diss., School of Oriental and African Studies, London, 2003).

[8] Meyers, "Feminism and Women's Autonomy."

[9] Chandran Kukathas, *The Liberal Archipelago* (Oxford: Oxford University Press, 2003).

in an almost diametrically opposed reading, Will Kymlicka represents autonomy as the very reason to support multicultural policies, even when these threaten to elevate the requirements of the group over the rights of the individual. In line with most contemporary liberals, Kymlicka understands autonomy as the capacity to assess and, when we feel it appropriate, revise our existing ends. In contrast to Kukathas, Kymlicka argues that being free to question and examine our beliefs is *as important as* being free to live our lives in accordance with those beliefs. His initially surprising, though by now quite widely endorsed, argument is that an individual's capacity to live a questioning and choosing life depends on the moral resources provided by a reasonably stable structure of values, obligations, and beliefs. Securing cultural stability is not then at odds with individual autonomy but is one of the conditions for autonomy to flourish, for "when the individual is stripped of her cultural heritage, her development becomes stunted."[10] If this is so, then the very value that liberals attach to autonomy requires them to support policies aimed at protecting and sustaining cultures that might otherwise fall apart. People who don't know who they are or where they are going are much less able than those with a strong sense of identity to think reflectively, make choices, and plan their lives. We need our cultures in order to become autonomous beings.

Kymlicka has been criticised for a "static and preservationist" understanding of culture that attaches cultures to language and locates them in a specific geographic space.[11] He has been said to operate with a rather holistic understanding of culture, and many have questioned whether this can be made compatible with individual autonomy in the way he hopes and suggests. Kymlicka does not, however, present *culture* as an especially strong determinant of individual action; if he did, his notion about societies needing to practice multiculturalism in order to promote individual autonomy would look rather strange. Rather, his argument centres on the need for a secure and strong *cultural community* as the context in which people are enabled to develop as autonomous beings, and he goes to some lengths in his earlier writing to distinguish a stable cultural community from a stable or unchanging culture. He clearly envisages individuals using the moral resources of their community to question and modify their culture's practices and beliefs. It is the community that is to be sustained rather than specific practices or beliefs.[12] This promises neatly to

[10] Will Kymlicka, *Liberalism, Community, and Culture* (Oxford: Clarendon Press, 1989), 176.

[11] Seyla Benhabib, *The Claims of Culture: Equality and Diversity in the Global Era* (Princeton, NJ: Princeton University Press, 2002), 67.

[12] Kymlicka, *Liberalism, Community, and Culture*, chap. 8.

resolve any tensions between caring about individual choice and supporting multicultural policies: the reason why societies ought to sustain other-
wise-threatened cultures is that this gives the individuals who make up
the cultural community a more secure basis from which to make choices
and live autonomous lives.

It is not my object here to settle whether Kymlicka's squaring of the
circle is as successful as he hopes—though my inclinations are towards
those who see his reluctance to condone external intervention in the activities of any subnational minority as weakening his supposed defence of
gender equality. The point that interests me at this stage is that in his
account, culture appears as enabling: it makes it more possible for people
to be more autonomous beings. This contrasts with a further account—
one that has been particularly influential in the jurisprudence regarding discrimination—where the case for multicultural accommodation
comes to depend on the fact that cultures *constrain* choice. In this third
account of the relationship between culture and autonomy, it is precisely
because living a particular culture can make it difficult for people to
adopt a certain course of action or apply for a particular job that societies
ought to modify their laws or regulations. This is the account that concerns me here.

Culture as Constraint: As an Argument for Multiculturalism

This third argument works within and at the limits of the discrimination
paradigm, the central point being that societies seeking to ensure equality
need to go beyond the initially race-, ethnicity-, and culture-blind measures of antidiscrimination towards a stronger recognition of difference.
The classic antidiscrimination approach considers treating people as
equals to be a matter of disregarding what ought to be deemed irrelevant
differences of gender, culture, and race—and not, therefore, discriminat-
ing against individuals because of these irrelevant characteristics. By contrast, the multicultural approach to discrimination legislation claims that
when cultural difference is disregarded, this will often deny people their
equality of opportunity. It is argued, in other words, that differential treatment will sometimes be necessary to ensure that people really are being
treated the same.

In *Rethinking Multiculturalism*, Bhikhu Parekh puts the case with particular clarity. Parekh argues that equal opportunity has to be interpreted
in a culturally sensitive way because an opportunity remains "mute and
passive" if an individual "lacks the capacity, the cultural disposition or

the necessary cultural knowledge to take advantage of it."[13] He refers to a number of cases that came before the English courts, including the landmark *Mandla v. Dowell Lee* (1983), where the school uniform prescribed by a private school was deemed discriminatory in its effects because the proportion of orthodox Sikhs who could comply was smaller than the proportion of non-Sikhs who could. (Basically, the school required boys to cut their hair short and wear caps. Since it is part of Sikh tradition not to cut one's hair, and for older boys and men to cover their hair with a turban, it was particularly difficult for a Sikh schoolboy to meet this requirement.) The issue for Parekh is the gap between offering a formal equality of opportunity and making that equality meaningful. As he puts it, "A Sikh is in principle free to send his son to a school that bans turbans, but for all practical purposes, it is closed to him. The same is true when an orthodox Jew is required to give up his yarmulke, or the Muslim woman to wear a skirt, or a vegetarian Hindu to eat beef as a precondition for certain kinds of jobs."[14] Under such circumstances, there are compelling reasons of equality for exempting members of particular religious or cultural groups from regulations that seem perfectly reasonable when imposed on other citizens.

The judgment in *Mandla v. Dowell Lee* revolved mostly around whether Sikhs constituted an ethnic group, for there was at that point no legislation in the United Kingdom against religious discrimination, and the case depended on the definitions of discrimination in the 1976 Race Relations Act. In relation to autonomy, the key clause was that discrimination is deemed to have occurred if the proportion of people from one racial group who "can comply" with a requirement or condition "is considerably smaller than the proportion of persons not of that racial group."[15] As the Appeal Court judges noted, when "can comply" is construed literally, then Sikhs are as capable as anyone else of refraining from wearing turbans, and there are no grounds for claiming discrimination. But the judges were guided by a decision in *Price v. Civil Service Commission* (1978), which had been heard under the similarly worded Sex Discrimination Act.[16] In the *Price* case, the question was whether a Civil Service rule that set an age limit of twenty-eight for applicants to the executive grade of the Civil Service discriminated against women. The judges decided that it did because the condition "is in practice harder for women to comply with than it is for men." Taking their cue from this,

---

[13] Bhikhu Parekh, *Rethinking Multiculturalism: Cultural Diversity and Political Theory* (London: Palgrave Press, 2000), 241.

[14] Ibid., 241.

[15] *Mandla v. Dowell Lee* [1983] 2 AC 548.

[16] *Price v. Civil Service Commission* [1978] I All ER.

the judges in the *Mandla* case interpreted "can comply" as "can in practice" or "can consistently with the customs and cultural traditions of the racial group."

The argument about cultural incapacity parallels more familiar ones about economic or social incapacity: the idea, for example, that people do not have an equal opportunity to vote if the polling station is situated in a place accessible only by those with a car, or that the equal opportunity to study remains "mute and passive" if the price of schooling is set beyond the average family's means. In these instances, it seems reasonable to say that the lack of a car prevents the individual from voting or that the lack of money prevents the child from studying. The more insouciant among us might object that a truly determined voter would get up the night before and walk the necessary miles, or that a truly determined student would find work or a patron to support her. But we can presumably agree that the lack of money and transportation *are* obstacles, and that it would take a particularly determined individual to overcome them. The real disagreement will then be about how much responsibility the state has to remove these obstacles.

As applied in the case for multicultural policy, however, the argument seems to involve a more contentious thesis about the power of culture and the great difficulty individuals would have in changing some culturally prescribed aspect of their lives. It represents (at least some) cultural conventions or values as so much bound up in one's identity as to become beyond one's control. Implicitly, it therefore represents culture as curtailing the individual's choice. The obstacle is not something external to yourself—the lack of a car or money—that you can overcome if you are enormously determined. It is something more internal that is said to make it virtually impossible for you to act otherwise. In Kymlicka's account, culture was seen as enabling. In the alternative one suggested by Parekh and enacted in a number of legal judgments, culture seems to incapacitate people. It is precisely because a culture can make it so difficult for individuals to choose a particular course of action or job that societies need to modify their laws or regulations to accommodate differences of culture. Parekh is not claiming that people are unable to modify *any* of their existing cultural practices, and he distinguishes between those "cultural inabilities that can be overcome with relative ease by suitably reinterpreting the relevant cultural norm or practice," and those that so much constitute the individual's sense of identity that they "cannot be overcome without a deep sense of moral loss."[17] But while he prefers to describe people as

---

[17] Parekh, *Rethinking Multiculturalism*, 241.

"deeply shaped" rather than "determined" by their cultures, he sees this second kind of cultural inability as coming close to a "natural inability."[18]

Richard Ford has analysed similar (though unsuccessful) attempts to extend antidiscrimination law in the United States. In the case of *Renee Rogers et al. v. American Airlines. Inc.* (1981), an African American woman sought $10,000 damages against her employer for prohibiting her from wearing her hair in cornrow braids.[19] Rogers claimed that braided hair "has been and continues to be part of the cultural and historical essence of Black American women." Her argument thus paralleled Parekh's formulation about some cultural norms so much constituting the individual's sense of identity that they cannot be overcome without a deep sense of loss. She lost the case, rightly in Ford's view, because she chose to base it on what he regards as the spurious grounds of cultural essence. Had she been able to establish that a no-braids policy was being employed to screen out black women from the workforce, that would have been a different matter, and Ford favours tightening antidiscrimination legislation to prohibit policies on behaviour that can be shown to operate as proxies for racial discrimination. But antidiscrimination laws should be reserved for what he considers the paradigmatic ones of race, colour, sex, disability, and sexual orientation, not extended to include discrimination on the basis of culture. Discrimination on the basis of immutable characteristics is clearly indefensible, but if the characteristics are of the kind that individuals can—and do—change, then they become, in his account, cultural "preferences" and not a legitimate object of antidiscrimination law. Describing cornrows as the essence of black womanhood turns the cultural practice of some black women into a supposedly hegemonic one for all, and claims a hairstyle that could be (and subsequently has been) adopted by some white women as "essentially" black. It "en-

[18] Ibid., 336, 241. I don't want to overdo the contrast between Kymlicka and Parekh. Kymlicka uses both the enabling and the incapacitating argument, and as anyone familiar with his work will know, it would be a serious misrepresentation to suggest that Parekh regards culture as a constraint on people's lives. Ultimately, the difference reflects different national situations. Kymlicka is formulating his arguments in the Canadian context, where he is thinking of the issues in relation to indigenous peoples as well as contemporary migration. The crisis for many indigenous people has been the loss of culture, the being stripped, as Kymlicka puts it, of one's cultural heritage. Parekh is writing in the European context and reflecting on cultural differences associated with the global migrations of the last sixty years. The discourse across Europe is not so much of people losing their cultures but of cultural traditions that have retained their strength, and then precisely because of this, present a challenge to the indigenous traditions.

[19] *Renee Rogers et al. v. American Airlines, Inc.*, 527 F. Supp. 229 (1981). My discussion of this is based on Richard T. Ford, *Racial Culture: A Critique* (Princeton, NJ: Princeton University Press, 2005), 23–29.

courages black women to wear cornrows while making them off-limits or at least peculiar for non-blacks."[20]

It might be said that these are very different cases: that the first involves religious, not just cultural, injunctions about not cutting one's hair, while the second involves only matters of fashion. But the judgment in *Mandla v. Dowell Lee* did not depend on religion. There was no legislation at that point forbidding discrimination on the grounds of religion, so Sikhs qualified as an ethnic, rather than a religious, group. Meanwhile, describing the second case as simply a matter of fashion prejudges the arguments, for this is precisely what was at issue. Setting to one side more technical differences in the way the legislation of the two countries is drawn up, the cases seem to raise much the same question. Is it appropriate, for the purposes of antidiscrimination policy, to treat culture on a par with more immutable characteristics like sex or the colour of one's skin? Or do charges of discrimination on the grounds of culture give too much credibility to the notion that their culture makes them do it, that individuals are defined through and by their culture, and are at the mercy of what their culture dictates? If so, do supporters of multiculturalism really want to represent culture in this way—as something that swallows up individuals to such a degree that they are now powerless to do anything else?

Importing the language of incapacity or inability into an argument about cultural difference is a risky business. If we think of ourselves as choosing—or at any rate endorsing—our religious beliefs and cultural practices, then any analogy with physical disabilities seems strained. People might still have grounds for claiming discrimination if the choices they make rule out a wider range of opportunities than the choices others make—if American Airlines embraces me with my punk hairstyle but rejects you with your cornrow braids, or if the state finances classes in my religion or language but refuses to finance them in yours. In two later cornrow cases, for example, the complainants did win compensatory damages, and their employers were instructed to change their hairstyle policy, because it was possible to establish that the policy was enforced only against African American women and /or that it had a disparate effect on them.[21] For instance, Hyatt Hotels had banned what it termed

---

[20] Ford, *Racial Culture*, 28. Ford suggests that the courts should assess whether provisions contribute "as a whole" to the exclusion or segregation of a particular group. If banning cornrows, for example, could be shown to correlate with a workforce in which African Americans were significantly underrepresented, then this might constitute grounds for legal action. But if the employer had succeeded, perhaps by virtue of other policies of inclusion, in achieving a fair representation of African Americans, then the fact that the employer also bans a hairstyle that is more likely to be favoured by African Americans should be deemed irrelevant.

[21] The cases—*Pamela L. Mitchell v. J. W. Marriott Hotel, Inc. and Marriott Corporation* (1988) and *Cheryl Tatum and Cheryl Parahoo v. Hyatt Hotels Corporation and Hyatt Re-*

"extreme or unusual hairstyles," but then allowed employees to wear their hair in spikes and permitted Latino men to wear ponytails, while insisting that African American women wear wigs over their cornrows. It was the employer's take on the hairstyles, rather than the women's choice of how to wear their hair, that effectively reduced their opportunities. But some reductions in opportunities are just built intrinsically into the choices. To use an example offered by Brian Barry, if I decide to become a pacifist, I thereby lose my chance of a brilliant military career, but I can hardly claim this as evidence of discrimination against pacifists. Barry argues that beliefs "are not to be conceived of as some sort of alien affliction," and that "somebody who freely embraces a religious belief that prohibits certain activities will rightly deny the imputation that this is to be seen as analogous to the unwelcome burden of a physical disability."[22] Although a religious belief arguably occupies a different territory from a cultural practice, this parallels Ford's assertion about choosing to wear your hair in a certain way being a matter of personal choice.

Barry's own position on this is a rather abrupt take-it-or-leave-it: if you knew what you were doing, and knew the likely consequences, you cannot now complain.[23] This underplays the problem of institutional bias, for in many cases, it will not be the religious belief or cultural practice per se that closes down an opportunity but the fact that the society we live in has adopted some other religious belief or cultural practice as its norm. I do not mean by this that the privileging of one set of beliefs and practices is always discriminatory, for there might be good historical reasons for this or just overwhelming practical difficulties that prevent the society from being evenhanded. (There are limits to how many languages can be given official status, for example, or how many religious festivals can be made into public holidays.) I mean only that people *could* still have grounds for complaint against a cultural bias even if they made their choices with their eyes fully open. The fact that we knew about a bias when we decided to adopt a particular way of life does not in itself justify the inequity. In Turkey in the late 1990s, there were mass dismissals of university teachers and students for wearing or supporting the wearing of Islamic headscarves. The fact that the women involved knew the risks when they decided to cover their heads does not in itself mean they had no right to complain.

---

gency Crystal City (1988)—are discussed in Alison Renteln, *The Cultural Defense* (New York: Oxford University Press, 2004), chap. 8.

[22] Brian Barry, *Culture and Equality: An Egalitarian Critique of Multiculturalism* (Cambridge, UK: Polity Press, 2001), 36, 37.

[23] As Susan Mendus sums it up, "When we choose to lead a certain kind of life, we also, and thereby, choose to pick up the bill for it"; "Choice, Chance, and Multiculturalism," in *Multiculturalism Revisited*, ed. Paul Kelly (Cambridge, UK: Polity Press, 2002), 43.

It is possible, then, to talk of discrimination even when the individuals concerned are acting voluntarily and in full knowledge of the likely consequences. But it is undoubtedly easier—and more common in discrimination cases—to follow Parekh's suggested line of argument, which represents culture as a matter over which individuals have little or no control. A Sikh schoolboy cannot comply with his school's dress code because to do so would undermine his ethnocultural identity; an African American woman cannot comply with her employer's dress code because to do so would threaten the very essence of her being. Both claims depend on a contentious thesis about the power of culture over the members of a cultural group. Since the arguments will, by definition, only be employed for members of a minority group (otherwise there would be no grounds for claiming discrimination), they give sustenance to what is already the popular representation of people from minority groups as more swallowed up in their cultural, ethnic, racial, or religious identity than the average member of a majority cultural group.

That being said, the policy consequences of representing culture as constraint have not been particularly severe. The courts have been cautious in applying notions of incapacity, and where they have employed them, could mostly have arrived at the same conclusion without suggesting that culture made it impossible for people to act in any other way. The relevant cases largely depend on notions of indirect discrimination that are widely considered legitimate for gender. While I share Ford's concerns about the misapplication of culture in circumstances where it is more appropriate to talk of racial discrimination, I see no reason in principle why notions of indirect discrimination should not be applied in the same way to culture. I would only argue that it ought to be the *same* way.

When lawyers maintain that setting an age limit for entry to particular occupations disadvantages women, for example, they are not saying that the gender norms that regulate the distribution of child care mean that women simply *cannot* embark on a career in their early twenties. More to the point, they are not saying that a woman who decides to embark on a career in her early twenties rather than have children, to embark on a career and place her children in a nursery, or to embark on a career while her partner looks after the children thereby threatens her sense of femininity or becomes less of a woman. All they argue—all they have to argue—is that women are less likely than men to be able to meet the requirement, and hence, that it indirectly discriminates against them. In a similar fashion, lawyers contesting what they see as discriminatory dress codes, work hours, or health and safety regulations do not have to claim that their client simply *cannot* conform to these, as if no individuals with those religious beliefs or that cultural history could make such a compromise of their values and beliefs. Nor do they have to claim (and think how insidious it would be if they did) that if their clients did conform, they would no longer be able to think of themselves as Jewish, Muslim, Hindu, or Rastafarian. The first claim makes the case vulnerable to evidence that other people sharing the client's religion or culture have nonetheless managed a compromise. The second implies that those others are betraying their religion or culture. It is not necessary to make either of these claims in order to establish a prima facie case as regards discrimination. What is required is to demonstrate that it is harder—though not impossible—for people from one cultural group to meet the requirement.

Establishing that a regulation has a disparate effect on those attached to a particular cultural and/or religious group is, moreover, only the first step. As Parekh has carefully delineated, a number of other issues then come into play.[24] Where the regulation involves a dress requirement, say, it may still be that there are compelling safety reasons for insisting that all abide by it, or it may be that the symbolic significance attached to the dress code justifies retaining it for all. When the British government exempted turban-wearing Sikhs from the requirement to wear a safety helmet when working on a building site, they first took advice from scientific experts about the level of protection afforded by a turban. The willingness to agree to the exemption therefore depended partly on the assurance that turbans offered some degree of safety protection. When the Royal Canadian Mounted Police finally agreed to allow Sikhs to wear turbans instead of the distinctive Mountie Stetson, a group of retired officers challenged the decision in the courts, alleging that the turbans undermined the nonreligious nature of the force. Though Parekh concludes (as did Canada's Supreme Court) that the objection was specious and discriminatory, he sees it as a legitimate concern to want to hold on to a cherished national symbol. By implication, he considers that there might be instances in which this would override equality concerns. Establishing that a regulation has a disparate effect on different groups is a necessary but not sufficient condition for establishing that it is discriminatory.

Culture as Constraint: As Argument against Multiculturalism

In the arguments *for* multiculturalism, I reach much the same policy conclusions as those who represent culture as incapacitating, but object to the way the case has been made. My objections to culture as constraint may then look rather academic, for what difference do they make? The main worry is that an overly determinist understanding of culture in the theoretical or legal literature can feed cultural stereotypes in popular dis-

---

[24] Parekh, *Rethinking Multiculturalism*, esp. chaps. 9 and 10.

course. In *Racial Culture*, Ford notes that the object of his criticism is not so much the laws or the law reform proposals associated with a discourse of culture, for he supports many of these, if usually for different reasons. What concerns him is the style of thinking expressed in contentions about the right to difference, and the political consequences that can flow from this.[25] In similar vein, my objection to the way culture has been deployed in some of the antidiscrimination cases is not so much to the legal or policy outcomes, most of which I support. What concerns me is that the arguments used in these cases threaten to sustain, rather than unsettle, cultural stereotypes.

When culture as constraint is employed as part of the argument *against* multiculturalism, there are also real problems with the policies that flow from this. This has been especially the case in those issues that hinge around tensions between multiculturalism and women's equality. In some of the most testing of these, it seems to be the women themselves who are making the cultural demand: girls and women saying that they want to cover their heads in school or at university, that they want the right to abort a foetus that has been diagnosed as female or want to marry an as-yet-unknown partner from their parents' country of origin. Critics of multicultural accommodation commonly discount this, claiming that these women are victims of their patriarchal culture, that what is being represented as their wish has been imposed on them by the men in their community and can therefore be safely ignored. In an increasing number of cases, governments have acted on these worries about cultural coercion by banning an entire practice.

Veiling

The term veiling covers numerous forms of Islamic dress, including the hijab, modest dress, usually interpreted as a headscarf covering the head and shoulders; the jilbab, a headscarf and gown that leave only the face and hands exposed; and the niqab that additionally covers the face. The hijab is not so different from the headscarf that was a mainstay of female dress in Europe up until the 1960s—and is sometimes described just as a headscarf—but has been banned in public institutions in Turkey, in public schools in France, for public officials in courtrooms in Austria and the Netherlands, and in numerous other contexts. The French *affaire du foulard* dates back to 1989, when three Muslim schoolgirls (acting, incidentally, against the advice of their parents) were excluded from school for wearing the hijab. After much public debate over the meaning of *laïcité*—a particularly militant version of secularism that allows no special status

---

[25] Ford, *Racial Culture*, 13–17.

for religion—and considerable variation between school authorities in the way they implemented this, a commission was set up to investigate how the principles of laïcité should be interpreted. In its 2003 report, the commission recommended new legislation to prohibit the wearing of "ostensible" items of dress that "manifest religious or political affiliation" in the public schools. An overwhelming majority of the legislature (494 to 36) passed the law in 2004.

In Belgium, where the state has pursued a policy of evenhandedness between religions rather than the stricter separation of church from state, the minister of internal affairs welcomed the French initiative and provoked extensive public debate with an article declaring that "forced veiling is unacceptable."[26] In Germany in 2003, the Federal Constitutional Court ruled in favour of Fereshta Ludin, a schoolteacher of Afghan origin who had lost her post in a secondary school in Baden-Württemberg because she insisted on wearing her headscarf to work. The ruling, however, effectively passed the buck to the state legislatures, for it revolved around the fact that there was no state legislation explicitly banning headscarves. By 2004, six states in Germany, including Berlin, had either passed or drafted legislation banning teachers from wearing headscarves in public schools. In the Netherlands in 2001, a Muslim law student was denied employment as a court clerk because she insisted on wearing her headscarf during court sessions. Although the Equality Commission defended her rights, the minister of justice ruled that religious symbols should not be permitted in the neutral arena of the courtroom. In Italy in 2004, a Muslim trainee teacher was asked to remove her headscarf on the grounds that it might frighten the children. In a case heard before the European Commission for Human Rights—*Karaduman v. Turkey* (1993)—the commission upheld the right of the Turkish government to deny a student her degree certificate because she refused to remove her headscarf for an identity photograph. In later cases heard before the European Court of Human Rights—*Dahlab v. Switzerland* (2001) and *Sahin v. Turkey* (2004)—the court upheld the right of the Swiss school authorities to forbid a convert to Islam to wear her headscarf in the classroom, and of the Turkish government to exclude a headscarf-wearing student from class.[27]

[26] Patrick Dewael, "Elke dwang tot sluieren is onaanvaardbaar" ["Forced Veiling Is Unacceptable"], *De Morgen*, 10 January 2004.

[27] Titia Loenen notes that in the second case, the teacher had worn her headscarf to work for three years with no complaints from parents. The court apparently found it "difficult to reconcile wearing a headscarf with the message of tolerance, of respect for others and most of all of equality and non-discrimination" that was expected of the public schools; "Family Law Issues in a Multicultural Society: Abolishing or Reaffirming Sex as a Legally Relevant Category? A Human Rights Approach," *Netherlands Quarterly of Human Rights* 20, no. 4 (2002): 433.

In the United Kingdom, schools commonly permit both students and teachers to wear headscarves, but in the case of *R v. Head Teacher and Governors of Denbigh High School* (2006), discussed earlier, the court upheld the school's right to refuse entry to a schoolgirl wearing the jilbab.

The primary justification for these decisions lies in the secular separation of church from state, and the belief that religion should not intrude into the public institutions deemed most important in securing the neutrality of the state. But it is women, of course, who are the main object of the bans. And as the Belgian discussion about "forced veiling" indicates, there is typically a secondary justification that represents the hijab as a symbol of women's subordination and particularly at odds with secular, egalitarian principles. When the women object, as many of them do, that it is *their* choice to cover their heads, their voices are often discounted as simply reflecting community pressure. It is presumed that no woman would *really* choose to abase herself in this way.

There is large literature on veiling, and while much of this condemns the practice as a symbol of women's subordination, a considerable amount also represents it as an expression of women's agency.[28] Research in societies where it has been a common practice certainly casts doubt on the notion that *adult* women who veil thereby demonstrate their lack of autonomy. In one particularly subtle account of a Bedouin society in Egypt in the late 1970s, Lila Abu-Lughod argues that the deference expected of women (and most visibly expressed in veiling) was part of a social system that attached a high value to autonomy in men and scorned docility in women. "Those who are coerced into obeying are scorned, but those who voluntarily defer are honourable."[29] This was clearly a double-bind situation—women were expected to veil, but were also expected to do it voluntarily—and Abu-Lughod does not present the life of Bedouin women as one of great self-determination. To the contrary, she shows how women have expressed their feelings of anger, frustration, or unhappiness in a subversive tradition of poetry that they shared only with other women. This was not a life of freedom and gender equality, yet it was also not a life of passive submission. Representing these women simply as constrained by their culture does not begin to capture the complexity of their choices.

[28] For a thoughtful overview, see Nancy J. Hirschmann, "Western Feminism, Eastern Veiling, and the Question of Free Agency," *Constellations* 5, no. 3 (1998): 345–68. See also Fatima Mernissi, *Beyond the Veil: Male-Female Dynamics in a Modern Muslim Society* (Cambridge, MA: Schenkman Publishing Co., 1975); Nilüfer Göle, *The Forbidden Modern: Civilization and Veiling* (Ann Arbor: University of Michigan Press, 1996).

[29] Lila Abu-Lughod, *Veiled Sentiments: Honor and Poetry in a Bedouin Society* (Berkeley: University of California Press, 1986), 105.

Later research by Arlene MacLeod into the "new veiling" of lower-middle-class women in Cairo in the mid-1980s tells a similarly complicated story.[30] The women she interviewed were not notably religious, few of them had any time for the radical politics of the Islamist groups, a number of them had decided to start wearing a headscarf and gown against the wishes of their fiancés or husbands, and all of them insisted that the decision was meaningless unless it came from the woman herself. Again, the decision hardly added up to a great act of self-determination: the clothing *was* restrictive, it was not best suited to the heat of Cairo, and what at the beginning of the 1980s was a recognisably women's initiative had become more a matter of bowing to male pressure by the end of the decade. But it would be seriously misleading to represent these women as at the mercy of cultural dictates or their stated wishes as not really "their own." It would also be misleading to represent these women as subordinating themselves to men. It is worth stressing, for example, that in the new veil movement (in Egypt and elsewhere), women do not see their head coverings as protecting them from the gaze of male strangers but rather as a sign of modesty and submission to God, and do not therefore remove them at all-women gatherings.[31]

But even if we acknowledge the agency of these women, what of schoolgirls, pressured by their parents, clerics, and as seems increasingly to be the case, the newly devout young men in their communities? In a study published in 1995, Françoise Gaspard and Farhad Khosrokhavar had argued that there were three distinct patterns of hijab wearing in France: older women who had moved to France in the 1960s, had been wearing the hijab since adolescence, and saw it as part of their ethnic/cultural identity; younger women, aged sixteen to twenty-five, who had adopted the hijab—often against their mother's preference and example—as part of an affirmation of their Muslim identity; and younger girls at school or college who wore it at their parents' insistence, but thereby bought the freedom to go out by themselves, attend college, and continue their education.[32] Though this third group was, in a sense, being coerced into something they would not otherwise have chosen, Gaspard and Khosrokhavar stressed the freedom their compliance brought them, and noted that most of these young women stopped wearing the hijab a few years after leaving

---

[30] Arlene Elowe MacLeod, *Accommodating Protest: Working Women, the New Veiling, and Change in Cairo* (New York: Columbia University Press, 1991).

[31] Dawn Lyon and Debora Spini, "Unveiling the Headscarf Debate," *Feminist Legal Studies* 12 (2004): 333–45. See also the illuminating study of the women's piety movement in Cairo in Saba Mahmood, *Politics of Piety: The Islamic Revival and the Feminist Subject* (Princeton, NJ: Princeton University Press, 2005).

[32] Françoise Gaspard and Farhad Khosrokhavar, *Le foulard et la république* (Paris; Le Decouverte, 1995), chap. 3.

school. Official statistics indicate only twelve hundred cases of girls wearing headscarves to school in 2003, thirty court cases, and four exclusions, a surprisingly low number in a country whose Muslim population is estimated at four million.[33]

Yet when the Stasi Commission produced its report in 2003, it claimed that there had been a resurgence of sexism in France's Muslim communities, and that young women were now exposed to high levels of verbal, psychological, and physical pressure.[34] (It also queried those statistics, suggesting that they represented the tip of the iceberg.) For many young women, it reported, covering one's head in public places—including at school—was becoming the only way to avoid being stigmatised as sexually loose or a heretic. For those who refused, the fact that others of their age group were wearing the hijab made them even more vulnerable to accusations of impurity. The commission therefore doubted whether young girls really were choosing the headscarf, and this perception made it easier for it to conclude that school students should not be permitted to wear conspicuous religious or political symbols, including large Christian crosses, the Jewish yarmulke, and the Muslim headscarf. Significantly, the commission did not recommend a similar ban for universities. Though this difference of treatment mostly reflects the role attributed to schools in educating future citizens into the ideals of the republic, it also reflects the view that adults should be assumed to know their own minds.

In the commissioners' view, the fact that some young girls had testified to the psychological and physical pressures exerted on them to get them to conform lifted the issue out of the realm of religious freedom and into the world of public order. "La république ne peut rester sourd au cri de détresse de ces jeunes filles."[35] I do not at all doubt that some young girls are being coerced; I believe that the public authorities have a responsibility to protect people from coercion; and I recognise the difficulties in protecting individuals from the kind of hidden and private coercion that goes on inside families and communities, hence the attraction of a simple ban. But when the republic stops pupils from wearing any ostensible religious symbols, it can also be seen as closing its ears to those others who insist that they are choosing what their religion recommends as modest dress. A blanket ban is here employed as a rough-and-ready way to protect anyone who might be a victim of coercion. No young woman

---

[33] Emmanuel Terray, "Headscarf Hysteria," *New Left Review* 26 (2004): 121.

[34] Bernard Stasi, *Laïcité et République. Rapport de la commission de réflexion sur l'application du principe de laïcité dans la république* (Paris: La Documentation Francaise, 2004), sec. 3.3.2.1.

[35] Ibid., sec. 4.2.2.1.

is to be permitted to wear a headscarf to school because some are being pressured to do so.

Forced Marriage

This blanket ban approach is increasingly becoming the standard policy response in Europe to the problem of forced marriage. I noted in chapter 2 that arranged marriage, where parents or the larger family play a leading role in selecting marriage partners for the younger generation, had been a relatively common practice among families that had migrated from parts of North Africa, the Indian subcontinent, Turkey, East Asia, and the Middle East. The nature of the practice has been changing rapidly (in countries of origin as well as those of destination), mostly in ways that allow the potential spouses a greater say. The literature on the United Kingdom, for example, suggests that there has been an overall decline in the number of marriages that are arranged, and that in those still described as arranged, the young people often make their selection from a short list of approved candidates, or choose their future partner themselves and then seek parental approval.[36] The chances of being forced into a marriage are of course especially high in a society that practises arranged marriage, for it is when it is the norm for parents to make the decision that the temptation to insist is most likely to arise. The chances of being forced into marriage against one's will may also increase as the practice of arranged marriage wanes, for parents may become more strident about their right to dictate the choice of spouse precisely because the young people are becoming more insistent on their own right to choose. There is some evidence that this is the case in contemporary Europe. As mentioned earlier, young people have been tracked down by bounty hunters, kidnapped, and held prisoner until they "agreed" to a marriage; less dramatically, but also effectively, they have been subjected to months of threats and emotional blackmail. Studies in the United Kingdom suggest that rates of suicide and self-harm are higher than average among South Asian women of marriageable age, and it is widely believed that the threat of forced marriage is part of the reason for this.[37] Across Europe, a

[36] We refer to some of this material in Anne Phillips and Moira Dustin, "UK Initiatives on Forced Marriage: Regulation, Exit, and Dialogue," *Political Studies* 52 (2004): 531–51. See also Yunas Samad and John Eade, *Community Perceptions of Forced Marriage* (London: Community Liaison Unit, Foreign and Commonwealth Office, 2002).

[37] Hannana Siddiqui, "'It Was Written in Her Kismet': Forced Marriage," in *From Homebreakers to Jailbreakers: Southall Black Sisters*, ed. Rahila Gupta (London: Zed Press, 2004); Khatidja Chantler, Erica Burman, Janet Batsleer, and Colsom Bashir, *Attempted Suicide and Self-Harm (South Asian Women)* (Manchester, UK: Women's Studies Research Centre, 2001).

number of high-profile cases of lives destroyed by forced marriage have drawn public attention to the issue.[38] By the end of the 1990s, a number of European governments had recognised this as an important area of concern.

Most then pursue some combination of four policy approaches: prosecute the offenders; assist those trying to escape a forced marriage; persuade religious and community leaders to take a more vocal stand against forced marriage; and/or make it harder for parents to force young people into marriage with an overseas partner by setting a high minimum age for *all* such marriages. The first is problematic because children mostly don't want to see their parents in prison.[39] This was one of the main objections in a consultation exercise run by the UK government to help it decide whether to create a specific offence of forcing someone to marry.[40] Existing laws relating to kidnapping, child abuse, and so on cover pretty much all that is required to prosecute someone trying to coerce another party into marriage (so there is no need for a new law), but also people do not want to see their parents charged with a criminal offence, and it is feared that they will be less willing to approach public authorities for help if they perceive this as exposing their parents to prosecution. So far, Norway is the only European country to have introduced specific legislation against coercing people into marriage, but at the time of writing, there has only been one prosecution under this law.[41] The second approach has been pursued to particularly good effect in the United King-

---

[38] Unni Wikan, *Generous Betrayal: Politics of Culture in the New Europe* (Chicago: University of Chicago Press, 2002), was particularly influential in prompting public debate in Norway. See also Sherene Razack, "Imperilled Muslim Women, Dangerous Muslim Men, and Civilised Europeans: Legal and Social Responses to Forced Marriages," *Feminist Legal Studies* 12 (2004): 129–74.

[39] When Ghulam Rasool, for example, was charged with kidnapping his stepdaughter in order to prevent her marriage to a non-Muslim, the young woman said in court that she was reconciled with her family and wanted neither her stepfather nor his coaccused to be prosecuted. Despite this, her stepfather was sentenced to two years' imprisonment, her mother was given a conditional discharge, and her brothers were ordered to perform community service. Rasool's sentence was confirmed on appeal. *R v. Ghulam Rasool*, [1990–91] 12 Cr. App. R (S.) 771.

[40] The consultation document and results of the consultation exercise are available on the Foreign and Commonwealth Office Web site, http://www.fco.gov.ac. A majority of respondents, including a majority of police respondents, felt the disadvantages associated with creating new legislation outweighed the advantages. At the time of writing, it is not clear what the government will decide, but it looks unlikely that it will now favour creating a specific offence of forcing someone to marry.

[41] In May 2005, the father and brother of a seventeen-year-old girl were sentenced to eight and ten years respectively for forcing her, under threat of death, to travel to Northern Iraq and marry a man chosen by her uncle. They also threatened to kill her when she later said she wanted a divorce. Reported in *Norway Post*, 22 May 2005.

dom, where the government's Forced Marriage Unit has established an impressive helpline for young people seeking to escape an unwanted marriage, now dealing with 350 cases each year, including up to 200 each year where the unit helps repatriate people taken abroad for marriage. The success of this depends, however, on people having the confidence to approach the relevant public authority and knowing that these helplines exist. The third approach steers a complicated path between conciliation and legitimation, for the "community leaders" identified by governments tend to be on the conservative side and may seek to extract promises of support in other policy areas as their price for speaking out against forced marriage.[42] It is no surprise, then, that a number of governments have turned to the fourth option: "protecting" young people from coercion into marriage with an overseas partner by making it difficult for them to marry overseas partners at all.

By no means all instances of forced marriage involve spouses from overseas, but some of the most dramatic examples have involved young people being tricked into travelling to their family's country of origin, only to discover that a marriage has been arranged. A marriage with an overseas spouse is particularly likely to involve an unknown partner, which increases the possibility that the marriage will be unwanted by at least one of the potential spouses. Since family reunification is one of the few remaining ways for non-Europeans to qualify for the right to live and work in Europe, a marriage with an overseas spouse also comes under suspicion as being primarily a way for nonnationals to get citizenship rights. For a combination of such reasons, it has become commonplace in both official and popular thinking to equate forced with overseas marriage: to think that most forced marriages involve partners from the family's country of origin, and that most marriages involving such partners are forced.[43] The easy response is then to prevent or delay *all* such marriages.

A number of European governments have introduced a higher age minimum for marriages involving overseas partners, usually defined as part-

---

[42] Siddiqui describes a 1999 press release from the Union of Muslim Organisations of the United Kingdom and Eire declaring that forced marriages are against the letter and spirit of the Sharia, and simultaneously welcoming what it took to be a Home Office commitment to expedite the introduction of Muslim family law to the Muslim community in the United Kingdom; "It Was Written in Her Kismet," 75. Whether an implicit bargain was struck is unclear. I don't think there was much likelihood of Muslim family law being introduced in the United Kingdom in 1999, and there is no likelihood at all after 2001, but a lot of politics is about implicit bargains, so the example is not implausible.

[43] Commenting on some of the Norwegian literature, Razack notes that "it is simply assumed that marriages contracted with partners of the same ethnic background who live outside Norway *necessarily* involve coercion." "Imperilled Muslim Women, Dangerous Muslim Men," 136.

ners from outside the European Union. Denmark took the first step in 2002, when it amended its Aliens Act to make it impossible to employ the right to family reunification to bring in overseas spouses or cohabitees when either party is under the age of twenty-four.[44] The legislation is framed in race-neutral terms, applying to everyone except citizens of the European Union and other Nordic countries. As critics have observed (this has been one of the major points of criticism within Denmark), it then catches in its net Danes seeking to bring in partners from Canada or the United States as well as those attempting to bring in partners from Africa or Asia. Inspired partly by this initiative, the United Kingdom introduced an immigration rule in 2003 prohibiting citizens under the age of eighteen from acting as sponsors for the entry of their overseas spouses. In 2005 this was extended, so that those applying to enter the United Kingdom as fiancé(e)s or spouses must also be at least eighteen years old. New immigration rules in Norway from 2003 mean that those under the age of twenty-three cannot use the right to family reunification to bring in overseas spouses unless they can establish that they are able to support their spouses financially. There has been public discussion, from the late 1990s onwards, about Norway raising the age for family reunification to twenty-four, with politicians from a range of parties voicing enthusiasm for the Danish approach, but at the time of writing, there has been no final decision on this. France, meanwhile, has raised the minimum age for *all* marriages to eighteen (before 2006, the minimum was eighteen for young men, but fifteen for young women), and ministers have described this as part of an initiative to address the problem of forced marriage. This more creditable policy follows the immigration-neutral route proposed in 2005 by the Council of Europe, and does not differentiate between marriages with partners inside or outside the European Union.[45]

The rationale for all these policies is to protect the youngest and most vulnerable from coercion, the not unreasonable presumption being that an eighteen, twenty-one, or twenty-four year old is in a better position to

[44] For a good discussion of the Danish and Norwegian legislation, see Anja Bredal, "Tackling Forced Marriages in the Nordic Countries: Between Women's Rights and Immigration Control," in *"Honour": Crimes, Paradigms, and Violence against Women*, ed. Lynn Welchman and Sara Hossain (London: Zed Books, 2005).

[45] The Parliamentary Assembly of the Council of Europe, representing forty-one countries across Europe, adopted an immigration-neutral approach in 2005 that calls on governments to raise the statutory age for *all* marriages to eighteen in order to combat forced and child marriages; Council of Europe, Parliamentary Assembly, "Forced Marriages and Child Marriages," Recommendation 1723 (2005). See also the preceding report, "Forced Marriages and Child Marriages," Document 10678 (2005), which notes the differential ages for marriage in France (fifteen for young women, and eighteen for young men) as a serious anomaly.

resist family pressures than a young person of sixteen. The effect of the Danish or UK policies, however, is a two-tier system in which those choosing partners from within the European Union can get married and live together at the legal age of marriage, while those seeking partners from outside must wait until they have arrived at a more demanding standard of maturity. Readers with teenage children will probably think that sixteen or eighteen is a ridiculously young age for anyone to decide to marry, but most governments are not proposing to raise the general age for marriage—perhaps for good liberal reasons, perhaps because young girls do get pregnant and it is thought better that they can choose to get married as well. The point to note is that *all* marriages with young overseas spouses are being banned because *some* of them might involve coercion. This echoes the main defence liberals have offered for a ban on wearing the hijab to school: that *all* headscarves must be banned because *some* are being worn under duress.

Sex Trafficking

The third example comes from outside Europe. International campaigns against sex trafficking have revealed a disturbing trade in girls and young women, many of whom are persuaded to seek employment outside their own countries by false promises of work in hotels or restaurants or as domestic servants. As with forced marriage, it is difficult to assess the precise scale of the problem. It is hard, that is, to know how many of the women know they are going to work as prostitutes and how many are being tricked into this. Ratna Kapur argues that the way the campaigns have been formulated draws on widespread images of women in the postcolonial world as victims in need of protection, and that this has encouraged a number of states to address the problem of sex trafficking by imposing a blanket ban on women workers seeking any kind of employment abroad.[46] For example, the government of Burma responded to a Human Rights Watch report on the trafficking of Burmese girls and women into Thailand's sex industries by prohibiting *all* women between the ages of sixteen and twenty-five from travelling without a legal guardian. In 1998, the government of Bangladesh banned women from going abroad as domestic workers. The Nepalese government prohibited the issue of employment licenses to women seeking to work overseas except where they had the consent of a husband or a male guardian. The pattern begins to look rather familiar. As with the European initiatives regarding the hijab and marriage, these measures respond to (legitimate and pressing)

---

[46] Ratna Kapur, *Erotic Justice: Law and the New Politics of Postcolonialism* (London: Glasshouse Press, 2005), 100.

worries about the coercion of vulnerable young women by imposing a total ban on all.

The argument goes something like this. Some girls who show up to school in the hijab are being forced into this by peer pressure and threats. Some young women who apply for entry visas for their husbands or fiancés are being forced by their families into marriage. Some young women from Bangladesh and Burma are being tricked into prostitution by false promises of other kinds of employment. Therefore, let us protect those subject to coercion by making it illegal for *anyone* to wear a headscarf in school, for *anyone* under a specified age to bring in a spouse from overseas, and for *any* young women to travel abroad without a legal guardian. These draconian policy responses catch in their net many individuals who are not being coerced but are simply going about their chosen business, trying to live autonomous lives. The policy measures are also oddly indirect, for instead of targeting and assisting those who *are* subject to coercion, they ban certain practices for all.

This is not a normal policy response. In most other cases where an entire practice is banned, it is because that practice is considered dangerous or unacceptable for everyone, or sufficiently dangerous for the average person to justify banning it even for those whose physiological makeup might mean they would suffer no harm. It is highly unusual to ban something for one subgroup that is permitted for all others or to ban something for all subgroups because *some* of those practising it might turn out to be doing it under duress. The most common example of the first is when something is banned for children but permitted to adults. Here, there are plausible grounds for some difference in treatment, though enormous difficulties in settling the precise age of maturity or consent. An example of the second might be when colleges ban all sexual relationships between staff and students because of a fear that some of these relationships involve an abuse of power.[47] I'm not convinced that this kind of blanket ban is any more justifiable than banning all headscarves because of a fear that some are being worn under duress—I favour regulations requiring staff to inform their head of department of such a relationship and remove themselves from their assessment role—but at least in the college case, students are being singled out for differential treatment because of their position in an institutional hierarchy and not because of some characteristic imputed to them as people. College authorities are not saying that the kind of people who become students are particularly lacking in judgment or unusually slow to spot sexual predators and thus need special protection. They are merely saying that the position students

---

[47] I am grateful to Samuel Scheffler for suggesting this example.

occupy in relation to their teachers makes them more vulnerable. Teachers do have power over students, the power to pass or fail, to give good or bad references, so while it potentially insults the integrity of the teacher and maturity of the student to say that all sexual relationships must be banned, at least the ban doesn't rest on a claim about students being less capable than others of asserting themselves. What, by contrast, is it about Muslim girls wearing headscarves to school or young people taking marriage partners from their family's country of origin that makes it seem appropriate simply to ban the practice for all?

Part of the answer may be that concerns about protecting vulnerable young women cloak a more interventionist agenda, and that what governments really want is to discourage the transnational loyalties that sustain marriages with overseas partners, encourage all citizens to adopt the higher marriage age that has become the norm across Europe, or encourage all citizens into a more secular way of life. It may also be that public authorities feel they lack the necessary knowledge to assist young girls from minority cultural communities in a more direct way. They have not trained enough teachers or social workers with a knowledge of and routes into these communities; they fear that if they make a wrong move, they will inflame the situation; and they know that the young girls in question do not sufficiently trust the neutrality or good will of the authorities to bring their problems to them. (That answer in itself raises questions about why governments have not acted more effectively in this field.) But the explanation also lies in a discourse of culture as constraint that makes it easier for governments to adopt a blanket ban approach when dealing with girls and women from ethnocultural minorities. When culture is taken as something that dictates what girls and women must do, it becomes that much easier to generalise from evidence that *some* girls and women are being coerced to the conclusion that pretty much *all* of them are. It then becomes easier to justify banning an entire practice because of evidence that some individuals are being coerced.

To clarify, I am not arguing that societies should act on the presumption that all actions are autonomous, except when the individual expressly says they were not. This would attach too little weight to the pressures that can make us think we have no other option, and would mean treating any acceptance of what we have come to view as inevitable as if it were an active choice. I am not, for example, entirely happy with Uma Narayan's account of autonomy, which she offers as an alternative to images of the Other woman as either a prisoner or dupe of patriarchy. In her version, "a person's choice should be considered autonomous as long as the person was a 'normal' adult with no serious cognitive or emotional impairments, and was not subject to literal or outright coercion from others. On this account, a person's choice could be autonomous even if made under considerable social or cultural pressure, and even if it were the only morally palatable option open to her."[48] My reading of this depends very much on what is intended by "literal or outright" coercion. If the implication is that a choice should be regarded as autonomous so long as no one is threatening you with physical violence or proposing to lock you up (as in the test applied in the English courts until the 1980s to cases of forced marriage, which required applicants to establish that their will had been "overborne by genuine and reasonably held fear caused by threat of immediate danger . . . to life, limb or liberty"),[49] then I think this involves too rigid a definition of coercion. If literal and outright coercion includes the complexities of emotional and moral pressure, then the account may be fair enough. But if not, I think the counter claims about agency are being taken too far.

So my point is not that public authorities should stop worrying about levels of coercion, or always accept it at face value when people say that dressing modestly according to Islamic principles, marrying an unknown partner selected by their parents, or seeking employment abroad is their own choice. But it ought to be possible to recognise the relevance of culture without concluding that it dictates all actions, and it ought to be possible to recognise that *some* individuals are coerced by cultural or religious pressures without concluding that *all* individuals are. It has proved reasonably easy to manage this manoeuvre in relation to class or gender. It ought to be possible to do this with culture as well.

Culture, Gender, and Class

I return now to the question I raised at the end of the last chapter: why can't culture be regarded in the more nuanced way that has become commonplace with gender or class? If we take multiculturalism as an approach to public policy that is sensitive to cultural diversity, works to avoid the unthinking imposition on all citizens of what turn out to be the values and practices of the majority or dominant group, and appreciates that equality sometimes means recognising rather than disregarding cultural differences, then multiculturalism clearly involves some thesis about people being shaped by their cultures. If it did not involve this, then societies could simply concentrate on making people equal as individuals, re-

[48] Uma Narayan, "Minds of Their Own: Choices, Autonomy, Cultural Practices, and Other Women," in *A Mind of One's Own: Feminist Essays on Reason and Objectivity*, ed. Louise M. Anthony and Charlotte E. Witt (Boulder, CO: Westview Press, 2002), 429.

[49] This was the judgment in the case of *Szechter v. Szechter* [1971] 2 W.L.R. 170, and was employed as the test in forced marriage cases until the mid-1980s.

gardless of any cultural difference. In my view, this modestly defined multiculturalism is right—but it is right in much the same way as parallel statements about how to treat differences of gender, race, or class. There is, by now, a lengthy literature on equality and difference that argues that societies will not achieve equality between citizens if they simply disregard all such differences. So long as gender, race, and class do position people differently and unequally in practice, shaping their life chances and sense of themselves, then pretending that the differences do not exist (or declaring in some high-minded way that they should not) will not in itself bring about equality. Much the same points apply to cultural difference. If societies disregard all differences associated with culture or pretend that these are of minimal importance, they are unlikely to achieve an equality of treatment. They will more probably end up with a formal equality of treatment that in practice favours some over others.

But when we talk about people's life chances or sense of themselves being shaped by their sex or class, this is not usually taken as denying their autonomy. As Gerald Dworkin observed years ago, you do not have to be the sole author of your actions to count as autonomous, and you do not have to arrive at your principles or beliefs entirely uninfluenced by anyone around you. All of us are "deeply influenced by parents, siblings, peers, culture, class, climate, schools, accident, genes and the accumulated history of the species."[50] At that point in time (this was in the late 1980s), Dworkin listed culture as one of the many influences—and failed to mention gender. Anyone drawing up the list today would almost certainly add gender, but might find it strange to have culture slipped in alongside the influence of siblings or schools. Culture has come to loom considerably larger than these other influences. As noted repeatedly through this book, culture is commonly represented as *more* determining and *less* compatible with autonomous action than either gender or class.

One of the reasons for this, to repeat, lies in the tendency to associate culture with non-Western or minority cultural groups, and to represent people in these groups as driven by their cultural values and traditions in ways that would seem alien to their counterparts in majority groups. When we talk of the influences of gender or class, we mostly appreciate that these have been influences on everyone, whatever their sex or class position. We do not divide the world into the more cosmopolitan members of the species who have freed themselves from all vestiges of class origin and managed to make their gender irrelevant, and those less favoured individuals who are still immersed in their class and gender formation. But then precisely because we do see class and gender as influ-

[50] Gerald Dworkin, *The Theory and Practice of Autonomy* (New York: Cambridge University Press, 1988), 36.

ences on everyone, we are less inclined to regard them as undermining a person's capacity for autonomy or status as a moral agent. (If they did undermine it, there would be no moral agents left.) The notion of culture, by contrast, has become increasingly exoticised, perceived as something that grips others, not me. In the process, it has become possible to think that the world divides into those at the mercy of their culture and those who have set themselves free. Culture and autonomy then become more mutually exclusive.

One indication of the contrasting approaches to culture, gender, and class is that there is widespread distrust of Parekh's "inability" argument when it is applied to gender or class. This is not because people feel that they have chosen their gender and class, nor because they feel that they have risen above all the early influences on their lives, nor in most cases because they have never felt their class and gender as a constraint. The objection, rather, is that saying that gender or class make it *impossible* for people to act any differently is felt to stereotype and patronise. It is felt to group too many individuals together into a single camp.

Consider smoking, which is clearly influenced by both gender and class. A number of countries have now introduced bans on smoking in public places. One counterargument to such initiatives is that this policy is unfair to working-class people because it fails to take into account the way that class affects the capacity to give up smoking. It is easy enough, it is said, for the middle classes, most of whom have already given up smoking and whose lifestyle is increasingly smoke free, to support a ban; but for someone who is out of work or living on the poverty line, being able to smoke may be one of the few remaining pleasures in life. By what right, then, do the complacent middle classes impose their own view of the healthy life on others? John Roemer provides a more theoretical version of this in his discussion of equality of opportunity.[51] He maintains that if the propensity to smoke is statistically correlated to sex, race, and class, such that a black male steelworker is more likely to be a heavy smoker than a white female college professor, then the steelworker can be said to have had less *opportunity* not to smoke than the professor. He should therefore be seen as less accountable for a failure to give up smoking. So if the society decides that heavy smokers must pay their smoking-related medical expenses, the steelworker should not be expected to pay as much as the (more culpable) heavy-smoking professor.

This line of argument has clear echoes of the cultural incapacity one, in that it is saying that the costs to one group of giving up smoking are significantly higher than those to another group, that it is much harder

---

[51] John E. Roemer, *Equality of Opportunity* (Cambridge, MA: Harvard University Press, 1998).

in practice for working-class than middle-class people to comply, and that legislation banning smoking in public places or making all heavy smokers pay the costs of their medical expenses is therefore unfair. It strikes me, however, that people do not take readily to this kind of argument when it is offered in relation to class. In some cases, they reject it because they see it as stereotyping working-class people, representing them all as forty-a-day smokers, unconcerned about their own or their children's health. In other cases, they reject it because they see the suggestion that being working class makes you *less capable* than others of giving up smoking as insulting or patronising. They do not necessarily contest the statistical evidence that middle-class people are on average less likely to be heavy smokers than working-class people, but accepting this is not the same as accepting Roemer's gloss on it, which represents working-class people as having *less opportunity* to give up smoking. To my knowledge, no one argues for a class exemption, along the lines of a cultural one, that would allow people, on production of the appropriate class certificate, to circumvent a general ban on smoking in public places. Apart from the obvious practical difficulties, a class exemption would be regarded as enormously insulting.

In respect to gender, there is a similar recognition that gender makes a difference, combined with a widespread refusal to take this as meaning that a woman cannot do what a man can do. There is considerable support for the kind of argument that underpinned the *Price v. Civil Service Commission* judgment, and it is not usually thought insulting to women to point out that many of them may be bringing up children in their twenties and hence not able to embark on their careers until a later date than men. On the other hand, it *would* be regarded as insulting (and in most countries, against the law) for an appointments committee to *presume* that a woman was going to spend her twenties rearing children and was therefore not a good candidate for the job. In the courtroom, there are many instances where a defence team represents its female client as less responsible for a crime than her male accomplice because he was the dominant partner in their relationship. There are also many cases where the judge is asked to take into account the defendant's dire socioeconomic circumstances. But it would not be assumed in such cases that a woman was less responsible *just because* she was a woman (though that was the assumption in English law for many years, at least as regards a married woman, who could not be tried independently for a crime if her husband was present at the time). Nor would it be assumed that a young offender was less blameworthy *just because* he was working class. Generalisations about gender and class always have to be filled in with specific evidence about the particular individual—what it is about *this* woman or *this* young offender that makes it unfair to hold them fully responsible for their acts?

On the whole, notions of inability are not now used in relation to either gender or class. You don't hear people saying, "I can't do this because I am working class," or (except sometimes, tongue in cheek), "I can't do this because I am a woman." Few would deny the constraints associated with gender and class, but there is a willingness to accept that people act autonomously even as they bow to gendered or class constraints. There is much less willingness to accept that people are acting autonomously when the constraint reflects culture.

Sawitri Saharso provides a particularly illuminating example of this when reporting a discussion of sex-selective abortion in the Netherlands (as it turned out, more an issue that gripped people's anxieties than something that was happening on any significant scale).[52] A television programme in the late 1990s had suggested that the Dutch abortion law was too lax, and that the wording of the act, which allowed women to have an abortion if they found themselves in a "critical situation," could be interpreted as permitting the abortion of a female foetus. The then minister of health—a feminist and a liberal—responded that in her view, sex-selective abortion was permissible under Dutch law, for she could imagine a situation in which "a woman from a foreign culture" might find herself in a critical situation if she were expecting another girl child and this put her marriage or even her life at risk. Many were horrified by this interpretation of the act and called for a tightening of the legislation to prohibit sex-selective abortion.

In the course of the discussion, it became clear that the constraints associated with class were being viewed differently from those associated with culture. In a standard "class" scenario, a woman requests an abortion because of her poverty. In what was being suggested as a standard "culture" scenario, she might request an abortion because the importance that her culture attaches to boys means she cannot "afford" to have another girl child. Both these are clearly choices made under constraints, and in each case, the woman might have reached a different decision had the circumstances been more favourable. But in the first instance, this is not normally taken as invalidating a woman's choice. We tend to think of a decision driven by economic considerations as still the woman's own; in the Netherlands, a majority then think of it as a decision the woman has a right to make. When, however, a woman is seen as responding to patriarchal norms that will make her life a misery if she has another girl, the decision to abort the foetus is less likely to be regarded as her own; she is

---

[52] Sawitri Saharso, "Feminist Ethics, Autonomy, and the Politics of Multiculturalism." *Feminist Theory* 4, no. 2 (2003): 199–215.

more likely to be represented as the victim of patriarchal norms, giving in to what one journalist described as a "culturally imposed demand."[53]

This is a hugely complicated issue, much discussed among feminists in India, where levels of sex-selective abortion and female infanticide are disturbingly high.[54] I am not arguing that sex-selective abortion should be regarded as a matter of a "woman's right to choose." Yet there is something odd about treating the decision not to have another child because the social inequalities of contemporary capitalism mean the family will be condemned to poverty as a sad but legitimate choice, and the decision not to have another *girl* child because the gender inequalities of one's culture mean the family will be condemned to poverty as an unacceptable capitulation to misogyny. There is a willingness to accept that people are acting autonomously even when bowing to economic necessity, but not a parallel willingness when they bow to cultural expectations. This puts the influence of culture in a completely different category from the influence of class.

The point I am stressing is that it has proved difficult in the debates around multiculturalism to allow for the *relevance* of culture without making culture a *determinant* of action, and that this is perplexing, given the relative ease with which law courts, governments, and popular opinion have come to differentiate influence from determination in regard to gender or social class. In discussions of the latter, we have become adept at talking about influences without suggesting that these determine behaviour. Indeed, in much of the current academic literature, people employ a language of negotiation rather than causation, and speak of people acting out (or performing) their class and gender identities, rather than being acted on. This is also increasingly standard talk in the sociological literature on culture, but popular discourse—also, I think, the literature in political theory—lags behind. Culture continues to be employed in a less differentiated and more stereotypical way. The easy finessing of free will and determinism that is becoming part of the common sense on gender and class is much less evident in relation to culture. More precisely, it is less evident in relation to minority or non-Western cultures, for it is in respect to these—not hegemonic cultures—that it has become so common to read individuals from their culture, and attribute all quirks of thought and action to membership in a cultural group.

---

[53] Cited in ibid., 204.

[54] See, for example, Nivedita Menon, "The Impossibility of 'Justice': Female Foeticide and Feminist Discourse on Abortion," in *Social Reform, Sexuality, and the State*, ed. Patricia Uberoi (New Delhi: Sage, 1996); Rajeswari Sunder Rajan, *The Scandal of the State: Women, Law, and Citizenship in Postcolonial India* (Durham, NC: Duke University Press, 2003).

The understanding of cultural difference and cultural influence would be much enhanced if multicultural societies could learn to treat culture in the more nuanced way that has become the norm in terms of gender and class. At present, culture remains too much an all-or-nothing phenomenon. Individuals are either in their culture (whether by birth or choice), in which case they are considered at the mercy of its prescriptions and prohibitions, or they exercise their powers of reflection and creativity, and can then no longer be considered authentic members of the cultural group. We are often told that the threat of ostracism is one of the ways in which cultures maintain their hold over their members, forcing people to swallow their criticisms on pain of being excluded from their cultural group. I sometimes think it is those outside the group who find it so hard to recognise nonconformists as "still" authentically aboriginal, Muslim, Sikh, Chinese, and so on. The preconceived images remain strong, making autonomy seem incompatible with culture.

Instead of viewing culture as something that *requires* individuals to do X or makes it *impossible* for them to do Y, it would help to think of the power of culture in ways more analogous to the power of gender or class. This shift in understanding would not significantly affect the policy outcomes in the kinds of cases discussed by Parekh, for as cases involving gender discrimination demonstrate, it is possible to make a convincing claim about indirect discrimination without deploying a determinist account of gender. Where it matters most is in relation to issues like overseas marriage or wearing the hijab, where it is sometimes offered as the reason for government action that girls and women are being forced to behave in ways that go against their own wishes and needs. It is never easy to determine who is being coerced, who claims to be acting for herself but is in reality being coerced, and who is genuinely making up her own mind. Where there *is* evidence of coercion, governments clearly have a responsibility to act. It is also reasonable to assume that there are plenty of cases of unproven coercion, and that limiting public assistance to those where there is self-evident coercion is therefore an inadequate response. But public authorities should be wary of presuming that culture makes people behave in a certain way, and extremely wary of presuming that some cultural groups are less capable of autonomy than others. Blanket bans, introduced in the name of protecting the weak and the vulnerable, should be regarded as particularly suspect.

CHAPTER FIVE

Exit and Voice

IN PREVIOUS CHAPTERS I have argued against determinist understandings of culture that represent women and girls from minority cultural groups as controlled or coerced by their cultures, and treat them as less than autonomous beings. The implication, in relation to cultural defence, is that courts need to be aware of the stereotyping and simplifications that attend references to culture, and recognise the many individual variations that culture talk tends to obscure. In relation to public policy, the main implication is that governments should stop justifying prohibitions on female behaviour on the often-spurious ground that they are protecting girls and women from coercion. Governments have a responsibility to protect individuals from coercion, but individuals also have rights, and some of the current prohibitions sacrifice the rights of individuals to their so-called protection. Thus, I suggest a less interventionist and more rights-driven approach to cultural diversity.

I turn at this point to what would be an even less interventionist approach: a version of multiculturalism that relies on the individual's right to exit as the main protection against undue cultural pressures. To anticipate, I do not regard this as providing sufficient protection, and part of my objection (perhaps surprisingly) is that it does not attach *enough* significance to cultural belonging. Where much of the argument so far has stressed the dangers of treating culture as more important, more overwhelming, and more all-encompassing than it is, I focus here on some of the dangers on the other side. I point to the risks of treating culture as something that can be readily put on or taken off.

My overall object, to repeat, is a multiculturalism that does without reified or essentialised notions of culture, but retains enough substance to differentiate itself from cosmopolitanism. I reject the idea of culture as thing, mainly because culture is not like that, but I arrived at this position via feminist concerns about cultural leaders abusing static conceptions of culture to preempt claims about women's rights. In my own thinking on these issues, the critique of reified notions of culture therefore went hand in hand with a critique of supposedly traditional practices that subordinate women. I start the chapter with what, from this perspective, is an oddity: a position in the literature that is also sceptical about culture, but argues for a level of toleration for cultural groups that would allow them to override most women's rights' claims. In *The Liberal Archipelago*, Chandran Kukathas rejects the notion of cultures as incommensurable, represents group identity as a political rather than cultural construct, and argues that human beings are guided by the same basic principles of human behaviour, no matter what their cultural group. He sees culture and ethnicity as fluid—people trade, migrate, marry individuals from other cultural and ethnic groups, and borrow ideas—and views identity as inescapably political. In a comment that might be taken from any number of contemporary feminist texts, Kukathas argues that "the most seductive and dangerous move in politics is that move which asserts identity to be *not* political but, somehow, natural or original. But identity is not natural, or original, or permanent, or even necessarily particularly enduring. It is fluid, ever-changing (to varying degrees) and inescapably political."[1]

In the feminist literature, the representation of culture as political or fluid helps challenge misogynist readings of a culture, making it harder for group leaders to impose what they claim to be their culture's cherished traditions. Uma Narayan stresses the selectivity with which particular practices are deemed core, and the tendency to rate in this way practices that keep women in their place. Leti Volpp asserts that courts need to hear the variety of interpretations of what are contested and shifting practices, not just accept one canonical reading. The group Women Living Under Muslim Laws disseminates information about the different ways Muslim law is interpreted in different Muslim countries, and uses this to encourage women to press for more progressive interpretations.[2] In Kukathas's argument, by contrast, women derive no great benefit from the fluidity of culture. The fact that people can and frequently do change their cultural practices does not significantly diminish the authority of the cultural group. It just supports an almost-exclusive reliance on exit as what protects the individual against cultural pressures.

So far as is possible, Kukathas wants cultural associations to be left alone to live as they choose. This includes being left alone to impose what restrictions they consider appropriate on the members of the association. The only significant protection he allows for dissident or dissatisfied members is that they must be free to leave one kind of association and join or set up another. If, in other words, they no longer accept the rules of the association, it must be possible for them to leave. This deliberately elides leaving a cultural "association" with other kinds of decisions like leaving a trade union or changing a job. Kukathas never claims that it is *easy* to

---

[1] Chandran Kukathas, *The Liberal Archipelago* (Oxford: Oxford University Press, 2003), 90.

[2] See their Web site, www.wluml.org.

leave one's culture or change one's beliefs, but his treatment of cultural groups as just another kind of association and his perception of cultures as constituted by the actions of individuals (not, as some other theorists would see it, the other way round) helps sustain an overly confident reliance on exit.

Kukathas rejects the idea that culture has an intrinsic value and criticises those who have represented an individual's well-being as bound up with the persistence of a particular culture. In doing so, he echoes some of the new anthropology's points about culture as a political construct. "The world is not," Kukathas declares, "arranged around groups with pervasive cultures; rather, groups have settled around social and political institutions and have acquired much of their cultural distinctiveness and shape because of these political formations . . . the most important fact about the way our world is organized is that it is, first and foremost, *politically* rather than culturally organized."[3] Part of his scepticism therefore comes from his recognition of the role of history, accident, and politics in "creating" ethnic or cultural groups. This combines with a rational actor tradition he traces back to David Hume that sees human beings as much the same the whole world over, "driven by the same motives which have marked human conduct over the millennia."[4] In this constructivist account of culture and universalist account of human nature, cultural groups are best understood "simply as associations of individuals."[5] We form associations because we find it in our interest to do so, and since we form them under different circumstances, we develop different practices and sensibilities. Since the motivating sources of human action have a cross-cultural universality, the resulting diversity does not mean that the practices of one culture will appear totally mysterious to those from another. In terms that recall Gananath Obeyesekere's critique of what he considered Marshall Sahlin's overly mythologised account of the killing of Captain Cook, Kukathas notes that "we have no experience of people who differ from us inasmuch as they act without motivation, do not rank options and make trade-offs, and have no taboos."[6] Nevertheless, differences in circumstances mean that ways of living and notions of morality or justice will be highly diverse. Since all individuals have the right to live their lives according to the dictates of their conscience (a foundational principle for Kukathas), there can be no justification for imposing the principles of one association on those who have chosen to live in another.

---

[3] Ibid., 198.
[4] Ibid., 42.
[5] Ibid., 97.
[6] Ibid., 66.

Though individuals rather than groups provide the basic units in this theory, this does not translate into any strong protection for individual rights. There will, no doubt, be associations that operate on the basis of an impeccably egalitarian charter of individual rights. But there will be others that regard men and women as fundamentally different, and see it as inappropriate for women to hold property in their own name or be educated in the same skills as men. There will be yet others that consider the notion of children's rights as an oxymoron and regard physical chastisement as the best way to discipline children. In Kukathas's argument, we have no basis for saying that one of these is more legitimate than the others. So long as the individual members of the association acquiesce in the practices (and that basically means so long as they stay in the association), we should assume that they consider these practices right and just. A member's right to exit then becomes the only really fundamental right. So long as individuals have the right to leave their community—and have decided not to exercise it—we should assume that they are living according to principles of their choice.

In contrast to those whose multiculturalism is premised on the intrinsic value or encompassing nature of cultures, Kukathas thus offers what could be described as a multiculturalism without culture—a regime of strong toleration that dispenses with strong notions of culture. In most of the feminist literature, weakening the claims of culture has also meant weakening the authority of the cultural group. According to Kukathas, it combines with a laissez-faire liberalism that could, in his own words, involve "significant harms" being visited on the most vulnerable members of a community.[7] He acknowledges that his own noninterventionist brand of multiculturalism might indeed mean tolerating communities that bring up children unschooled and illiterate, force young people into unwanted marriages, or inflict cruel and unusual punishment. His position therefore offers minimal protection to the individual—and is what one would more readily expect from theorists who insist on the rights of the cultural group. His representation of this as a specifically *liberal* theory depends very much on the validity of his position on exit.

Right of Exit

The right of exit figures, in some way, in every resolution of multicultural dilemmas and is one of the few uncontested rights in these debates. Even the strongest advocate of cultural rights will not say that groups have the right to detain individuals against their will or force them to live according

---

[7] Ibid., 135.

to prescriptions they no longer accept. In fact, in most instances those policing the membership of cultural groups do not want the right to hold on to recalcitrant members and are all too happy to get rid of them. The more common problem, addressed later in this chapter, is that people who continue to identify with their group, but break *some* of its cultural prescriptions, may find themselves excluded against their wishes. Churches cannot force people who repudiate their beliefs to remain members, but they can and do excommunicate those they see as promoting beliefs incompatible with church membership. The threat of exclusion is one of the pressures brought to bear on people resisting an arranged marriage, who are often made to feel that they will be cutting themselves off from their community and culture if they persist in refusing a particular marriage partner. Susan Moller Okin describes as "involuntary exit" the case of a pregnant teacher in a Christian fundamentalist school whose employment contract was terminated because the school board believed women with young children should not go out to work.[8] Madhavi Sunder discusses the case of a New Jersey scoutmaster whose membership in the Boy Scouts of America was revoked when the organisation discovered that he was gay, and who then fought an unsuccessful legal battle against the exclusion, taking his case as far as the Supreme Court.[9] As the examples indicate, there has been disagreement about—and even legal challenges over—whether and when groups have the right to force a member to leave. There is no such disagreement about whether individuals have the right to go.

The point at issue, then, is not whether people should have the right to leave their cultural community or group, but whether having this right can ever be enough of a protection against cultural pressures. It is clear why some liberals might want to present it as such. The alternatives mostly involve a schedule of basic human rights that sets the limits of toleration and provides the wider society with the necessary guidelines for deciding which activities should be banned. Given the real possibility that what are conceived of as basic human rights or universal principles of rectitude might be more parochial reflections of a particular social history, this could mean imposing the values of one group on the others. For principled as well as pragmatic reasons, it can therefore seem a good idea to put the onus of decision on the individual. Instead of governments intervening in a heavy-handed manner to protect individuals from their cultural group, why not concentrate on ensuring that individuals

[8] Susan Moller Okin, "'Mistresses of Their Own Destiny': Group Rights, Gender, and Realistic Rights of Exit," *Ethics* 112 (January 2002): 205–30.

[9] Madhavi Sunder, "Cultural Dissent," *Stanford Law Review* 545 (December 2001): 495–567.

retain their right to leave? As Brian Barry puts it, "If you remain in some association that you have the power to leave, that establishes a presumption that the perceived benefits of staying are greater than the benefits of the most attractive alternative."[10] The fact that someone else thinks your situation is intolerable does not seem sufficient reason for a government to intervene.

If the right to exit is the *only* restriction a society places on the activities of a cultural group, however, this requires maximum toleration of a maximum diversity of practices—some of which might be deeply at odds with gender equality. This suggests a strong version of multiculturalism. The oddity is that it is a multiculturalism that depends on a rather cavalier attitude towards the capacity of individuals to leave their cultural group, and to that extent, on a weak representation of culture. This is one of the paradoxes in the exit approach. What I have previously described as strong or reified notions of culture overstate the power that culture exerts over the individual, and sometimes rely on this overstatement to justify cultural concessions. Exit approaches to cultural diversity suffer from the opposite problem, in that they seem to understate culture's power. They misrepresent exit as easier than it is, and staying as more of an expression of acceptance. Because they make exit the main way to address oppression, they also reduce the pressure on cultural groups to engage in internal change.

The literature on this has identified two main difficulties with exit. The first is that saying one has the right to leave one's cultural group or community may turn out to be empty talk, begging major questions about the substantive conditions that make the right of exit real. What, for example, of a community like the Amish that removes its children from schooling at the age of fourteen and leaves them ill equipped for life outside? What of communities that practice communal ownership of land and thereby tie their members into financial dependence? What of the psychological costs of exit: the fear of ostracism by family and friends, the potential loss of identity, or just the generalised fear of change? Given the many reasons why people might find it difficult—in some cases, even inconceivable—to live outside their cultural group, how much can we really assume from an individual's decision not to leave? Jacob Levy neatly sums up these points when he observes that "everything about a culture is an exit barrier. To have a culture whose exit is entirely costless (not just beneficial all things considered, but *costless*) is to have no culture at all."[11]

---

[10] Brian Barry, *Culture and Equality: An Egalitarian Critique of Multiculturalism* (Cambridge, UK: Polity Press, 2001), 149.

[11] Jacob T. Levy, *The Multiculturalism of Fear* (Oxford: Oxford University Press, 2000), 112.

Some of my illustrations draw, again, on the example of forced marriage. I have noted that one favoured policy response is to set age restrictions on the entry of overseas spouses. But immigration control is not the only or even dominant response. In the United Kingdom, much of the policy emphasis has been on enabling young people to refuse or escape a forced marriage: helping them get out of a marriage they entered against their will, or before they reach that point, get away from the family and community that is exerting pressure on them. Following the 1999 report of the Working Group on Forced Marriage, the government set up the Community Liaison Unit (later relaunched as the Forced Marriage Unit), with the remit to coordinate initiatives against forced marriage. This unit helped draw up guidelines for police officers, social workers, and teachers, and provides an impressive (if somewhat shoestring) helpline for individuals, dealing with an average of 350 cases each year. Working in cooperation with police forces, courts, and embassy staff in the Indian subcontinent, the unit has helped a significant number of young people extricate themselves from the threat of an unwanted marriage, including assisting in their repatriation if their families have taken them abroad. Working in cooperation with nongovernmental organisations and women's refuges in the United Kingdom, it has also helped young people find alternative accommodation away from the families who are pressuring them. Some of the domestic police forces have been active as well, and their initiatives, too, are often literally focused on exit: directing people to alternative accommodation and sometimes even organising a police escort to enable people to escape from the family home. The difficulties that surround these initiatives therefore provide a particularly good illustration of the general problems in ensuring "realistic" rights of exit.

The second set of difficulties picks up on Albert Hirschman's distinction between exit and voice, and his suggestion (applied, in his work, to the relationship between a customer and a firm) that an infatuation with exit can discourage internally generated change. Voice, for Hirschman, meant trying to alter rather than escape an objectionable state of affairs—for example, customers or shareholders challenging the practices of a firm rather than simply taking their money elsewhere. At the time of his writing (in the late 1960s), he assumed that the exit option was "ordinarily unthinkable, though not always wholly impossible, from such primordial human groupings as family, tribe, church, and state."[12] His worries about the preference for "flight rather than fight,"[13] however, have been echoed in recent literature on cultural change, where feminists have been particu-

---

[12] Albert O. Hirschman, *Exit, Voice, and Loyalty* (Cambridge, MA: Harvard University Press, 1970), 76.
[13] Ibid., 108.

larly prominent in arguing the importance of contesting discriminatory practices from within, and have often explicitly linked this to a critique of cultural essentialism.

Making Exit Real

What makes the exit option real? When Marx analysed the "free labour" of capitalism, he noted that unlike the slave or feudal serf of earlier times, wage labourers belonged to neither owner nor land, and were free to leave their employers when they liked. Although Marx did not use this term, the wage labourer had an exit option, and this was an important new phenomenon. The freedom to leave one's employer, to move around the country in search of better employment conditions, to move even to a different country, is not a negligible freedom, and though later generations of socialists often spoke of workers as "wage slaves," Marx insisted on the differences between slavery and wage labour. But so long as selling one's labour (or more technically, in Marxist language, one's labour power) to *some* employer is the only means of subsistence, wage labourers cannot leave the entire class of employers. The wage labourer belongs, as Marx put it, not to this or that capitalist but to the capitalist class as a whole. Saying that one has the *right* of exit does not, in other words, tell us enough. If we are to take the act of staying as indicating acquiescence, we have to consider further questions about what makes the exit option real. Four of these commonly arise in the literature. Is there anywhere else for you to go? Do you have access to the minimal resources without which you cannot realistically leave? Is the cost of leaving set unacceptably high? And of particular pertinence when considering exit from a culture, is it possible for you even to conceive of going?

Everyone accepts the importance of the first question. If there were only one kind of society in the world—say, all six and a half billion of us lived under an identical regime of state communism—it would make no sense to say we had indicated our acquiescence in the system of government by virtue of not going elsewhere. Dissenters have to have somewhere to go; this is one of the conditions set by Kukathas, the other being that associations should not be legally authorized to prevent them from leaving.[14] But while this condition seems at first glance straightforward (either there is or there isn't somewhere else to go), it remains a matter of degree. As

---

[14] William Galston also argues that "in circumstances of genuine pluralism, individual freedom is adequately protected by secure rights of exit coupled with the existence of a wider society open to individuals wishing to leave their groups of origin"; "Two Concepts of Liberalism," *Ethics* 105 (April 1995): 533.

we have seen, Marx suggests that wage labourers are free to leave their employers, but in the deeper sense of leaving the capitalist class as a whole, have nowhere else to go. The same would apply to a bunch of anarchists weighing up which country to move to. If you are profoundly disenchanted with *any* of the existing systems of government, you might feel justifiably irritated if your decision to exchange one system of oppression for another is taken as evidence that you acquiesce in the new one. There is in one sense somewhere to go; in another, all places are the same.

Needing somewhere else to go has been axiomatic in relation to domestic violence, and here too there are crucial matters of degree. Women's refuges are often underfunded and overcrowded. They provide security, but sometimes at the cost of privacy, and they may have difficulty balancing the need to protect residents from renewed contact with violent partners against the need to sustain contact between fathers and their children. Given these difficulties, it is not surprising that some women who urgently need a way out of their domestic situation still turn down the offer of a place in a refuge. When considered as places of safety for young people escaping an unwanted marriage, these problems are compounded by the fact that most refuges were not set up with this in mind. Women's refuges are more likely to be organised around the needs of women with children and women who have experienced severe physical violence, and may not be particularly attuned to the religious and/or cultural needs of those escaping a forced marriage. The United Kingdom's Forced Marriage Unit reports a number of instances of people "rescued" from the threat of a forced marriage and placed in secure alternative accommodation, but drifting back to their families because of the loneliness; some of these contact the unit a second or even third time because their families start coercing them again into marriage. In a strict sense, someone escaping a forced marriage always has somewhere else to go. They can always find *somewhere*, however unwelcoming or unsatisfactory, that provides an alternative to living with the family pressuring them into marriage or living with an unwanted spouse. Having the right somewhere to go, though, is more a matter of degree.

This is also true in relation to the second question: are there certain resources without which you cannot, in practice, leave? Some cultural—and particularly, some religious—communities organise the education of their young people in ways that make it especially hard for them to uproot themselves and live elsewhere. This is true, for example, of the Old Order Amish, an Anabaptist group that fled to North America to escape religious persecution in Europe, and now live in small communities across the United States and western Canada. A U.S. Supreme Court decision in the case of *Wisconsin v. Yoder* (1972) granted them (on the basis of parents' rights to guide the religious future and education of their children) the unusual right to withdraw their children from school at the age of fourteen. Since the economy of these communities is organised primarily around farming and the young Amish leave school with no formal quali-fications, it is reasonable to assume that they are poorly equipped to seek employment and independence outside their community. Similar prob-lems—Jeff Spinner-Halev suggests, even greater problems—arise for ultra-Orthodox Jews, who regard the study of religious texts as the core of a boy's education.[15] This also is not a great preparation for dissidents who want to try their hand at living a different kind of life. The Hutterites of western Canada (another Anabaptist group that fled religious persecu-tion in Europe) live in small farming communities where all the land and resources are communally owned. Anyone leaving the community leaves with nothing. In many countries and cultures, women have lower literacy rates than men, and girls are more likely than boys to be withdrawn from school. It is somewhat misleading to represent this as a cultural or reli-gious phenomenon, because the presumption that the schooling of boys matters more than the schooling of girls has been a characteristic of pretty much all countries and cultures up until the 1970s. The fact remains that in many communities, girls and women are ill equipped educationally to start life afresh in another. They are also less likely to own property.

In the case of people seeking to leave a forced marriage, resource con-straints loom particularly large for women married against their will to European citizens and then brought into the country as spouses. In the United Kingdom, these women do not qualify independently for most forms of public funding until they have been granted indefinite leave to remain, and under current regulations, they must live in the country for at least two years before becoming eligible for this.[16] They rely, moreover, on their husbands to make the application on their behalf, and there are cases where women have remained in limbo for years because their hus-bands preferred not to submit the applications. Campaigning by women's

---

[15] "Some Ultraorthodox Jewish boys know a great deal about Jewish texts, but little else"; Jeff Spinner-Halev, *Surviving Diversity: Religion and Democratic Citizenship* (Balti-more, MD: Johns Hopkins University Press, 2000), 78.

[16] The Forced Marriage Unit's Guidelines for Social Workers puts it thus:

If the young person has not got indefinite leave to remain (ILR), exceptional leave to remain or a right of abode in the UK then they are likely to have a restriction on receiv-ing public funds. Public funds include income support and housing benefit. This means that they will not automatically get access to a refuge (although some refuges will offer places). As a result individuals may experience tremendous difficulty in finding alterna-tive accommodation and a means by which to live. This may lead individuals to feel they have no option but to remain in the marriage and to feel unable to co-operate with social services or anyone they see as being in "authority."

groups has produced what is known as the "domestic violence concession," whereby those who can prove that they are victims of domestic violence can speed up the process of getting the independent right to remain in the country. But the standard of proof is high, and these women still have no access to public funds until their immigration status is resolved.[17] When we add to this that many of them will not yet be fluent in English, and may have no friends or contacts outside the family of their spouse, it is clear that the opportunity for leaving an unwanted marriage is severely curtailed.

The tough response to these objections is to say that people *do* leave, even when the conditions seem least propitious. Despite the many difficulties, some of the women trapped in unwanted marriages find their way to a supportive women's group or sympathetic member of Parliament; indeed, it is only because some do escape the trap that we know such cases exist. Spinner-Halev notes that despite their seeming lack of qualification for life outside the Amish community, a steady number of Amish do leave.[18] Kukathas adds that those who leave are often the ones who would be thought of as the most vulnerable. The rich and the powerful have less of an incentive to leave their community, for things are mostly going their way, and it is commonly the poor and the powerless who exit: "Amish elders do not commonly defect. Nor are the world refugee camps filled with members of political elites."[19] The suggestion here is that people are more ingenious than is credited by those who anguish about their vulnerability. If we are being really tough-minded, those who leave can be taken as proof that the others also could. This is too complacent, but it does usefully remind us that people retain agency even when their lives are severely circumscribed. It also reinforces the point about realistic rights of exit being a matter of degree.

---

[17] Pieces of evidence that are now deemed acceptable are a medical report from a hospital doctor, a letter from a general practitioner, an undertaking to a court, a police report, a letter from social services, or a letter from a women's refuge. An applicant needs two pieces of evidence, however, if she does not have one of those specified under the original concession, and the Women's Aid Federation reports that the success so far has been limited; Women's Aid Federation, "Briefing on the Key Issues Facing Abused Women with Insecure Immigration Status to Entering the UK to Join Their Settled Partner," 2002, www.womensaid.org.uk.

[18] Jeff Spinner, *The Boundaries of Citizenship: Race, Ethnicity, and Nationality in the Liberal State* (Baltimore, MD: Johns Hopkins University Press, 1994), 102. This leaves him open to criticism by Barry, who argues that he simultaneously claims the proportion leaving (around 20 percent) as high enough to undercut worries about the Amish not having the capacity to survive outside and too low to trigger concerns about them not being sufficiently prepared; Barry, *Culture and Equality*, 242–43.

[19] Kukathas, *The Liberal Archipelago*, 108.

Because of this, some have rephrased the question about whether people are able to exit (do they have the minimum resources necessary to leave?) into one of costs. In the absence of physical coercion, it is assumed that people can leave, and this assumption is confirmed by the evidence that some people do. It is also assumed that any decision carrries costs with it, and that sometimes the costs of leaving one's community will be high. For Kukathas, this is pretty much the end of the question, because he sees costs as having nothing to do with the freedom to leave. "Cost may have a large bearing on the decision taken; but it has no bearing on the individual's freedom to take it."[20] As an illustration, he imagines himself being offered a billion dollars not to leave his position as a chief executive officer to become a university professor, and notes that while this makes exit extremely costly, it would be odd to say that he was no longer free to leave. But the example works partly because it translates costs into monetary terms—and even in poor societies, people tend to view money as something one can have more or less of, rather than something without which one cannot be alive. The example might be less convincing if the cost were linked to identity, to something without which you cannot continue to be the person you think you are. Strictly speaking, someone whose sense of herself is profoundly bound up with being a Catholic *is* still free to choose an abortion, just as someone whose self-definition depends on being a good and loving daughter is still free to refuse the marriage partner that her parents have chosen. But the cost involved in changing your sense of who you are is significantly different from that involved in refusing a billion dollars you do not currently have. Saying cost has "no bearing" on the freedom to make a decision only makes sense if you refuse, in principle, to think of freedom as open to gradations.

That all-or-nothing conception of freedom is not, in my view, helpful, nor is it in line with current UK jurisprudence on forced marriage. Under an all-or-nothing definition, anyone who gets married due to parental pressure has agreed to the arrangement, for all marriages require at least the semblance of consent, and young people are not being carried kicking and screaming to the ceremony.[21] With important exceptions, these are not cases of parents disposing of their children to the highest bidder or using them to cement a business deal. More commonly, the parents may genuinely believe they are acting in the best interests of their children, and

---

[20] Ibid., 107.

[21] This is perhaps too sanguine a statement. In the case that prompted the Norwegian government to introduce specific legislation against forced marriage, the young woman was lured to Pakistan and married at gunpoint; Hege Storhaug and Human Rights Service, *Human Visas: A Report from the Front Lines of Europe's Integration Crisis* (Oslo, Norway: Human Rights Service, 2003).

since the children remain (understandably) unwilling to break off family ties, many young people will succumb to moral pressure and consent. Up until the 1980s, the English and Scottish courts took this as evidence of free consent. Anyone applying for the annulment of a marriage on the grounds of coercion had to establish that they had been frightened into the marriage by threats to "life, limb, or liberty," and this rule was rigorously applied even in a case like *Singh v. Singh* (1971), where the petitioner was a seventeen-year-old Sikh girl who had gone through a civil marriage ceremony, but subsequently refused to confirm it through a religious ceremony or have anything to do with her husband.[22] The judges decided she would have been willing enough to continue with the marriage had the man in question been (as promised) handsome and educated. In what now seems an extraordinary trivialisation of her dilemma, they concluded that when she saw him for the first time, "she did not like what she saw" and therefore changed her mind after the ceremony. Despite her age, her obvious vulnerability to parental pressure, and the fact that the two young people had not met before the ceremony, this was accepted as a marriage based on free consent.

In the landmark case of *Hirani v. Hirani* (1983), the Court of Appeal adopted a more nuanced position. The petitioner this time was a nineteen-year-old Hindu woman who had gone through both civil and religious ceremonies, and lived with her husband (though in an unconsummated marriage) for six weeks before leaving him. On this occasion, her age and financial dependence on her parents were taken as relevant factors, while the fact that her parents had arranged the marriage in order to prevent her association with a young Muslim man was taken as a clear enough indication that she was an unwilling participant. The court concluded that the crucial question was not whether she was in genuine fear for her life or liberty but "whether the mind of the applicant (the victim) has in fact been overborne, howsoever that was caused."[23] The Scottish case of *Mahmud v. Mahmud* (1993) further established that a thirty-year-old man, living apart from his family and not financially dependent on them, could have his consent "vitiated by pressure amounting to force"—in this case, by being made to believe that his persistent refusal to marry had brought about his father's death, and was bringing shame and degradation on his family.[24] The judge argued that in cases of moral pressure,

[22] *Singh v. Singh* [1971] All ER 828.

[23] *Hirani v. Hirani* [1983] 4 F.L.R. 232.

[24] *Mahmud v. Mahmud* [1994] S.L.T. 599. The man had been living for some years with a non-Muslim woman, with whom he already had one child and was expecting another, and the cousin brought over from Pakistan for the marriage had already been deported by the immigration authorities at the time of the case. It seems likely that these factors had an important effect.

there was "no general basis for expecting the male to be stronger than the female or the thirty-year-old to be less swayed by conscience than the twenty-four-old," and granted a decree of nullity.[25] If freedom is conceived of as something we either have or don't, then the kinds of costs referred to in these cases—the threatened loss of financial support, the supposed responsibility for the death of one's father, or the inability to continue thinking of oneself as a good daughter or loving son—should have no bearing. The courts have decided otherwise, establishing a more nuanced definition of free consent.

In the theory literature, costs have either been detached from the freedom to act (Kukathas) or turned into a question of compensation. The main focus has been whether the cost of leaving has been set unacceptably high—so not whether the cost has become, in the strict sense of the word, prohibitive but more that it may have become unfair. As regards the case of people leaving a Hutterite community, for example, there seems to be something of a consensus (at least among political theorists) that people should be able to take something from the communal property when they leave. Spinner-Halev suggests that the Hutterites should set aside an exit fund for members leaving the community, and mentions a few thousand dollars per individual as a possible sum.[26] Barry believes the Hutterites should make payments to those they expel, though not, so far as I can tell, to those who leave voluntarily.[27] Even Kukathas accepts that Hutterites leaving their community have some moral and legal claim to a share of the communal property, although he finds it hard to see how this claim might be quantified.[28] It is perhaps pertinent to note that this issue came to the fore because of a lawsuit in 1970, when four brothers forced to leave because of their conversion to a different religion claimed a share of the colony's assets.[29] Given the context, subsequent discussion has focused not so much on whether people *can* leave without some share of the assets but whether it is fair for them to be expected to do so. The discussion has shifted, that is, from whether exit is a realistic option to whether it is fair, and then shifted further into a question of compensation.

This move is particularly apparent in Barry's discussion of what he terms the intrinsic, associative, and external costs of exit. These are not distinguished according to the kinds of obstacles they would present to

---

[25] Key later cases, both from the Scottish courts, include *Mahmood v. Mahmood* [1993] S.L.T 589; *Sohrab v. Khan* [2002] SCLR 663.

[26] Spinner-Halev, *Surviving Diversity*, 77.

[27] Barry, *Culture and Equality*, 164.

[28] Chandran Kukathas, "The Life of Brian—or Now for Something Completely Difference-Blind," in *Multiculturalism Reconsidered*, ed. Paul Kelly (Cambridge, UK: Polity Press, 2002), 201–2.

[29] *Hofer v. Hofer* (1970) 13 DLR (3d) 1 (Supreme Court of Canada).

someone deciding whether to leave (on a scale of more to less difficult) but according to whether the liberal state could legitimately reduce the costs.[30] Nothing, Barry argues, can be done about intrinsic costs, for these are ones that are inherent to the loss of membership, and arise out of associations doing things they must be permitted to do. He illustrates this (perhaps oddly) with a case of *involuntary* exit: excommunication by the Catholic Church. We cannot say it is unfair for the individual to have to carry the costs of this exclusion, because that would mean denying churches the right to determine what beliefs are compatible with church membership. So no case for compensation here. Associative costs come about as a result of people doing things no liberal state could compel them to do: for example, refusing to have anything to do with lapsed members, or refusing to speak to one's daughter if she marries outside her cultural or religious group. Here the freedom of group members to associate with whom they choose comes up against the potential delinquent's freedom from coercion. Sadly, there is not much the state can do here either. The point at which it can act is when individuals face what Barry calls the external costs of exit. Governments can make it illegal, for instance, for organisations to sack ex-members from their jobs, except where it can be shown that the work needs someone of that particular cultural or religious persuasion. They can also require associations to compensate ex-members who have suffered serious financial hardship as a result of a boycott by their erstwhile colleagues.

Barry is clearly concerned about what makes exit a real option. He notes that "if the possibility of exit were to be understood as no more than the absence of locked doors or chains, its value as a safeguard against oppression and exploitation would be extremely scant," and goes on to stress the value of education in equipping people both to choose and to leave.[31] He presents his discussion of exit costs as a way of establishing when membership in a group is really voluntary: in essence, membership can be regarded as voluntary so long as the costs of exit are not excessive. But because excessive is understood as more than is fair, this gets tangled up with what it is legitimate for individuals and governments to do, and this moves the discussion away from whether exit is a realistic option. To a devout Catholic (as Barry observes) the costs of excommunication are almost beyond calculation, but since it is legitimate for a church to impose these costs, it hardly makes sense to describe them as excessive. Barry then has nothing interesting to say about whether Catholics who are at odds with the church over core components of its teachings can be described as free to leave. In a move that mirrors much recent theorising

---

[30] Barry, *Culture and Equality*, 150–54.
[31] Ibid., 239–40.

about equality and justice, the attention shifts from prior constraints on action to after-the-event calculations about compensation.

When is Exit Even an Imaginable Option?

The feminist literature has been less focused on calculations of cost or compensation, and more on the fourth question about whether people can even imagine life outside their cultural group. Describing the right of exit as important but "inherently problematic," Okin has observed that "those most likely to need it are those least likely to be able to employ it. Neither may they see it as a desirable or even an imaginable option."[32] I have reported numerous criticisms of Okin for representing women from non-Western cultures as "victims without agency," but her underlying argument about oppression stultifying the imagination should not really be controversial in feminist circles. It has been one of the formative beliefs that women who are encouraged to see themselves as of lesser value than men will put up with worse treatment than those who regard themselves as equals—hence the energy that feminists from Mary Wollstonecraft onwards have put into challenging myths of female inferiority. Similar points apply to children, who are likely to put up with worse treatment if they have been persuaded to believe that young people should be seen but not heard than if they have been encouraged to think in terms of children's rights. The effects of socialisation are never secure, for people everywhere question, subvert, and challenge (and it may be that Okin does not sufficiently acknowledge this). But if you have been taught to regard respect for your elders as one of life's central values, you are less likely to question your parents' decisions—including those about whom you should marry—than if you have been taught to consider the older generation as hopelessly out of date. You may not even experience their control as control.

I do not, therefore, reject Okin's suggestion on principle, for I share her belief that horizons are drawn in relation to what is perceived as possible, and that years of being told there is no alternative can have a paralysing effect. And yet in relation to forced marriage, the suggestion that people might be so conditioned by the expectations of their culture that they simply don't see themselves as coerced fails to ring true. This is partly because there *is* no cultural expectation as regards forced marriage, only, in some cultures, an expectation that marriages will be arranged. But the suggestion also misses the mark because people *do* know the difference between wanting and not wanting a particular marriage partner. None of the evidence indicates that people cannot imagine life in any other way

---

[32] Okin, "Mistresses of Their Own Destiny," 205.

or that they are unaware of being pressured into something against their will. Rather, the problem is that the right to exit leaves them with too stark a choice, for when the alternatives are between rejecting an unwanted marriage partner or being rejected in turn by one's family (and as many experience it, then having to abandon one's religious or cultural identity), the costs are set almost impossibly high. It is too cavalier in this context to say that no decision is costless, and profoundly unhelpful to take the act of staying as evidence of acquiescence.

"Exit—the door with the glowing red sign—marks the road not taken that proves we chose our path."[33] In a particularly effective critique of what she sees as the *ideology* of exit, Martha Mahoney looks at the way it has been employed to deny the existence of abuse. Her main example is when Anita Hill's testimony against Clarence Thomas, in the Senate hearings to consider his appointment to the U.S. Supreme Court, was discredited by her willingness to continue working with him. Mahoney links this to the way women's claims about domestic violence are discredited by their willingness to persist with their relationship with the supposed abuser. "Once exit is defined as the appropriate response to abuse, then staying on can be treated as evidence that abuse never happened."[34] If things were are bad as they alleged, why did they not leave?

What is especially interesting in Mahoney's analysis is that her critique of the exit ideology does not depend on saying that women have no choice, are trapped in violent relationships, or have nowhere else to go. The idea that people simply *cannot* leave an oppressive situation seems implausible in the case of Anita Hill, a well-qualified lawyer, who could certainly have decided to change her job. But it also, Mahoney argues, fails to capture the experiences of many women living in violent relationships, who mostly refuse to describe themselves as helpless victims, and whose sense of agency is often quite strong. Mahoney suggests that "this strong sense of agency reflects both sound self-knowledge and denial of the impact of structures of power."[35] Women experiencing domestic violence tend to minimise the extent and effects of that violence—and to that degree, may be said to be fooling themselves—but they often also have a well-grounded sense of themselves as capable of endurance, caring for their children, and able to make tough decisions under pressure. Moreover, those who think their men will change are not being entirely self-deceiving, for significant numbers of men do stop the violence in order to hold on to the relationship. In her exploration of this, Mahoney draws

[33] Martha R. Mahoney, "Exit: Power and the Idea of Leaving in Love, Work, and the Confirmation Hearings," *Southern California Law Review* 65 (1991): 1283.

[34] Ibid., 1285.

[35] Ibid., 1309.

attention to the double bind associated with exit. *Either* it takes away your grounds for complaint (if things were that bad, you surely wouldn't have stayed) *or* it represents you as so helplessly subordinated that you were simply unable to go.

This is the problem with making the debate about exit turn exclusively on what makes the right to exit real. If the debate remains only on this terrain, it presents us with what may be two unpalatable alternatives. On the one hand, we have the formal understanding of exit represented in the work of Kukathas, who is well aware that some people find it easier than others to leave a marriage, family, association, or country, but refuses to grade chances of exit according to the costs they impose or the obstacles in their way. This offers a highly attenuated understanding of consent and is at odds with current legal understandings of the term. Against this, we have the position articulated by Okin or Martha Nussbaum, who have stressed the effects of socialisation in making women accept what in other cultures would be regarded as unacceptable conditions, and the way this can render exit not just difficult but unthinkable.[36] Their reading of this captures something important about learnt preferences and stultified imagination, but seems in some more fundamental way to deny women agency, and especially to deny the agency of women in non-Western groups. In a comment that echoes some of the anthropological distinctions between an "egocentric" Western self, characterised by a clear differentiation between self and other, and a "sociocentric" non-Western one, Okin argues that "without a cultural context that allows one to develop a sound sense of self, it is difficult to imagine a woman being able even to conceive of exit as an option."[37] It is as if we have to choose between pretending away the effects of oppression—the Kukathas option—or representing women as so thoroughly oppressed that they have lost the capacity to act. Mahoney's point is that this unhappy either/or choice comes about because we have taken exit as the test of agency. "When agency is equated with exit, failure to exit must be a sign of a positive choice or a symptom of such subjugation that agency no longer exists."[38]

Ayelet Shachar on Transformative Accommodation

The alternative approach is well set out by Shachar, who argues that "the right of exit rationale forces an insider into a cruel choice of penalties:

---

[36] See her discussion of preference formation in Martha C. Nussbaum, *Women and Human Development: The Capabilities Approach* (Cambridge: Cambridge University Press, 2000).

[37] Okin, "Mistresses of Their Own Destiny," 220.

[38] Mahoney, "Exit," 1309.

either accept all group practices—including those that violate your fundamental citizenship rights—or (somehow) leave."[39] Shachar's bracketed "somehow" refers back to the feasibility issues: the emotional, economic, or educational obstacles that can make exit a near impossibility. The real centrepiece of her argument, however, is that exit puts all the burden of resolving conflict on to the individual, and relieves both the group and the state of any responsibility for promoting change. It should, she argues, be possible for those who bear the brunt of oppressive practices—the "at-risk group members," many of them women, who carry "a disproportionate share of the costs of multiculturalism"—to stay and fight for change.[40]

Shachar's position on this reflects what one might describe as a strong but not essentialist conception of culture. In *Multicultural Jurisdictions*, she uses the term nomoi communities interchangeably with identity groups to refer to religiously defined groups or people that "share a unique history and collective memory, a distinct culture, a set of social norms, customs, and traditions, or perhaps an experience of maltreatment by mainstream society or oppression by the state."[41] These groups have a "comprehensive world view that extends to creating a law for the community."[42] They are differentiated from other groups by "their unique cultural and legal understanding of the world."[43] They have what Shachar clearly regards as a legitimate concern with determining who counts as a group member, and what she describes as "normatively and legally justifiable interests in shaping the rules that govern behavior."[44] Nomoi groups are therefore pretty solid entities. They are distinct, unique, defined by religion rather than the more diffuse culture, and they seek (justifiably, it seems) to control their members' lives. They also command enormous loyalty—hence Shachar's dissatisfaction with Okin, who seems not to appreciate the importance women themselves attach to their cultural membership.

But Shachar also insists that people have multiple identities and affiliations, that no one, for example, is "just" a member of a nomoi group or a citizen of the state, but both of these at the same time. And while she seems willing to talk of "the essential traditions that constitute a group's *nomos*," she stresses the fluidity of these traditions, arguing (in terms that recollect Narayan) that the way they are interpreted and coded often

---

[39] Ayelet Shachar, *Multicultural Jurisdictions: Cultural Differences and Women's Rights* (Cambridge: Cambridge University Press, 2001), 41.

[40] Ibid., 17.

[41] Ibid., 2n.

[42] Ibid., 2n. She is quoting here from Abner S. Greene, "*Kiryas Joel* and Two Mistakes about Equality," *Columbia Law Review* 96, no. 4 (1996): 4.

[43] Shachar, *Multicultural Jurisdictions*, 17.

[44] Ibid., 118.

works to the detriment of women, and that there is far more scope for redefining essential traditions than is commonly allowed.[45] Her target here is the notion of culture as all or nothing, the idea that women must put up or shut up, that they must either accept all the practices represented to them as crucial to their group "or (somehow) leave."

What she proposes is a system of joint governance between nomoi groups and the state that builds in incentives for change. Most of the existing ways of dividing jurisdictions between group and state are, she argues, too static. For example, in what she calls the temporal accommodation of the *Wisconsin v. Yoder* case, the state retains authority over the education of Amish children up to the age of fourteen and then turns jurisdiction over to the group. This helps the group maintain its distinctiveness, but does nothing to ease the difficulties individuals face in navigating between two jurisdictions and contains no dynamic towards reform. In Shachar's "transformative accommodation," jurisdiction is divided between group and state in ways that permit individuals to move between them, thus setting up an incentive system for both to improve their act. Exit reappears here as a notion of "partial" or "selective" exit, always coupled with possibilities of reentry.[46] The religious group might, for example, assume authority over matters of marriage and divorce, but if members who fail to get what they regard as fair treatment (say, women in a divorce case) can submit to the jurisdiction of the state *without* thereby leaving the group entirely, this will put pressure on the group to get its own house in order. Faced with members who withdraw from parts of their jurisdiction—and the threat that they might leave the jurisdiction entirely—groups will come under pressure to modify their harsher rules. This kind of accommodation therefore allows "cultural difference to flourish, while creating a catalyst for internal change."[47]

Shachar's starting point is compelling. It surely ought to be possible to refuse the choice between "my culture or my rights," and reject that harsh injunction that requires you either to accept all the practices represented as crucial to your group or (somehow) leave. She has difficulty, however, conjuring up real-world illustrations, and all those she gives differ in some important respects from what she has in mind.[48] Much of the material is

[45] Ibid., 40.
[46] "Clearly delineated and selective 'entrance,' 'exit' and 're-entry' options are thus a crucial component in improving the situation of traditionally vulnerable group members"; ibid., 124.
[47] Ibid., 118.
[48] For instance, Shachar (ibid., 132–33) discusses the Malaysian Islamic Family Law (Federal Territories) Act of 1984, which is a good illustration in two respects but not in a third. Here, the state and the group share authority over family law: the religious courts make the decisions regarding the division of property on separation or divorce, but they are instructed by the state to incline towards an equality of division. This system of joint governance has,

taken from countries like Israel or India that already practice some system of joint governance between the state and religious groups, and hence is most useful as an argument for moving existing models of joint governance in a more dynamic direction. It is unclear what relevance this has for contemporary Europe, where joint governance between the state and religious bodies is not a likely outcome. It is also unclear whether the incentive structure that Shachar envisages really could have such positive effects. In one challenging critique, Oonagh Reitman suggests that community leaders could become even more determined in their commitment to their hierarchical and patriarchal practices as their dissident members leave. Citing the example of Orthodox Judaism, she notes that "Orthodox leaders want to ensure ideological purity and the pursuit of what is perceived to be God's command. They may have little interest in bolstering numbers as such, preferring to soldier on with those whose commitment is beyond question."[49]

What is additionally intriguing is that Shachar combines a strong sense of the distinctiveness and uniqueness of different religio-cultural traditions with a rational actor view of the world. The language is all of incentives, costs, and risk-reduction strategies, the goal being "to make in-group subordination more costly to the group" and "create incentives for the group to transform the more oppressive elements of its tradition."[50] Vulnerable group members are described (in thoroughly market-driven terms) as exercising their selective exit and reentry options, raising the stakes of failure, and posing credible threats of exit. Nomoi groups are portrayed as engaging in a competitive relationship with the state for the loyalty of their constituents, having an interest in overstating their jurisdiction over members, and opting for the risk-reduction strategy of compromise over the perils of losing out altogether. This depiction of a world of rational calculators sits oddly in a discussion of groups defined by "their *unique* cultural and legal understanding of the world" (emphasis added). It is an oddity that Shachar shares with Kukathas, for when it comes to the sources of human motivation, both theorists depict the individual in abstractly ahistorical terms. There is nothing inherently contradictory about this: it is entirely coherent to say that individuals and orga-

---

it seems, encouraged transformation, with the courts actively reinterpreting a pre-Islamic Malay custom to give women even stronger protection. But there is no mechanism of partial or selective exit putting pressure on the group—so it isn't clear why this counts as an example of transformative accommodation.

[49] Oonagh Reitman, "On Exit," in *Minorities within Minorities: Equalities, Rights, and Diversity*, ed. Avigail Eisenberg and Jeff Spinner-Halev (Cambridge: Cambridge University Press, 2005), 199.

[50] Shachar, *Multicultural Jurisdictions*, 126; pages 122–26 are particularly written in the language of the marketplace.

nisations behave much the same the whole world over, and that one of the things they have in common is a desire to do things in their own way. But the positions these two reach on exit—the key protection for the individual for Kukathas, and the key leverage on groups for Shachar—reflect a rational actor view of the world that flattens out much of the cultural difference. This is particularly ironic given that both theorists would count as strong multiculturalists.

Voice Rather than Exit: Cultural Dissent

Though Shachar wants to strengthen the bargaining position of women and encourage processes of internal reform, she regards it as entirely reasonable that members of identity groups might want to be bound by group traditions rather than state law. Part of what qualifies Shachar as a strong multiculturalist is that she so readily concedes that a nomoi group should have the right to determine its own membership rules, though she favours separating out the demarcating function from the distribution of resources, and regards the rules of membership as also open to internal contestation and change. As applied to the religiously defined groups that are her main focus, this right to determine one's own membership rules has some immediate plausibility. Certainly, if a church draws up articles of faith and announces that only those abiding by these articles can be regarded as members of the church, it is hard to see how any outside body would have the right to object. Things look more complicated, however, when the membership is by birth rather than belief—for example, in Judaism, where membership is transmitted through the mother, and children of fathers who have married outside the religion only get membership through conversion, or in the much-debated case of the Santa Clara Pueblo Indians, where membership is transmitted through the father, and children of mothers who marry outside the group do not qualify for the health and other benefits of living on the reservation.[51] In these cases, too, Shachar defends the right of the group to determine its own membership rules. Her solution is to detach demarcation from distribution, so that children born outside the group can access resources from the state if the group fails to provide for them.

But this, of course, is one of the issues. Just how much right has a cultural group (which usually means a cultural elite) to decide who does

---

[51] This case is discussed, inter alia, in Will Kymlicka, *Multicultural Citizenship: A Liberal Theory of Minority Rights* (Oxford: Clarendon Press, 1995); .Shachar, *Multicultural Jurisdictions*; Judith Resnik, "Dependent Sovereigns: Indian Tribes, States, and the Federal Courts," *University of Chicago Law Review* 56 (1989): 671–759.

and doesn't belong? In an analysis of cultural dissent, Madhavi Sunder explicitly draws on the new anthropology to stress internal diversity and challenge notions of culture as thing, and sees it as one of the effects of globalisation that people "are moving away from imposed cultural identities towards a conception of cultural identity based on autonomy, choice, and reason."[52] She shares with Shachar the idea that cultural membership matters to people, hence that offering them the right to exit barely begins to engage with their concerns. Yet her understanding of the terms on which people now demand cultural membership goes a long way beyond Shachar's recognition that group members may have different and conflicting interests, or that group traditions are open to change. It also goes a long way beyond Kukathas, who has little to say about internal diversity and explicitly rejects the idea that autonomy matters to people across all cultures. Sunder argues that more and more people are claiming the right to remain as members of a group, but define what that cultural membership means to them more on their own terms. She cites as examples gay Irish Americans claiming their right to march in the annual Saint Patrick's Day parade, Muslim women demanding new interpretations of their religion that will foster gender equality, lesbians, gays, and bisexuals in India celebrating their Indian heritage alongside their sexuality, and Catholics who continue to see themselves as good Catholics even while practising contraception and supporting the right to an abortion. This poses new questions about who has the right to decide membership terms.

In a useful departure from normal practice, Sunder chooses the case of *Boys Scouts of America v. Dale* (2001) for her exploration of cultural survival and dissent.[53] James Dale was an exemplary Scout. He joined the Cub Scouts at the age of eight, progressed to an Eagle Scout at eighteen, and volunteered as an assistant scoutmaster while attending college in New Jersey. When the local council of the Boy Scouts discovered that he was gay (from a newspaper article referring to his membership in a gay student group), Dale's Scout membership was revoked. He sued for reinstatement, citing New Jersey's prohibition of discrimination on the grounds of sexual orientation. The final judgment from the Supreme Court held that freedom of association protects a minority association's right to be distinct from the majority and that opposition to homosexuality was part of the association's message, and it therefore decided on behalf of the Boy Scouts. As Sunder documents, this decision involved refusing to accord significance to evidence that had been presented to the lower court demonstrating a range of opinions on homosexuality within the association, and considerable internal disagreement. In effect, the Su-

---

[52] Sunder, "Cultural Dissent," 517.
[53] *Boy Scouts of America v. Dale*, 530 U.S. 649 (2001).

preme Court accepted that the association's leadership had the right to determine its view of homosexuality, rather than the members. Sunder reads this as a case of the law imposing an essentialised version of Boy Scout culture: "by treating culture as homogeneous, freedom of association law helped transform the Boy Scouts from a heterogeneous community in which meanings are plural, contested, and changing, into a commodity or 'cultural essence' that represents a false image of the real."[54]

Part of the normative claim here is that "cultural outsiders (women, gays, lesbians, bisexuals, the unorthodox) have just as much of a right to culture, community and association as do cultural elites."[55] This brings me back to the difference between multicultural and cosmopolitan perspectives, and the reasons why I have chosen a multiculturalism that rids itself of mistaken notions of culture over a cosmopolitanism that grafts on to itself a better understanding of cultural diversity. From a cosmopolitan perspective, Sunder's cultural outsiders would probably be best advised to leave their oppressively conformist communities. They will probably always retain some vestiges of their initial cultural influences—the Boy Scout will continue to engage in challenging outdoor activities, and for the rest of his life, may seek out situations where he can work as part of a team—but basically, these people should move on. Sunder's point is that this resolution leaves the original associations at the mercy of their more conservative interpreters, while denying to their dissident members their own right to culture, community, and association.

And why, one might ask, is moving on always to be considered the more progressive option? In a later discussion of the organisation Women Living Under Muslim Laws (which she takes as a prototype for cultural dissent), Sunder identifies a "transition narrative" that regards Muslim campaigns for women's rights as illustrating a strategic accommodation: a canny political adjustment to the constraints of living in a theocratic society or community, but not to be understood as having any normative value of its own.[56] In this transition narrative, engaging with religious texts or arguments in order to establish the basis for a more progressive treatment of women is presented as a bowing to necessity, something imposed on people by the fact of living in a Muslim country or needing to engage with a Muslim community. The expectation, however, is that organisations like Women Living Under Muslim Laws will eventually free themselves from this constraint and situate themselves more straightforwardly on the terrain of secular rights. It is as if religious assertions can

[54] Sunder, "Cultural Dissent," 533.
[55] Ibid., 565.
[56] Madhavi Sunder, "Piercing the Veil," *Yale Law Journal* 112 (2003): 1399–472.

only be understood as strategic. The implication is that no one who cared about rights or equality could really take them seriously.

Like Sunder, I have been struck by the prevalence of this view as regards religion. Liberal-minded people living in broadly secular societies too often treat religious belief as superstitious nonsense, a collection of weirdly unscientific claims that must surely be swept away over time by the greater powers of reason. Forgetting, perhaps, that it was secular rather than religious ideas that inspired the more barbaric episodes of the twentieth century, they also represent religions as peculiarly responsible for wars and violence. Given the number of believers in the world today, there is a strange kind of arrogance in this. It also offers what seems to me an implausible reading of the likely directions of future change. My own view is that while globalisation may well erode many of the *cultural* differences between people, ultimately rendering redundant much of the debate that takes place in the name of multiculturalism, the same processes are likely to sustain and even strengthen religious belief. Certainly, if globalisation continues on its present path towards greater inequality and heightened environmental damage, a lot of people are going to be looking for alternatives to materialism and individualism. This is guesswork, and I wouldn't want to be judged on it. But however this history unfolds, it seems clear that offering exit as the main option encourages the view so unfortunately formulated in Okin's phrase about some women perhaps being better off if the culture they were born into were "to become extinct."[57] The right to exit does not provide enough protection to people living in oppressive conditions, but it also does not offer enough of a solution to those with a strong normative commitment to their cultural or religious group. Voice matters as well as exit. The right to leave has to be complemented by the right to stay.

---

[57] Susan Moller Okin, "Is Multiculturalism Bad for Women?" in *Is Multiculturalism Bad for Women?* ed. Joshua Cohen, Matthew Howard, and Martha C. Nussbaum (Princeton, NJ: Princeton University Press, 1999), 22.

CHAPTER SIX

Multiculturalism without Groups?

THE MAIN BURDEN of Madhavi Sunder's argument is that when the courts get into the business of legitimating and confirming cultural associations, they thereby freeze cultures and make them less available to internal reform. "However difficult, cultural boundaries are scalable; legal boundaries are much less so."[1] I take it that she would extend this warning also to government initiatives that codify or in some way institutionalise cultural groups, and I am very much with her on this point. But it is not always easy to distinguish between acknowledging the rights of the individual—who seems, from the discussion in chapter 5, to value her cultural heritage, and be willing to do battle with others over the meanings and definitions of her culture—and acknowledging the authority of the group. After all, this was where much of the recent literature on multiculturalism or minority rights began: with the idea that acknowledging the rights and autonomy of the individual might mean acknowledging and legitimating the authority of the cultural group. In this chapter, I offer some final clarification on my own position regarding the relationship between the individual and the group, and indicate some remaining and unresolved issues.

My starting point is the distinction between regulation, exit, and dialogue, which I take as the three most common approaches to contested matters of cultural diversity in the practices of contemporary states. As we have seen, governments will sometimes *regulate*, perhaps by reference to a schedule of basic human rights that is considered the necessary minimum for all. This approach (some elements of which are endorsed in this book, but much of which is at odds with my position) is the least shaped by multicultural considerations. It is relatively unconvinced by the epistemological or normative problems associated with cultural difference, and asserts, without incurring too much self-doubt, that particular principles of behaviour are right. The subsequent implementation of these principles may be more or less vigorous, for even in cases where a contested practice is criminalised (this would be the strictest kind of regulation), public officials might still consider it undesirable to intervene in a heavy-handed manner against specific groups because of the risk of contributing to a

---

[1] Madhavi Sunder, "Cultural Dissent," *Stanford Law Review* 545 (December 2001): 503.

backlash against them. What most characterises the regulation approach is not, then, its insensitivity to cultural difference in the process of implementation, but its relative confidence in determining what is right.

Laws against female genital cutting offer a good illustration here, because they have been formulated in ways that lend themselves to accusations of cultural bias, and because countries have varied in the vigour of their implementation. When legislation against what was then termed female circumcision was first proposed in Britain in 1985, the medical associations were concerned that as originally formulated, the law would make it an offence to operate on girls or women who had developed an anxiety about the shape or size of their genitalia, thereby making it illegal to perform cosmetic surgery in order to alleviate mental distress. An amendment was added that permitted genital surgery "where necessary for physical or mental health," but precluded taking account of "any belief . . . that the operation is required as a matter of custom or ritual."[2] One way of glossing this would be to say that a girl or woman can have surgery to enable her to conform to Western norms prescribing a particular kind of female body, but not to enable her to conform to norms from Somalia or the Sudan.[3] The prohibition on the second was to be absolute, but this was not felt to raise any especially troubling issues about permitting the first.

In the event, there were no prosecutions under this legislation, which then served more as a statement of what was unacceptable than an active regulation. The later Female Genital Mutilation Act (2003) extended the prohibition to make it illegal to take a girl or woman abroad to be excised or infibulated, yet retained the caveat about mental health along with the reference to custom or ritual. RAINBO, an African-led international nongovernmental organisation, recommended that the bill be amended to prohibit operations on *all* minors, whether the reasons were "cosmetic" or "customary," and not to prohibit operations for *any* consenting adult, again regardless of whether the reasons were cosmetic or customary. Though this begs the question of how to determine consent, it looks like a plausible recommendation, and one that might have circumvented

---

[2] The final act made it an offence to excise, infibulate, or otherwise mutilate the whole or any part of the labia majora, labia minora, or clitoris with the exception of cases when: "2(1)(a) it is necessary for the physical or mental health of the person on whom it is performed and is performed by a registered medical practitioner." The qualification to this is: "2(2) In determining for the purposes of this section whether an action is necessary for the mental health of a person, no account shall be taken of the effect on that person of any belief on the part of that or any other person that the operation is required as a matter of custom or ritual." Prohibition of Female Circumcision Act, 1985.

[3] I am grateful to Moira Dustin for drawing my attention to the peculiarities of the British legislation.

concerns about cultural bias. (It was not taken up.) The later legislation has a wider remit than the first, but is also largely symbolic. Pressed on whether they anticipated that immigration officials would carry out genital inspections on young girls returning from vacation in parts of Africa, supporters acknowledged that they neither anticipated nor desired this, and confirmed that they did not expect many new prosecutions. In other countries, by contrast, there has been a greater willingness to consider implementing legislation through intrusive programmes of inspection in schools. In others, specific legislation against female genital cutting has been deemed unnecessary: France is the country in Europe that has most vigorously pursued prosecutions against those carrying out the operations, but does not have specific laws against it.

Where regulation is deemed inappropriate or too intrusive, governments may stress the right of individuals to *exit* from their group and focus policy initiatives on support programmes that enable this. This is not necessarily incompatible with criminalisation—governments could adopt primarily an exit strategy in relation to forced marriage or genital cutting while still having legislation on the statute books that makes the practice illegal—but it concentrates energies on enabling oppressed individuals to leave their situation or group. Just as regulation may be more or less intrusive, so, too, may exit be more or less proactive. I have noted as one of the accusations against multiculturalism that it can encourage social workers, teachers, or the police to hold back from interfering in what they deem to be a community's internal affairs. Where this happens, this could be taken as a particularly inactive version of the exit strategy, which simply leaves it up to individuals to decide if or when to leave, and refrains from providing them with any guidance or support. But as the discussion of initiatives against forced marriage indicates, exit may also be pursued in a more proactive manner, involving the distribution of information about support services, the provision of income support and alternative accommodation, or help in repatriation.

The objection to regulation is that it is insufficiently sensitive to differences in cultural norms and moral values. The objection to exit (rehearsed in the previous chapter) is that it puts the onus on the individual, who then has to choose between accepting the practices and norms of the community or getting out. On the face of it, it looks as if the third option, *dialogue*, can meet both these objections, for it is more willing than regulation to recognise that the people disagreeing about norms and practices might all have valid concerns, and more willing than exit to address the norms that are generating the difficulties as well as how these might be challenged and changed. Theoretically, it maps on to a literature on the role of intercultural deliberation in resolving normative disputes that has been characterised by a greater willingness to recognise the validity of different points of view and a greater optimism about ways of promoting intercultural understanding—the kind of arguments developed by Bhikhu Parekh, Seyla Benhabib, or Monique Deveaux, all of whom stress the importance of giving reasons for favoured practices and engaging in public debate.[4] At its best, this dialogic alternative offers the prospect of mutual exchange and modification between people from majority and minority groups, in ways that can dislodge cultural stereotypes and secure a better understanding all around. It also offers the prospect of internal transformation of the kind favoured by Ayelet Shachar and Madhavi Sunder, for it opens up disputed practices to internal scrutiny and makes it easier for dissident voices to press their own point of view.

In its more messy practice, however, the dialogic approach has tended to encourage the sedimentation of cultural groups and communities, and the selection of specific spokespeople (generally male) who are then in a position to represent their own readings of their culture or community as if these were generally agreed on. In other words, it brings us back to what was the starting point of the feminist critique: that it is usually the more powerful members of a minority community who are called on to act as gatekeepers between majority and minority communities, and their version of the community's practices that figures most prominently in intercultural debates. Public agencies commonly consult with community leaders, particularly when trying to mobilise them to convey the appropriate message to their constituents (that terrorism is against Islam, that forcing young people into marriage is against all moral and religious principles, or that honour killing is a crime). Sometimes, though more rarely, this becomes a two-way engagement, such that some of the consultation then modifies official views. This kind of consultation is a top-down version of "dialogue," of course, and not what most theorists have in mind when they speak of a dialogic encounter. But it is in practice what tends to come out of the notion of engaging with cultural groups.

It is always easiest, in public consultations, to search out the leaders—easier to call on those heading national rather than local networks, those who have been around the longest, and those claiming some formal authority, perhaps by virtue of their religious role. Deliberately or not, this focuses attention on the more established and often also the more conservative elements within a community, leaving Sunder's cultural outsiders feeling that their views are once again being ignored. In the aftermath of

[4] Bhikhu Parekh, *Rethinking Multiculturalism: Cultural Diversity and Political Theory* (London: Palgrave Press, 2000); Seyla Benhabib, *The Claims of Culture: Equality and Diversity in the Global Era* (Princeton, NJ: Princeton University Press, 2002); Monique Deveaux, *Cultural Pluralism and Dilemmas of Justice* (Ithaca, NY: Cornell University Press, 2000).

the July 7, 2005, bombings in London, the government was keen to engage in discussion with British Muslims, and started talking of Britain's Muslim communities (plural) as part of its recognition that it was misleading to assume there was a single unified group. Comments from younger Muslims suggest that the government was not entirely successful in making this change. "People are saying take me to your leaders—it's a colonial thing," said Shahedah Vawda, founder of an Islamic peace group. "The government doesn't talk to young people," said Andleen Razzaq, a teacher. "At a community consultation meeting I went to, there were only three youths. The government only talks to older Muslims."[5] The exit strategy threatens to treat people as individuals without cultural attachments. The dialogue alternative threatens to relate to them through the perceived leaders of their group. What does this poverty of alternatives mean in terms of multicultural policy? More specifically, how should we understand the relationship between individual and group?

The Rights of Individuals, Not Groups

The multiculturalism defended in this book is grounded in the rights of individuals rather than those of groups. None of what I have argued implies that cultures have rights—to respect, funding, or survival—only that individuals do. I do not see cultures as all-inclusive ways of life that can be categorised according to their core beliefs or traditions, and I do not see multiculturalism as a way of distributing power and authority between different cultural groups. The literature on multiculturalism has been hampered by an overly holistic understanding of culture, which partly reflects its starting point in a literature on minority and indigenous rights. This encouraged the notion that what is at stake is a negotiation between two or more relatively distinct cultures, each operating as a self-reproducing whole.[6] As it developed in Europe, moreover, multiculturalism often

---

[5] The comments come from a group of young Muslims brought together in a discussion by the *Guardian* newspaper; "Islamic Voice of Reason Speaks out but the Anger Remains," *Guardian* (Manchester), 21 November 2005.

[6] Although partly responsible for this association, Will Kymlicka has worked hard to dispel it, repeatedly distinguishing between the self-government rights of national minorities (who might more closely approximate that image of distinct and separate societies) and what he regards as the lesser "polyethnic" rights of immigrant groups. It does not help, however, that Kymlicka has continued to describe the different sets of policies relating to immigrants, national minorities, and indigenous peoples all as examples of multiculturalism. The elision of difference brings us too readily to the notion that multiculturalism is a matter of recognising or accommodating *cultural groups*. See Keith Banting and Will Kymlicka, "Do Multiculturalism Policies Erode the Welfare State?" in *Cultural Diversity versus Economic Solidarity: Proceedings of the Seventh Francqui Colloquium*, ed. Philippe van Parijs (Brussels: De Boeck, 2004).

built on political structures set in place in the course of the twentieth century to deal with religious and/or linguistic divides. Many countries in Europe contained within them what seemed almost distinct societies: Belgium with its French-speaking Walloons and Dutch-speaking Flemish; Germany with its Catholics and Protestants; the Netherlands with its divisions between Calvinist, Catholic, Socialist, and Liberal; and Switzerland with its four language groups. Some countries established federal structures that devolved much of the decision making to regions, while others practiced what Arendt Lijphart described as consociational arrangements, which shared power between the different groups.[7] In these arrangements, government often involved a coalition between the various political parties rather than a winner-takes-all majoritarianism, and resources—including funding for churches and opportunities for employment in the public sector—were frequently distributed between the groups in rough proportion to their population share. This kind of power-sharing arrangement then provided one of the models for the treatment of new cultural and religious minorities in Europe.

In the Netherlands, for example, it seemed an obvious enough extension of previous policy to subsidise ethnic organisations, establish consultative councils to represent the views of the communities, and make proportionality the guiding principle in the distribution of housing, education, and jobs. In Belgium, where the Catholic, Protestant, and Jewish religions already had official status and received state subsidies, it seemed a self-evident extension to recognise Islam as an official religion, therefore also with government funding (though not with a proportionate share). This grafting of multiculturalism on to preexisting mechanisms of power sharing encouraged a version of multicultural policy that parcels out resources between communities and then has to seek out—or even create—community leaders to organise this process. It has been one of the standard criticisms of consociationalism that it relies too heavily on the role of elites, for it is the "leaders" of the communities who get together with one another to divide up resources and power between them. The other criticism is that it freezes relationships between communities, because in organising the distribution of resources via the groups, it sets up incentives for individuals to continue to attach themselves primarily to their group. Both of these have recurred as problems in the practices of multiculturalism.

The association with indigenous rights, on the one side, and consociational power sharing, on the other, helped promote an understanding of multiculturalism as the accommodation of or negotiation with cultural

---

[7] Arendt Lijphart, *Democracy in Plural Societies: A Comparative Exploration* (New Haven, CO: Yale University Press, 1977).

communities or groups—which then exposed it to the standard feminist critique of accommodating the interests of male elders falsely representing themselves as the voice of their group. The understanding of multiculturalism developed in this book rests, by contrast, on the rights and needs of individuals. It is grounded in the rights and needs of citizens, not of cultures or cultural groups, with culture entering as an attribute of the individual rather than the group. What have sometimes been depicted as cultural rights are better understood as elaborations of standard citizenship rights that ought to be enjoyed by all. Describing them as cultural rights is misleading, encouraging the view that these are rights enjoyed by a group, on the one hand, and that they are rights peculiar to minority or non-Western groups, on the other.[8]

Article 27 of the International Covenant of Civil and Political Rights (dating from 1966, and ratified by an overwhelming majority of the world's countries) states that "in those States in which ethnic, religious or linguistic minorities exist, persons belonging to such minorities shall not be denied the right, in community with the other members of their group, to enjoy their own culture, to profess and practise their own religion, or to use their own language." This lends support to multicultural policies, and has been further interpreted by the United Nations Human Rights Committee as creating a positive obligation on states to protect indigenous cultures.[9] Note, however, that it speaks in terms of the rights of "persons belonging to such minorities" rather than of minorities themselves: the rights of individuals belonging to particular groups rather than the rights of groups. This emphasis is reinforced by other articles in the covenant that talk almost exclusively in terms of individual rights, the two exceptions being Article 1, which refers to "peoples" having the right to self-determination, and Article 23, which portrays the family as "the natural and fundamental group unit of society" and "entitled to protection by society and the State." And even as regards this last, the covenant goes on to stress the rights of individuals within the family: the right of men and women of marriageable age to marry and start a

---

[8] In the multicultural literature, there has been considerable discussion about the relationship between individual and group rights, or between collective and corporate rights. It is not unusual within this to argue that cultural identities can be adequately protected by a regime of individual, not collective, rights. See Judith Baker, ed. *Group Rights* (Toronto: University of Toronto Press, 1994); Yael Tamir, "Against Collective Rights," in *Multicultural Questions*, ed. Christian Joppke and Steven Lukes (Oxford: Oxford University Press, 1999); Peter Jones, "Group Rights and Group Oppression," *Journal of Political Philosophy* 7, no. 4 (1999): 353–77.

[9] Human Rights Committee, "General Comment 23, Article 27, Paragraph 7," in *Compilations of General Recommendations adopted by Human Rights Treaty Bodies*, UN Doc HRI/GEN/1/Rev.7, 12 May 2004, 160.

family; the requirement that no marriage be entered into without the free and full consent of the intending spouses; and the requirement that parties to the covenant "take appropriate steps to ensure equality of rights and responsibilities of spouses as to marriage, during marriage and at its dissolution."

The rights that matter in developing a case for multiculturalism are those of individuals, not groups: the right to choose a marriage partner without interference from the state, to follow the dress code prescribed by one's religion or culture, or more generally, to live one's life in accordance with one's beliefs. None of these should be seen as unconditional, for like most rights, they depend on context and may need to be balanced against other rights. I cannot for the moment think of the conditions that would limit the right to choose a marriage partner from one's country of origin. It is relatively easy, by contrast, to envisage conditions that would limit the right to follow one's chosen dress code. I think that if the death toll for Sikh motorcyclists relying only on the protection of turbans rose significantly above that for motorcyclists with helmets, a responsible government would revisit legislation providing for exemptions and consider whether these should be retained. I believe it reasonable to expect citizens not to cover their faces in photographs taken for identity purposes, though I am unconvinced by the stronger claim that wearing a headscarf also poses an identification problem. (If headscarves are to be banned on the grounds of potentially masking identity, then all women should probably be banned from changing their hairstyles and colour.) I can see a case for banning the niqab (the face veil that leaves only the eyes visible) in schoolrooms, for teachers might reasonably claim that they need to be able to judge their pupils' understanding and reactions from their facial expressions. I can see no justification for the wholesale ban on wearing the niqab in public that was adopted by some Belgian councils in 2005.

On the more general right to live one's life according to one's norms, it is clear that there must be limiting conditions. Some of these derive from the broad principles set out in chapter 1: the requirement to prevent serious harm to minors, to prevent physical and mental violence, and to ensure that men and women are treated as equals. Others derive their legitimacy from the democratic process. For example, if laws have been passed establishing particular ages for leaving school, getting married, and having the right to vote, then the fact that different laws operate in different countries does not in itself give people who have migrated from these countries the right to continue with what was their normal—and previously legal—practice. What it does, more minimally, is pose the standard multicultural question: is existing legislation biased towards the cultural identities or religious beliefs of particular social groups, and if so, is this defensible? What Parekh terms the "operative public values" of a society may be defensible even if not universally shared. They may encapsulate values about children's rights, the age of maturity, or the freedom to practice one's sexuality that were long debated, hard fought, and now represent a considered consensus. The fact that they are not universal—in the literal sense of not being endorsed by everyone, from every country, class, or culture—is not a reason to drop them. But they may also encapsulate values that rely heavily on particular cultural experiences or religious beliefs, in ways that do undermine their general validity. That legislation was passed with due democratic process and the appropriate majority vote does much of the necessary work of legitimation, but appealing to this alone could mean ignoring the generally accepted risks of majority tyranny, and the way that risk increases when majority/minority divisions of opinion map on to majority/minority distinctions between ethnocultural groups. When opinions are polarised along racial, ethnic, or religious lines, the principle of majority rule is not enough of a protection. This was the main justification for consociational power-sharing arrangements, and it is widely accepted in democratic theory as one of the constraints on majority rule.[10] Even laws and rules that enjoy majority support may reflect a cultural bias. Recognising this possibility was the first step in formulating a multicultural policy. The second is to work out what, if anything, to do about it.

Distributing Powers to Groups

Grounding multiculturalism in individuals' rights and needs means it is *not* about distributing powers or resources to groups. This is not to say that governments should refuse to fund ethnocultural associations—refuse, for example, to fund the Turkish Cultural Centre or the Asian Women's Refuge. This kind of association makes its bid for resources partly on the basis of meeting needs that will not be met—or not fully met—in a generic centre. But it does not, and could not, claim to be *the* voice of *its* community, and it certainly could not claim any regulatory authority over community members. The bid more closely parallels that of a youth group that wants to focus on providing facilities and support for young people who are gay, lesbian, or bisexual, and argues that their needs will be better met when they have dedicated facilities and a safe place. In all these cases, there will be differences of opinion about whether it is better in the long run for people to make use of segregated facilities or integrate into a larger community, but none of the positions in these debates need

---

[10] See also Lani Guinier, *The Tyranny of the Majority: Fundamental Fairness in Representative Democracy* (New York: Free Press, 1994).

invoke notions of authenticity or of one option being the only option appropriate to members of that group. It is entirely coherent to support the funding of a Turkish Cultural Centre, for instance, without thereby suggesting that all Turks must in future use it or that those who prefer to socialise elsewhere are thereby betraying their Turkish heritage.

When I say multiculturalism is not about distributing powers or resources to groups, I also do not mean that societies should refuse to experiment with mechanisms for increasing the political representation of cultural or national groups—refuse, for example, to consider mechanisms to ensure a fair representation of French Moroccans in the Assemblée Nationale or German Turks in the Bundestag. To the contrary, I see such initiatives as welcome extensions of policies I strongly support for achieving the fair representation of women in politics.[11] My reservations about this kind of initiative are mostly practical, for it is harder to construct appropriate institutional arrangements for representing ethnocultural groups than for representing women, because the line of demarcation between cultural groups is less clear than that between women and men (there are lots of people situated between groups, by birth, marriage, and choice), and because there is a potentially bewildering number of subsets that could be identified as needing fair representation.

To go back to an earlier point about the way racial categories have been mobilised in politics, it would be almost a form of racism in itself to lump all minorities together as *the* group that needs better representation, as if Indians are interchangeable with Turks, who in turn are interchangeable with West Africans, Chinese, or Moroccans, and as if all of these can be said to be better represented when there are more people from just one of these groups in the legislature. But if we accept that as implausible, how should societies intent on equalising representation proceed? Should they draw up lists of groups differentiated by country of origin, religion, country of origin subdivided by religion, or country of origin subdivided by religion and sex? Let me stress: I do not see the practical difficulties that arise in addressing the underrepresentation of people from minority cultural groups as making this a worthless endeavour. To the contrary, I see it as one of the most important moves a democracy in a multiethnic and multicultural society can make. My point is simply that societies have to work harder to identify appropriate mechanisms that do not generate perverse effects.

There is a further point that applies also to the representation of women, and helps clarify my understanding of the relationship between individual and group. Increasing the proportion of French Moroccans,

[11] As I argue in *The Politics of Presence: The Political Representation of Gender, Ethnicity, and Race* (Oxford: Oxford University Press, 1995).

British Asians, or women does not mean there is now a better representation *of that group.* Strictly speaking, when political parties introduce candidate selection quotas to increase the proportion of women elected to national or local legislatures (as many now do), they are not increasing the representation of *women*—for what is this group called women, and how are these newly elected representatives supposed to know what this group called women wants? Strictly speaking, the initiatives simply increase the number of women serving as political representatives, the proportion of women in the legislature. The expectation, of course, is that this will bring a wider range of experiences and a different set of priorities into the political arena, and that the concerns of other women outside the legislature will thereby be better voiced. This expectation is largely confirmed by the empirical literature, though perhaps on a less dramatic scale than some of us had hoped.[12] But it would be a misnomer to label this a form of group representation, for there is no clearly delineated group called women, and even if there were, there is no obvious mechanism of accountability linking the representatives back to that group.

By the same token, if measures are introduced to raise the proportion of political representatives that belong to cultural minorities, this cannot be described as distributing power to cultural *groups.* It is necessary to bear in mind here the distinction between including or representing *a group,* and including or representing those deemed by themselves and others to constitute its members—that is, the distinction between a corporatist representation in which individuals serve as the authorised representatives of their group and are regarded as its authentic voice, and looser measures that seek to increase the representation of people sharing the markers and experiences of these groups. The former invokes the reified understanding of *the* group, *the* culture, or *the* community that has been my target in this book. What I endorse, rather, is the latter, which recognises the often-crucial significance of group difference in structuring our lives and aspirations, and the importance of achieving a system of representation that reflects more of that difference. While the markers of gender, race, ethnicity, culture, and religion continue so profoundly to shape our lives—and to shape the way others view us—they will continue to be associated with key differences in experience, values, interests, and aspirations that should then be represented in the decision-making process. This makes it a matter of pressing concern to ensure an equitable representation of the diversity of identities, interests, and perspectives, but it does not treat measures to achieve this goal as bringing about the representation of *a group.*

---

[12] For an authoritative survey of this evidence, see Joni Lovenduski, *Feminizing Politics* (Cambridge, UK: Polity Press, 2005).

So when I say multiculturalism should not be about distributing powers or resources to cultural groups, I am not objecting to either the funding of ethnocultural associations or measures to raise the political representation of people from minority cultural groups. My objection, instead, is to measures that enhance the regulatory authority of a group over its members, or elevate what some of its members claim to be their cultural norms over the beliefs and interpretations of others from the group. If the criticism of reified conceptions of culture is correct, *and* there are no convincing mechanisms by which members of a cultural group can establish democratic control over those who speak in their name, then measures that enhance the regulatory powers of a group over those deemed to be its members should be viewed as intrinsically authoritarian. Of course, there are countries that have formalised precisely this kind of regulatory power, though more commonly with reference to religion than culture. In Israel and India, for example, individuals are deemed—usually by birth, but sometimes by choice—to belong to particular religious communities, and thereby come under the operation of that community's laws as regards aspects of family and civil affairs.[13] I shall not comment on either of these examples, partly because I lack the necessary knowledge, but also because the issues that arise in Israel or India are not so much about enhancing those regulatory powers as modifying and curtailing those already in place. There are also numerous agreements—some in the form of historical treaties, and others of more recent date—that recognise the powers of an indigenous authority or the legitimacy of customary law. One of the staples of the multicultural literature is the case of *Santa Clara Pueblo v. Martinez* (1979), where the U.S. Supreme Court decided that the tribe had the authority to determine its own membership rules, even though these discriminated against the children of women who married outside the tribe, but not the children of men who did so. In South Africa, where the refusal to recognise customary law marriages was one of the injustices of the apartheid regime, the 1996 Constitution recognised African customary law, subject to the proviso that it be exercised in a manner consistent with the Bill of Rights. Precisely how this balancing act will work out in relation to women's equality is still being tested in the courts.[14] Again, I do not intend to comment on these, partly because I think questions relating to indigenous minorities should not be subsumed under the remit of multiculturalism, and partly because my primary focus is on the

---

[13] In India, they also have a nonreligious option. For further discussion of Israel and India, see Ayelet Shachar, *Multicultural Jurisdictions: Cultural Differences and Women's Rights* (Cambridge: Cambridge University Press, 2001).

[14] Lisa Fishbayn, "Litigating the Right to Culture: Family Law in the New South Africa," *International Journal of Law, Policy, and the Family* 13 (1999): 147–73.

multiethnic, multicultural societies formed through the mass migrations of the last fifty years. But both examples clearly raise issues pertinent to my discussion, including whether women's equality can be adequately secured by reference to a bill of rights (not, it seems, in the first example, yet possibly in the second) or by establishing a fair representation for women on the bodies that determine group rules.

The question of group power arises in its strongest form when groups claim the right to have matters regarding marriage, divorce, the division of property, or the custody of children regulated according to the precepts of their religion or culture. Throughout much of the 1970s, 1980s, and 1990s, the Union of Muslim Organisations of the United Kingdom pressed (without success) for official recognition of a separate system of Islamic family law, arguing that this should be the default legal system for British Muslims.[15] In Canada, there was an explosive debate in 2003–5 about the application of Islamic family law in Ontario, when it became clear that the Arbitration Act passed in 1991, and intended to allow for cheaper and less adversarial methods of settling civil disputes, also allowed religious bodies to set up arbitration courts to regulate family affairs. Jewish and Catholic organisations had used this legislation to establish arbitration tribunals from the early 1990s. When the Islamic Institute of Civil Justice announced in 2003 that it would now provide similar arbitration services under Islamic law, the really provocative point was the suggestion that good Muslims should in the future *only* settle civil and family disputes in this forum: that sharia courts, in other words, should become the main regulatory authority for Canadian Muslims. As Avigail Eisenberg has convincingly argued, what caused the furore was not so much the proposal to set up private arbitration services employing Islamic law but the suggestion that any Muslims who continued to opt for civil law procedures would be regarded as failing in their religious duties.[16] The Ontario government commissioned a report on the issue, which recommended that existing legislation be left in place, but with new safeguards to ensure that the interests of women were not endangered in the

---

[15] This proposal does not reflect majority Muslim opinion, nor is it supported by all Muslim scholars. When the idea of a separate legal system for British Muslims surfaced again at a meeting in 2004, Zaki Badawi, the main inspiration behind the London-based Muslim Law (Shariah) Council, argued that "uniformity of the law is central in ensuring that justice is served to all members of society" and that "there should be just one legal system which should be applied to all." Cited in Samia Bano, "Complexity, Difference, and 'Muslim Personal Law': Rethinking the Relationship between Shariah Councils and South Asian Muslim Women in Britain" (PhD diss., University of Warwick, 2004), 193–94.

[16] Avigail Eisenberg, "The Debate over Sharia Law in Canada," in *Sexual/Cultural Justice*, ed. Barbara Arneil, Monique Deveaux, Rita Dhamoon, and Avigail Eisenberg (London: Routledge, 2006).

resolution of disputes in family law. In the event, the premier decided to block the creation of Islamic family courts, and close down the Jewish and Catholic ones as well.

This is the point at which things become a bit more tricky. It is a clear enough implication from the arguments in this book that religious or customary authorities should not be able to claim the exclusive authority to adjudicate matters for their members, and that there should be no move in the direction of introducing different systems of law for different cultural or religious communities. Systems of customary or religious law are often interpreted in ways that make them less advantageous to women—providing them a less equitable settlement on divorce, for example, or not allowing women to act as judges in the courts—and a multicultural polity that empowers customary or religious authorities to regulate the family affairs of its members would be failing in its responsibilities to ensure equitable treatment between its citizens. On this point, I am at odds with Shachar, who is well aware that women can be disadvantaged in the operation of religious family law, and wants to curb this by bringing the regulation of the financial aspects under civil law, but still wants states to officially recognise the jurisdiction of the cultural or religious group.[17] Empowerment, however, does not come exclusively or even most commonly from state action. In many cases, it is the individuals themselves who "empower" customary or religious authorities because they want their lives to be regulated in ways that accord with their religions and customs. What, under these circumstances, is the appropriate response?

It would be difficult to argue that citizens as individuals do not have the right to follow the prescriptions of their religion, or that religious authorities do not have the right to offer authoritative interpretations of religious law. Catholics and non-Catholics alike have criticised the Catholic Church for its insistence that marriage is for life and sex for procreation, and its opposition therefore to divorce, contraception, abortion, and homosexuality. But even the most ardent critic of the church could not legitimately question the "right" of devout Catholics to consider themselves still married even after getting a civil divorce or their right to turn to the church authorities for advice on how to get a religiously sanctioned annulment. (The language of rights is barely appropriate here, but I employ it for extra emphasis.) Where people have a strong allegiance to customary or religious law—when they do not consider themselves properly married or divorced, say, unless they have gone through the pro-

---

[17] For a good critique of Shachar's proposals regarding the splitting of jurisdictions, see Oonagh Reitman, "On Exit," in *Minorities within Minorities: Equality, Rights, and Diversity*, ed. Avigail Eisenberg and Jeff Spinner-Halev (Cambridge: Cambridge University Press, 2005).

cedures enjoined by their religion or customs—it is hardly appropriate for a government to tell them they cannot think like this. By the same token, it is hardly appropriate to block their access to arbitration procedures authorised by their religion. This surely remains the case even if the resulting arrangements are going to be less favourable to them than the civil procedures.

I am, to repeat, opposed to multicultural policies that distribute powers to a cultural or religious group. But there is a distinction between that and preventing religious groups from offering mediation or arbitration services that their members appear to desire, or as one might put it, a difference between stopping the state from distributing powers to a group and stopping its members from distributing such powers. A study of the women using the mediation services of the London-based Muslim Law (Shariah) Council shows, first, that they were voluntarily applying (so not under pressure from male family members), and second, that they had felt disempowered by the secular social and legal services, partly because they thought that these engaged with them as members of an ethnic rather than a religious group.[18] They mainly turned to the council because they needed religiously sanctioned help in freeing themselves from their marriages. In Islam, as in Orthodox Judaism, it is difficult for a woman to obtain a divorce against her husband's wishes: under all five schools of Islamic law, the marriage contract can be unilaterally terminated by the husband in a *talaq* divorce, but at the wife's initiative only when the husband consents. There is also, however, provision for parties to write the wife's right to divorce into their initial marriage contract, and failing that, for a woman to appeal to a religious judge for a dissolution of the contract, on a range of grounds including desertion, abuse, or the husband's renunciation of Islam. The Muslim Law (Shariah) Council is made up of people representing all five schools of law, mostly with some formal training in Islamic jurisprudence, and one of its primary activities has been to act as a religious judge in disputes about marriage contracts. It has proved enormously helpful to British Muslim women.

Some of the women who approach the council are married only according to Islamic law, and thus have no recourse to the civil courts in trying to obtain a divorce; others may already be divorced under civil law, but have failed to persuade their husbands to pronounce a talaq divorce. The council will contact the husbands on the women's behalf, thereby putting pressure on the men to account for their behaviour or justify their refusal. Where this fails to bring about a resolution, the council will adjudicate on whether the circumstances justify dissolving the marriage. It

---

[18] Sonia Nurin Shah-Kazemi, *Untying the Knot: Muslim Women, Divorce, and the Shariah* (London: Nuffield Foundation, 2001).

would be doing these women no service to ban the council or tell them they would be better off applying to the civil courts. It is clearly important that people be made aware of alternative civil procedures, particularly where these can offer more equitable arrangements for resolving disputes or afford women better protection. When there is a range of sharia councils, as is the case in Britain, some of which offer more favourable (to women) interpretations of the law than others, it also matters that women be made aware of the range so that they can apply, when they wish, to the more progressive ones. Since all councils regard the reconciliation of husband and wife as the most desirable outcome of mediation, all of them "may eschew gender equality in favour of religious and communal homogeneity."[19] But I do not see how one can object to people seeking to regulate their lives according to the prescriptions of their religion, even where—and this is the difficult point—those prescriptions offend against a principle of gender equality.

We can moderate this point by noting that in some of the cases dealt with by the Muslim Law (Shariah) Council, the women were better able to retrieve property from a marriage than they would have been under civil law (because they were able to appeal to Islamic principles to recover the *mahr*, a sum of money set aside for the wife at the time of the marriage contract). Or we can finesse the point by recalling that notions of gender equality are highly contested, and that it is not therefore self-evident which system of law will be more equitable between the sexes. But this last assertion looks like a weasel way out of the difficulty. In truth, we seem to face here what Sawitri Saharso has described as a conflict between recognising women's equality and recognising autonomy, although it is an odd sort of autonomy because it depends on recognising the authority of their religion. The fact that one system of law puts women in a weaker position in relation to men than another does not, however, seem sufficient grounds for requiring women to comply with the system that is more favourable.

Women with dual citizenship are particularly likely to want—or at least need—their marriages or divorces to conform to the laws of their country of origin. Titia Loenen notes that in the Netherlands today, many Moroccan women want to conform to Islamic law, even though this is mostly less favourable to them than Dutch law.[20] The sociological evidence suggests that Dutch Moroccan women, especially those who are second- or third-generation Dutch, are far from submissive in their ideas about the

---

[19] Bano, "Complexity, Difference, and 'Muslim Personal Law,'" 272.

[20] Titia Loenen, "Family Law Issues in a Multicultural Society: Abolishing or Reaffirming Sex as a Legally Relevant Category? A Human Rights Approach," *Netherlands Quarterly of Human Rights* 20, no. 4 (2002): 427.

appropriate relationships between women and men. But they identify strongly with their Moroccan heritage. They also know that marriages and divorces carried out under Dutch law may not be recognised in Morocco, to the point where a divorced woman—divorced under civil but not yet Islamic law—visiting family in Morocco could in principle be prosecuted for adultery or leaving her husband. It may be that these women do not feel themselves properly married or divorced unless the process conforms to religious law; more simply, it may be that they need their marriages or divorces recognised under Moroccan law in order to get on with their lives. Whichever it is, the fact that Dutch law is more equitable may be beside the point. In some cases, women who have already divorced their husbands under Dutch law, but have not yet persuaded those husbands to pronounce a talaq divorce, have applied to the Dutch courts for a legal order requiring their (ex-)husbands to repudiate them. In some of these instances, the courts have obliged, citing principles of tort law.[21]

This is not a unique occurrence—similar cases arise across Europe—and it is notable that when the civil courts *have* decided to enforce some component of religious law or recognise some aspect of another country's legislation, this mostly assists women who would otherwise be left in a more vulnerable position. There have been cases, for example, where a court in Europe has ordered a husband to pay his wife the mahr that is a condition for the validity of a marriage under Islamic law, or has rejected a husband's claim that his religious wedding had no enforceable legal status when he has employed this to avoid the payment of child support.[22] It seems likely that these kinds of issues will continue to arise—indeed increasingly so, as dual citizenship becomes more common—and that situations will continue to spring up where it seems fairer to recognise a competing jurisdiction. Certainly, if *no* account were ever taken of religious law in the proceedings of the civil courts or of one country's legal system in the courts of another country, this could amount to unequal treatment. It would be like a ban on so-called cultural defences that left defendants from minority cultural groups at a disadvantage, and denied them the opportunity to provide the kind of information about social context and personal background that has been widely accepted as legitimate from other defendants.

There has been considerable confusion over these issues in recent debates, with critics of multiculturalism interpreting *any* acknowledgment

[21] Ibid., 428.

[22] See a number of cases discussed in Sylvia Maier, "Multicultural Jurisprudence: Muslim Immigrants, Culture, and the Law in France and Germany" (paper, Council of European Scholars conference, Chicago, 2004).

of customary, religious, or second-country law as establishing different legal regimes for different groups. This misperception reflects the reified conceptions of religion and culture that I have been attacking in this book, for it is partly that all-or-nothing understanding that makes the legal recognition of any aspect of religious law appear as evidence of a wholesale capitulation to an alternative legal system. Insisting on the dangers of reifying cultures and cultural communities, the rights of cultural dissidents also to determine the values and practices of their communities, and the internal contestations that mark every cultural group provides some of the theoretical equipment for querying this move. But the problem is not just one of perception. First, it accords with what have been the expressed demands of some minority organisations. Second, and more problematic from my point of view, the fact that some individuals choose to regulate their lives according to alternative legal principles will sometimes have the effect of putting pressure on others to take the same route. Where this happens, something that looks like a benign way of helping women reach a religiously sanctioned solution to their difficulties could have the effect of enhancing authoritarian powers.

This is presumably the worry that lies behind the otherwise-contradictory position adopted by Hege Storhaug and the Norwegian Human Rights Servicein their discussion of Muslim women trapped in unwanted marriages.[23] The Human Rights Service posts information about the Muslim Law (Shariah) Council on its Web site, and advises Norwegian women whose husbands are refusing to pronounce a talaq divorce to make use of its services. It has also recommended to the government that it compile and disseminate information to Muslim women about this and other such organisations in order to assist those seeking a divorce. Yet the Human Rights Service remains resolutely opposed to religious courts or councils setting up in Norway, arguing that classical Islamic law on divorce is "fundamentally discriminatory against women" and that separate religious family courts represent "a step towards a segregated society."[24] This looks pretty contradictory: so it's great that such councils exist in England, but under no circumstances should similar ones be established in Norway. The justification, I take it, is one that balances the need to address existing suffering against what are seen as the risks of reproducing that suffering in future generations. If women have no recourse to sharia councils, they

---

[23] Hege Storhaug and Human Rights Service, *Human Visas: A Report from the Front Line of Europe's Integration Crisis* (Oslo, Norway: Human Rights Service, 2003), chap. 9. For a critique, see Sherene Razack, "Imperilled Muslim Women, Dangerous Muslim Men, and Civilised Europeans: Legal and Social Responses to Forced Marriages," *Feminist Legal Studies* 12 (2004): 129–74.

[24] Storhaug, *Human Visas*, 206.

will remain at the mercy of their husband's decision over the termination of their marriage; but if they turn to such councils, they thereby legitimate and sustain what remains a sexually discriminatory system of Islamic law. The Human Rights Service is therefore relieved that London has a relatively progressive sharia council because this offers a way out for individual women seeking redress today. But it regards this only as a transitional measure, a temporary alleviation while Muslim women in Europe presumably adjust themselves to the superiority of civil law, and it refuses to support initiatives that might shore up the authority of Islamic law over other women in the future. The fact that women's use of these services is voluntary, that Muslim law is supplementing rather than displacing civil law, and that the interpretations of the law are clearly working to women's advantage is treated as irrelevant.

I do not see this as a defensible position, but it helps to highlight the difficulties in drawing a clear line between empowering an individual and authorising a group. It is not only state action that empowers or legitimates an organisation or a group but also the actions of those individuals who attribute significance to it. The entirely voluntary actions of some may then strengthen the authority of an organisation over others who did not regard it as so important. This was the problem reported to the Stasi Commission: that girls who did not themselves attach much weight to the injunction to cover their heads in school would be less able to defend themselves against accusations of impiety if they were surrounded by others wearing headscarves, and that what might be the voluntary actions of some could later operate as coercion on others. Faced with this problem, it seems disingenuous to rely on my distinction between recognising the rights and needs of individuals (good) and distributing powers and resources to groups (bad) as if that resolves all issues. We can aim at a multiculturalism without reified understandings of culture, but it would be unrealistic to think this will deliver us a multiculturalism without groups. And wherever there are groups, there is always the potential for coercion.

Coercion and Choice

The theme running through this book is the importance of treating people as agents, not as captives of their culture or robots programmed by cultural rules, and the problem that has recurred throughout is that this throws up difficult questions about what constitutes autonomy or consent. I have argued against treating the choices people make under conditions of social pressure as therefore inauthentic, as if there is some pure set of choices unsullied by social, economic, familial, or what is termed cultural pressure, and as if only this pure set counts. But I have also argued against an all-or-nothing understanding of freedom that takes the fact that people remain within a particular relationship or cultural group—the fact that they do not take the opportunity to exit—as evidence that they have consented to all its arrangements. I do not accept (and neither, now, do the English or Scottish courts) that young people who give in to sustained family pressure, threats of being thrown out of their family and community, or moral blackmail about having already caused the death of one parent and being likely to cause the death of the other can be described as giving their free consent to a marriage. Nor do I accept (and neither, again, will most courts) that those who have decided to stay with a violent partner can be depicted as consenting to their continued abuse. It is clear enough that people, especially young people, experience coercion, and that some of this is genuinely life-threatening even under the strictest definition. But some of the coercion comes via the recognised authorities of your religion (the priests, the rabbis, or the imams) or the local dignitaries you regard as the representatives of your community, whose recommendations about how you are to live your life may edge close to commands. Some of it is subtly linked to accusations of being sexually loose, bringing shame on your family, or betraying your culture or religion. What, then, marks out consent? At what point do we say that people are doing what they choose, that while it may not be what everyone would want, it is causing no great inconvenience or harm to others, and that there are therefore no grounds for intervention? (As John Stuart Mill might put it.) At what point do public agencies have a responsibility to leave things be? And at what point do they have a responsibility to act?

There is no answer to this that can catch all instances of coercion. To avoid the trap of treating certain groups of people—particularly women, and particularly women from non-Western or minority cultural backgrounds—as less capable of autonomous choice than others, we have to go primarily by what people say. With minors, there is a responsibility to protect, though as anyone involved in child protection will confirm, this lends itself to difficult judgments about the point at which what others see as in the children's best interests ought to override their stated wishes. Simply fixing a legal age of majority does not resolve this, not only because individuals vary in their emotional development, but because young people are capable of knowing what is best for them—or at least, of making as good a stab at this as those charged with their protection—considerably before they reach the legal age of majority. Social workers and family court judges now typically operate on this assumption. So what I argue leaves a large unsettled area as to where the protection of a child ends and respect for adult judgment begins. With children and adults alike, however, the clear policy implication is that institutions should be developed that will better enable individuals to articulate what they want.

Left as it is, "going primarily by what people say" is too lax, and needs to be supplemented by measures that make it easier for people to get *their* voices (not someone else's) heard. One important feature of the British guidelines on forced marriage is the insistence that police officers, social workers, and teachers should always give young people the opportunity to talk to them on their own, without the intermediaries from their family or wider community whose presence might constrain what they say. Guarantees of privacy and anonymity are usually crucial components when there is an issue of coercion, as is publicising the avenues through which people can seek support. Research suggests that few of those working in the agencies most likely to be dealing with instances of forced marriage are yet aware of the guidelines, so there is clearly room for action here.[25] It is also, of course, crucial that there *are* support services. On the whole, people do not want to denounce their family or community to police or social workers, and especially not if they come from a social group that is currently a target of racism. It is thus unlikely that they will report any coercion they are experiencing unless it has either become so extreme that they feel they have no other option or they can see that reporting it is likely to have some effect. If there *are* no support services, there is nothing to be gained.

In other words, there are a number of obstacles that discourage people from articulating their concerns about cultural pressures or practices, and there is much that can be done by governments and public agencies to remove these. There is also much that can be done to assist people in making their personal decisions about when to comply with family or community pressure and when to resist. In her discussion of hymen repair surgery, Saharso concludes that doctors should be prepared to carry out such operations (otherwise they are putting an ideological battle against the virginity rule above the women's mostly well-grounded fears of community reprisals), but recommends that any woman requesting the procedure be offered a confidential individual interview where alternative ways of solving the problem are discussed.[26] As regards forced marriage, teachers should be encouraged to discuss with their students the nature of marriage, the meaning of consent, and the difference between listening to parental advice and being forced against one's will. All this operates, how-

[25] Geetanjali Gangoli, Amina Razak, and Melanie McCarry, *Forced Marriage and Domestic Violence among South Asian Communities in North East England* (Bristol: University of Bristol, School for Policy Studies, 2006), 7.

[26] Sawitri Saharso, "Feminist Ethics, Autonomy, and the Politics of Multiculturalism," *Feminist Theory* 4, no. 2 (2003): 199–215.

ever, on the assumption that people do know—at some level—when they are being pressured against their will. None of these initiatives will help those who are so brainwashed by their oppression that they cannot even perceive that something is awry.

Personally, I do not believe there *are* many such individuals. There are plenty of people around who put up with aspects of their lives they dislike because of other aspects they value, and many of these will not voice their complaints until they can see some realistic prospect of change. This is different, however, from saying that they do not even know their life is hard. I do not think there are many people so ground down by their circumstances that they have entirely internalised its norms—but I also do not think there is a great deal that public agencies can do if they come up against the apocryphal tamed housewife, for if people are *entirely* tamed, *unambiguously* convinced that their life is the best one for them, it is hard to see the basis for public intervention. We can make the standard exception for slavery—public agencies ought to free slaves even if they protest that they are happy in their slavery—though I tend to think that the "happy slave" is also a figment of the overactive academic imagination. But a defensible multiculturalism has to put human agency at its core, and this limits the kind of protections that can be offered to individuals choosing what others may consider self-denying or self-destructive behaviour.

When multiculturalism is represented as the accommodation of or negotiation with cultural communities or groups, this encourages us to view the world through the prism of separate and distinct cultures. We see ways of life struggling to survive; we see clashes of cultures. If we are feminist critics, we may see the oppressed female victims of patriarchal ways of life. The individuals, in all their complexity, disappear from view. My object here is a multiculturalism without this conception of culture, a multiculturalism that dispenses with reified notions of culture or homogenised conceptions of the cultural group yet retains enough robustness to address cultural inequalities. Working out the precise implications in terms of policy relies heavily on the context: we should expect different policies to be more or less appropriate in different political and historical contexts, and should not imagine there to be only one morally permissible arrangement deducible from nonnegotiable general rules.[27] Working out the precise implications also depends on addressing the democratic deficit; it depends on electing a wider range and larger number of citizens from

[27] As argued in Joseph H. Carens, *Culture, Citizenship, and Community: A Contextual Exploration of Justice as Evenhandedness* (Oxford: Oxford University Press, 2000); Sawitri Saharso, "Culture, Tolerance, and Gender: A Contribution from the Netherlands," *European Journal of Women's Studies* 10, no. 1 (2003): 7–27.

minority cultural groups to participate in the country's legislative and deliberative processes, and hearing a wider range of voices in consultations with minority cultural groups. Solutions to multicultural dilemmas are best arrived at through discussion and dialogue, where people from different cultural backgrounds explain to one another why they favour particular laws or practices, and develop the skills of negotiation and compromise that enable us to live together. Too often, however, societies fall into the trap of thinking that this means a negotiation between clearly delineated groups, differentiated by extraordinarily different values and perspectives, led by spokespeople who will articulate "their" community's point of view. It is that group-based version of multiculturalism that I have primarily taken issue with here. Cultural difference is not as great as it is often said to be. It does not map neatly on to communities. It will not be resolved by ceding authority to cultural groups.

Bibliography

Abu-Lughod, Lila. *Veiled Sentiments: Honor and Poetry in a Bedouin Society.* Berkeley: University of California Press, 1986.

———. "Writing against Culture." In *Recapturing Anthropology: Working in the Present,* edited by Richard G. Fox. Santa Fe, NM: School of American Research Press, 1991.

Abu-Odeh, Lama. "Comparatively Speaking: The 'Honour' of the East and the 'Passion' of the West." *Utah Law Review* (1997): 287–307.

Ackerman, Bruce. "Rooted Cosmopolitanism." *Ethics* 104 (1994): 516–35.

Afshar, Haleh, Rob Aitken, and Myfanwy Franks. "Feminisms, Islamophobia, and Identities." *Political Studies* 53, no. 2 (2005): 262–83.

Anderson, Elizabeth. "Should Feminists Reject Rational Choice Theory?" In *A Mind of One's Own,* edited by Louise Anthony and Charlotte Witt. 2nd ed. Boulder, CO: Westview, 2001.

Appiah, Kwame Anthony. "Cosmopolitan Patriots." *Critical Inquiry* 23 (1997): 617–39.

Appiah, Kwame Anthony, and Amy Gutmann. *Color-Conscious: The Political Morality of Race.* Princeton, NJ: Princeton University Press, 1996.

Archibugi, Daniele. "The Language of Democracy: Vernacular or Esperanto? A Comparison between the Multiculturalist and Cosmopolitan Perspectives." *Political Studies* 53, no. 3 (2005): 537–55.

Arneson, Richard. "Feminism and Family Justice." *Public Affairs Quarterly* 11, no. 4 (1997): 345–63

Asad, Talal, ed. *Anthropology and the Colonial Encounter.* London: Ithaca Press, 1973.

Baker, Judith, ed. *Group Rights.* Toronto: University of Toronto Press, 1994.

Balibar, Etienne. "Is There a Neo-Racism?" In *Race, Nation, Class,* edited by Etienne Balibar and Immanuel Wallerstein. London: Verso, 1991.

Bano, Samia. "Complexity, Difference, and 'Muslim Personal Law': Rethinking the Relationship between Shariah Councils and South Asian Muslim Women in Britain." PhD diss., University of Warwick, 2004.

Banting, Keith, and Will Kymlicka. "Do Multiculturalism Policies Erode the Welfare State?" In *Cultural Diversity versus Economic Solidarity: Proceedings of the Seventh Francqui Colloquium,* edited by Philippe van Parijs. Brussels: De Boeck, 2004.

Barry, Brian. *Culture and Equality: An Egalitarian Critique of Multiculturalism.* Cambridge, UK: Polity Press, 2001.

Baumann, Gerd. *Contesting Culture: Discourses of Identity in Multi-Ethnic London.* Cambridge: Cambridge University Press, 1996.

Baumann, Gerd, and Thijl Sunier. "De-essentialising Ethnicity." In *Post-Migration Ethnicity: Cohesion, Commitments, Comparison,* edited by Gerd Baumann and Thijl Sunier. Amsterdam: Het Spinhuis, 1995.

Baumann, Gerd, and Thijl Sunier. eds. *Post-Migration Ethnicity: Cohesion, Commitments, Comparison*. Amsterdam: Het Spinhuis, 1995.

Benhabib, Seyla. *The Claims of Culture: Equality and Diversity in the Global Era*. Princeton, NJ: Princeton University Press, 2002.

Bhabha, Homi. *The Location of Culture*. London: Routledge, 1994.

Breckenridge, Carol A., Sheldon Pollock, Homi K. Bhabha, and Dipesh Chakrabarty, eds. *Cosmopolitanism*. Durham, NC: Duke University Press, 2002.

Bredal, Anja. "Tackling Forced Marriages in the Nordic Countries: Between Women's Rights and Immigration Control." In *"Honour": Crimes, Paradigms, and Violence against Women*, edited by Lynn Welchman and Sara Hossain. London: Zed Books, 2005.

Brubaker, Rogers. "Ethnicity without Groups." *European Journal of Sociology* 43, no. 3 (2002): 163–89.

Brubaker, Rogers, and Frederick Cooper. "Beyond 'Identity.'" *Theory and Society* 29 (2000): 1–47.

Butler, Judith. "Merely Cultural." *Social Text* 52–53 (1997): 265–77.

———. *Gender Trouble: Feminism and the Subversion of Identity*. London: Routledge, 1999.

Carens, Joseph H. *Culture, Citizenship, and Community: A Contextual Exploration of Justice as Evenhandedness*. Oxford: Oxford University Press, 2000.

Carline, Anne. "Zoora Shah: 'An Unusual Woman.'" *Social and Legal Studies* 14, no. 2 (2005): 215–38.

Castles, Stephen, Mary Kalantzis, Bill Cope, and Michael Morrissey. *Mistaken Identity: Multiculturalism and the Demise of Nationalism in Australia*. Sydney: Pluto Press, 1988.

Chakrabarty, Dipesh. "Modernity and Ethnicity in India." In *Multicultural States: Rethinking Difference and Identity*, edited by David Bennett. London: Routledge, 1998.

Chantler, Khatidja, Erica Burman, Janet Batsleer, and Colsom Bashir. *Attempted Suicide and Self-Harm (South Asian Women)*. Manchester, UK: Women's Studies Research Centre, 2001.

Chiu, Daina C. "The Cultural Defense: Beyond Exclusion, Assimilation, and Guilty Liberalism." *California Law Journal* 82, no. 4 (1994): 1053–125.

Cohen, Anthony P. *Self-Consciousness: An Alternative Anthropology of Identity*. London: Routledge, 1994.

Cohen, Joshua, ed. *For Love of Country: Debating the Limits of Patriotism. Martha C. Nussbaum with Respondents*. Boston: Beacon Press, 1996.

Cohen, Joshua, Matthew Howard, and Martha C. Nussbaum, eds. *Is Multiculturalism Bad for Women? Susan Moller Okin with Respondents*. Princeton, NJ: Princeton University Press, 1999.

Coleman, Doriane Lambelet. "Individualizing Justice through Multiculturalism: The Liberal's Dilemma." *Columbia Law Review* 96, no. 5 (June 1996): 1093–167.

Community Cohesion: Report of the Independent Review Team. London: Home Office, 2001.

Council of Europe, Parliamentary Assembly. *Forced Marriages and Child Marriages*. Document 10678. 2005. Available at http://assembly.coe.int/Documents/WorkingDocs/doc05/EDOC10678.htm.

———. *Forced Marriages and Child Marriages*. Recommendation 1723. 2005. Available at http://assembly.coe.int/Documents/AdoptedTexts/tu05/EREC1723.htm.

Deveaux, Monique. *Cultural Pluralism and Dilemmas of Justice*. Ithaca, NY: Cornell University Press, 2000.

Dumont, Louis. *Homo Hierarchicus: The Caste System and Its Implications*. Chicago: University of Chicago Press, 1980.

Dworkin, Gerald. *The Theory and Practice of Autonomy*. New York: Cambridge University Press, 1988.

Eisenberg, Avigail. "The Debate over Sharia Law in Canada." In *Sexual/Cultural Justice*, edited by Barbara Arneil, Monique Deveaux, Rita Dhamoon, and Avigail Eisenberg. London: Routledge, 2006.

Eisenberg, Avigail, and Jeff Spinner-Halev, eds. *Minorities within Minorities: Equality, Rights, and Diversity*. Cambridge: Cambridge University Press, 2005.

Elster, Jon. *Sour Grapes: Studies in the Subversion of Rationality*. Cambridge: Cambridge University Press, 1983.

Entzinger, Han. "The Rise and Fall of Multiculturalism: The Case of the Netherlands." In *Towards Assimilation and Citizenship: Immigrants in Liberal Nation-States*, edited by Christian Joppke and Eva Morawski. Basingstoke, UK: Palgrave, 2003.

Ezekiel, Judith. "Magritte Meets Maghreb: This Is Not a Veil." *Australian Feminist Studies* 20, no. 47 (2005): 231–43.

Fassin, Didier. "Culturalism as Ideology." In *Cultural Perspectives on Reproductive Health*, edited by Carla Makhlout. Oxford: Oxford University Press, 2001.

Fishbayn, Lisa. "Litigating the Right to Culture: Family Law in the New South Africa." *International Journal of Law, Policy, and the Family* 13 (1999): 147–73.

Flax, Jane. "Beyond Equality: Gender, Justice, and Difference." In *Beyond Equality and Difference*, edited by Gisela Bock and Susan James. London: Routledge, 1992.

Ford, Richard T. *Racial Culture: A Critique*. Princeton, NJ: Princeton University Press, 2005.

Fournier, Pascale. "The Ghettoisation of Differences in Canada: 'Rape by Culture' and the Danger of a 'Cultural Defence' in Criminal Law Trials." *Manitoba Law Journal* 29 (2002): 81–113.

Friedman, Jonathan. "Global Crises, the Struggle for Cultural Identity, and Intellectual Porkbarrelling: Cosmopolitans versus Locals, Ethnics, and Nationals in an Era of De-hegemonisation." In *Debating Cultural Hybridity: Multi-Cultural Identities and the Politics of Anti-Racism*, edited by Pnina Werbner and Tariq Modood. London: Zed Books, 1997.

Friedman, Marilyn. "Autonomy, Social Disruption, and Women." In *Relational Autonomy: Feminist Perspectives on Autonomy, Agency, and the Social Self*, edited by Catriona MacKenzie and Natalie Stoljar. New York: Oxford University Press, 2000.

———. *Autonomy, Gender, Politics*. Oxford: Oxford University Press, 2003.

Galston, William. "Two Concepts of Liberalism." *Ethics* 105 (April 1995): 516–34.

Gangoli, Geetanjali, Amina Razak, and Melanie McCarry. *Forced Marriage and Domestic Violence among South Asian Communities in North East England*. Bristol: University of Bristol, School for Policy Studies, 2006.

Gaspard, Françoise, and Farhad Khosrokhavar. *Le foulard et la république*. Paris: Le Decouverte, 1995.

Geertz, Clifford. " 'From the Native's Point of View': On the Nature of Anthropological Understanding." 1974. Reprint, *Culture Theory: Essays on Mind, Self and Emotion* edited by Richard A. Shweder and Robert LeVine. Cambridge: Cambridge University Press, 1984.

———. *Local Knowledge: Further Essays in Interpretive Anthropology*. 1983. Reprint, London: Fontana Press, 1993.

Gilroy, Paul. *The Black Atlantic: Modernity and Double Consciousness*. London: Verso, 1993.

———. *Against Race: Imagining Political Culture beyond the Color Line*. Cambridge, MA: Belknap Press, 2000.

Glazer, Nathan. *We Are All Multiculturalists Now*. Cambridge, MA: Harvard University Press, 1997.

Göle, Nilüfer. *The Forbidden Modern: Civilization and Veiling*. Ann Arbor: University of Michigan Press, 1996.

Guinier, Lani. *The Tyranny of the Majority: Fundamental Fairness in Representative Democracy*. New York: Free Press, 1994.

Gupta, Akhil, and James Ferguson. "Beyond 'Culture': Space, Identity, and the Politics of Difference." *Cultural Anthropology* 7, no. 1 (1992): 6–23.

Gutmann, Amy, and Dennis Thompson. *Democracy and Disagreement*. Cambridge, MA: Belknap Press, 1996.

Hall, Stuart. "Cultural Identity and Diaspora." In *Identity: Community, Culture, Difference*, edited by Jonathan Rutherford. London: Lawrence and Wishart, 1990.

Hesse, Barnor, ed. *Un/settled Multiculturalisms: Diasporas, Entanglements, Disruptions*. London: Zed Books, 2000.

Hirschman, Albert O. *Exit, Voice, and Loyalty*. Cambridge, MA: Harvard University Press, 1970.

Hirschmann, Nancy J. "Western Feminism, Eastern Veiling, and the Question of Free Agency." *Constellations* 5, no. 3 (1998): 345–68.

Hollinger, David A. *Postethnic America: Beyond Multiculturalism*. New York: Basic Books, 1995.

Hughes, Robert. *The Culture of Complaint: The Fraying of America*. New York: Oxford University Press, 1993.

Ignatieff, Michael. "Why 'Community' Is a Dishonest Word." *Observer* (Manchester), 3 May 1993.

Jaggar, Alison. "Globalizing Feminist Ethics." In *Decentering the Center: Philosophy for a Multicultural, Postcolonial, and Feminist World*, edited by Uma Narayan and Sandra Harding. Bloomington: Indiana University Press, 2000.

Jenkins, Roy. *Essays and Speeches*. London: Collins, 1967.

Jones, Peter. "Group Rights and Group Oppression." *Journal of Political Philosophy* 7, no. 4 (1999): 353–77.

Joppke, Christian. "The Retreat of Multiculturalism in the Liberal State: Theory and Policy." *British Journal of Sociology* 55, no. 2 (2004): 237–57.

Joppke, Christian, and Eva Morawska, eds. *Towards Assimilation and Citizenship: Immigrants in Liberal Nation-States*. Basingstoke, UK: Palgrave, 2003.

Kapur, Ratna. *Erotic Justice: Law and the New Politics of Postcolonialism*. London: Glasshouse Press, 2005.

Kastoryano, Riva. *Negotiating Identities: States and Immigrants in France and Germany*. Princeton, NJ: Princeton University Press, 2002.

Kim, Nancy S. "The Cultural Defence and the Problems of Cultural Preemption: A Framework for Analysis." *New Mexico Law Review* 27 (1997): 101–39.

Kukathas, Chandran. "The Life of Brian—or Now for Something Completely Difference-Blind." In *Multiculturalism Reconsidered*, edited by Paul Kelly. Cambridge, UK: Polity Press, 2002.

———. *The Liberal Archipelago*. Oxford: Oxford University Press, 2003.

Kuper, Adam. *Culture: The Anthropologists' Account*. Cambridge, MA: Harvard University Press, 1999.

Kymlicka, Will. *Liberalism, Community, and Culture*. Oxford: Clarendon Press, 1989.

———. *Multicultural Citizenship: A Liberal Theory of Minority Rights*. Oxford: Clarendon Press, 1995.

———. *Politics in the Vernacular: Nationalism, Multiculturalism, and Citizenship*. Oxford: Oxford University Press, 2001.

Levy, Jacob T. *The Multiculturalism of Fear*. Oxford: Oxford University Press, 2000.

Lijphart, Arendt. *Democracy in Plural Societies: A Comparative Exploration*. New Haven, CO: Yale University Press, 1977.

Lloyd, Genevieve. *The Man of Reason: "Male" and "Female" in Western Philosophy*. London: Methuen, 1986.

Loenen, Titia. "Family Law Issues in a Multicultural Society: Abolishing or Reaffirming Sex as a Legally Relevant Category? A Human Rights Approach." *Netherlands Quarterly of Human Rights* 20, no. 4 (2002): 423–44.

Lovenduski, Joni. *Feminizing Politics*. Cambridge, UK: Polity Press, 2005.

Lyon, Dawn, and Debora Spini. "Unveiling the Headscarf Debate." *Feminist Legal Studies* 12 (2004): 333–45.

Ma, Veronica. "Culture Defense: Limited Admissibility for New Immigrants." *San Diego Justice Journal* 3, no. 2 (1995): 461–84.

Mackie, Gerry. "Female Genital Cutting: The Beginning of the End." In *Female "Circumcision" in Africa: Culture, Controversy, and Change*, edited by Bettina Shell-Duncan and Ylva Hernlund. New York: Lynne Rienner, 2000.

MacLeod, Arlene Elowe. *Accommodating Protest: Working Women, the New Veiling, and Change in Cairo*. New York: Columbia University Press, 1991.

Madhok, Sumi. Autonomy, Subordination, and the "Social Woman": Examining Rights Narratives of Rural Rajasthani Women. PhD diss., School of Oriental and African Studies, London, 2003.

Magnarella, Paul J. "Justice in a Culturally Pluralistic Society: The Culture Defense on Trial." *Journal of Ethnic Studies* 19 (1991): 65–84.

Mahmood, Saba. *Politics of Piety: The Islamic Revival and the Feminist Subject.* Princeton, NJ: Princeton University Press, 2005.

Mahoney, Martha R. "Exit: Power and the Idea of Leaving in Love, Work, and the Confirmation Hearings." *Southern California Law Review* 65 (1991): 1283–319.

Maier, Sylvia. Multicultural Jurisprudence: Muslim Immigrants, Culture, and the Law in France and Germany. Paper presented at the Council of European Scholars conference, Chicago, 2004.

McColgan, Aileen. "General Defences." In *Feminist Perspectives on Criminal Law*, edited by Donald Nicolson and Lois Bibbings. London: Cavendish, 2000.

Mehta, Pratap Bhanu. "Cosmopolitanism and the Circle of Reason." *Political Theory* 28, no. 5 (2000): 619–39.

Mendus, Susan. "Choice, Chance, and Multiculturalism." In *Multiculturalism Revisited*, edited by Paul Kelly. Cambridge, UK: Polity Press, 2002.

Menon, Nivedita. "The Impossibility of 'Justice': Female Foeticide and Feminist Discourse on Abortion." In *Social Reform, Sexuality, and the State*, edited by Patricia Uberoi. New Delhi: Sage, 1996.

Mernissi, Fatima. *Beyond the Veil: Male-Female Dynamics in a Modern Muslim Society.* Cambridge, MA: Schenkman Publishing Co., 1975.

Meyers, Diana Tietjens. "Feminism and Women's Autonomy: The Challenge of Female Genital Cutting." *Metaphilosophy* 31, no. 5 (2000): 469–91.

Miller, David. *On Nationality.* Oxford: Oxford University Press, 1995.

Modood, Tariq. *Multicultural Politics: Racism, Ethnicity, and Muslims in Britain.* Edinburgh: Edinburgh University Press, 2005.

Modood, Tariq, Richard Berthoud, Jane Lakey, James Nazroo, Patten Smith, Satnam Virdee, and Sharon Beishon. *Ethnic Minorities in Britain.* London: Policy Studies Institute, 1997.

Narayan, Uma. *Dislocating Cultures: Identities, Traditions, and Third World Women.* London: Routledge, 1997.

———. "Essence of Culture and a Sense of History: A Feminist Critique of Cultural Essentialism." *Hypatia* 13, no. 2 (1998): 86–106.

———. "Undoing the 'Package Picture' of Cultures." *Signs* 25, no. 4 (2000): 1083–86.

———. "Minds of Their Own: Choices, Autonomy, Cultural Practices, and Other Women." In *A Mind of One's Own: Feminist Essays on Reason and Objectivity*, edited by Louise M. Anthony and Charlotte E. Witt. Boulder, CO: Westview Press, 2002.

Norton, Anne. "Review Essay on Euben, Okin, and Nussbaum." *Political Theory* 29, no. 5 (2001): 736–49.

Nussbaum, Martha C. "Patriotism and Cosmopolitanism." In *For Love of Country: Debating the Limits of Patriotism. Martha C. Nussbaum with Respondents*, edited by Joshua Cohen. Boston: Beacon Press, 1996.

———. *Women and Human Development: The Capabilities Approach.* Cambridge: Cambridge University Press, 2000.

Obeyesekere, Gananath. *The Apotheosis of Captain Cook: European Mythmaking in the Pacific.* Princeton, NJ: Princeton University Press, 1992.

Okin, Susan Moller. *Justice, Gender, and the Family.* New York: Basic Books, 1989.

———. "Feminism and Multiculturalism: Some Tensions." *Ethics* 108, no. 4 (1998): 661–84.

———. "Is Multiculturalism Bad for Women?" In *Is Multiculturalism Bad for Women?* edited by Joshua Cohen, Matthew Howard, and Martha C. Nussbaum. Princeton, NJ: Princeton University Press, 1999.

———. "'Mistresses of Their Own Destiny': Group Rights, Gender, and Realistic Rights of Exit." *Ethics* 112 (January 2002): 205–30.

Parekh, Bhikhu. *Rethinking Multiculturalism: Cultural Diversity and Political Theory.* London: Palgrave Press, 2000.

Pateman, Carole. *The Sexual Contract.* Cambridge, UK: Polity Press, 1988.

Phillips, Anne. *The Politics of Presence: The Political Representation of Gender, Ethnicity, and Race.* Oxford: Oxford University Press, 1995.

———. "Multiculturalism, Universalism, and the Claims of Democracy." In *Gender Justice, Development, and Rights,* edited by Maxine Molyneux and Shahra Razavi. Oxford: Oxford University Press, 2002.

Phillips, Anne. "Defending Equality of Outcome." *Journal of Political Philosophy* 12, no. 1 (2004): 1–19.

———. "'Really' Equal: Opportunities and Autonomy." *Journal of Political Philosophy* 14, no. 1 (2006): 18–32.

Phillips, Anne, and Moira Dustin. "UK Initiatives on Forced Marriage: Regulation, Exit, and Dialogue." *Political Studies* 52, no. 3 (2004): 531–51.

Pollitt, Katha. "Whose Culture?" In *Is Multiculturalism Bad for Women?* edited by Joshua Cohen, Matthew Howard, and Martha C. Nussbaum. Princeton, NJ: Princeton University Press, 1999.

Poulter, Sebastian. *English Law and Ethnic Minority Customs.* London: Butterworth, 1986.

———. "The Significance of Ethnic Minority Customs and Traditions in English Criminal Law." *New Community* 16, no. 1 (1989): 121–28.

———. *Ethnicity, Law, and Human Rights: The English Experience.* Oxford: Clarendon Press, 1998.

Rajan, Rajeswari Sunder. *The Scandal of the State: Women, Law, and Citizenship in Postcolonial India.* Durham, NC: Duke University Press, 2003.

Razack, Sherene. "Imperilled Muslim Women, Dangerous Muslim Men, and Civilised Europeans: Legal and Social Responses to Forced Marriages." *Feminist Legal Studies* 12 (2004): 129–74.

Reitman, Ooonagh. "On Exit." In *Minorities within Minorities: Equality, Rights, and Diversity,* edited by Avigail Eisenberg and Jeff Spinner-Halev. Cambridge: Cambridge University Press, 2005.

Renteln, Alison. *The Cultural Defense.* New York: Oxford University Press, 2004.

Resnik, Judith. "Dependent Sovereigns: Indian Tribes, States, and the Federal Courts." *University of Chicago Law Review* 56 (1989): 671–759.

Roemer, John E. *Equality of Opportunity*. Cambridge, MA: Harvard University Press, 1998.

Rowlinson, Matthew. "Re-Reading Criminal Law: Gendering the Mental Element." In *Feminist Perspectives on Criminal Law*, edited by Donald Nicolson and Lois Bibbings. London: Cavendish, 2000.

Runnymede Trust Commission. *The Future of Multi-Ethnic Britain*. London: Profile Books, 2000.

Saharso, Sawitri. "Culture, Tolerance, and Gender: A Contribution from the Netherlands." *European Journal of Women's Studies* 10, no. 1 (2003): 7–27.

———. "Feminist Ethics, Autonomy, and the Politics of Multiculturalism." *Feminist Theory* 4, no. 2 (2003): 199–215.

———. "Is the Freedom of the Will but a Western Illusion? Individual Autonomy, Gender, and Multicultural Judgment." In *Sexual/Cultural Justice*, edited by Barbara Arneil, Monique Deveaux, Rita Dhamoon, and Avigail Eisenberg. London: Routledge, 2006.

Sahlins, Marshall. "Goodbye to Tristes Tropes: Ethnography in the Context of Modern World History." *Journal of Modern History* 65 (March 1993): 1–25.

Samad, Yunas, and John Eade. *Community Perceptions of Forced Marriage*. London: Community Liaison Unit, Foreign and Commonwealth Office, 2002.

Sams, Julia P. "The Availability of the 'Cultural Defense' as an Excuse for Criminal Behavior." *Georgia Journal of International and Comparative Law* 16 (1986): 335–54.

Samuels, Alec. "Legal Recognition and Protection of Minority Customs in a Plural Society in England." *Anglo-American Law Review* 10, no. 4 (1981): 241–56.

Schlesinger, Arthur M. *The Disuniting of America*. New York: W. W. Norton, 1992.

Scott, David. "Criticism and Culture: Theory and Post-colonial Claims on Anthropological Disciplinarity." *Critique of Anthropology* 12, no. 4 (1992): 391–94.

———. "Culture in Political Theory." *Political Theory* 31, no. 1 (February 2003): 92–115.

Scott, Joan W. *Only Paradoxes to Offer: French Feminists and the Rights of Man*. Cambridge, MA: Harvard University Press, 1996.

Sen, Amartya. *Inequality Re-examined*. Oxford: Clarendon Press, 1992.

———. "Gender Inequality and Theories of Justice." In *Women, Culture, and Development*, edited by Martha Nussbaum and Jonathan Glover. Oxford: Clarendon Press, 1995.

———. *The Argumentative Indian: Writings on Indian History, Culture, and Identity*. London: Allen Lane, 2005.

Sen, Purna. "'Crimes of Honour': Value and Meaning." In *"Honour": Crimes, Paradigms, and Violence against Women*, edited Lynn Welchman and Sara Hossain. London: Zed Books, 2005.

Shachar, Ayelet. *Multicultural Jurisdictions: Cultural Differences and Women's Rights*. Cambridge: Cambridge University Press, 2001.

Shah-Kazemi, Sonia Nurin. *Untying the Knot: Muslim Women, Divorce, and the Shariah*. London: Nuffield Foundation, 2001.

Shapiro, Ian, and Will Kymlicka, eds. *Ethnicity and Group Rights NOMOS XXXIX*. New York: New York University Press, 1997.

Shweder, Richard A., and Edmund J. Bourne. "Does the Concept of the Person Vary Cross-culturally?" In *Culture Theory: Essays on Mind, Self, and Emotion*, edited by Richard A. Shweder and Robert LeVine. Cambridge: Cambridge University Press, 1984.

Siddiqui, Hannana, " 'It Was Written in Her Kismet': Forced Marriage." In *From Homebreakers to Jailbreakers: Southall Black Sisters*, edited by Rahila Gupta. London: Zed Press, 2004.

Sokefeld, Martin. "Debating Self, Identity, and Culture in Anthropology." *Current Anthropology* 40, no. 4 (1999): 417–47.

Song, Sarah. "Majority Norms, Multiculturalism, and Gender Equality." *American Political Science Review* 99, no. 4 (November 2005): 474–89.

Spelman, Elizabeth. *Inessential Woman: Problems of Exclusion in Feminist Thought*. Boston: Beacon Press, 1988.

Spinner, Jeff. *The Boundaries of Citizenship: Race, Ethnicity, and Nationality in the Liberal State*. Baltimore, MD: Johns Hopkins University Press, 1994.

Spinner-Halev, Jeff. *Surviving Diversity: Religion and Democratic Citizenship*. Baltimore, MD: Johns Hopkins University Press, 2000.

Spiro, Melford E. "Is the Conception of the Self 'Peculiar' within the Context of the World Cultures?" *Ethos* 21, no. 2 (1993): 107–53.

Spivak, Gayatri Chakravorty. "Subaltern Studies: Deconstructing Historiography." In *Selected Subaltern Studies*, edited by Ranajit Guha and Gayatri Chakravorty Spivak. Oxford: Oxford University Press, 1988.

Stasi, Bernard. *Laïcité et République. Rapport de la commission de reflection sur l'application du principe de laïcité dans la république*. Paris: La Documentation Francaise, 2004.

Stolcke, Verena. "Talking Culture: New Boundaries, New Rhetorics of Exclusion in Europe." *Current Anthropology* 36, no. 1 (1995): 1–24.

Stoljar, Natalie. "Autonomy and the Feminist Intuition." In *Relational Autonomy: Feminist Perspectives on Autonomy, Agency, and the Social Self*, edited by Catriona MacKenzie and Natalie Stoljar. New York: Oxford University Press, 2000.

Storhaug, Hege, and Human Rights Service. *Human Visas: A Report from the Front Line of Europe's Integration Crisis*. Oslo, Norway: Human Rights Service, 2003.

Sunder, Madhavi. "Cultural Dissent." *Stanford Law Review* 545 (December 2001): 495–567.

———. "Piercing the Veil." *Yale Law Journal* 112 (2003): 1399–472.

Sunstein, Cass. "Preferences and Politics." *Philosophy and Public Affairs* 20 (1991): 3–34.

Tamir, Yael. "Against Collective Rights." In *Multicultural Questions*, edited by Christian Joppke and Steven Lukes. Oxford: Oxford University Press, 1999.

Taylor, Charles. "The Politics of Recognition." In *Multiculturalism and the Politics of Recognition*, edited by Amy Gutmann. Princeton, NJ: Princeton University Press, 1992.

Terray, Emmanuel. "Headscarf Hysteria." *New Left Review* 26 (2004): 118–27.

Tostan. *Breakthrough in Senegal: The Process That Ended Female Genital Cutting in 31 Villages*. Washington, DC: U.S. Agency for International Development, 1999.

Tully, James. *Strange Multiplicity: Constitutionalism in an Age of Diversity*. Cambridge: Cambridge University Press, 1995.

Turner, Terence. "Representing, Resisting, Rethinking: Historical Transformations of Kayapo Culture and Anthropological Consciousness." In *Colonial Situations: Essays in the Contextualization of Ethnographic Knowledge*, edited by George W. Stocking Jr. Madison: University of Wisconsin Press, 1991.

———. "Defiant Images: The Kayapo Appropriation of Video." *Anthropology Today* 8, no. 6 (December 1992): 5–15.

———. "Anthropology and Multiculturalism: What Is AnthropologyThat Multiculturalists Should Be Mindful of It?" Reprinted in *Multiculturalism: A Critical Reader*, edited by David T. Goldberg. Cambridge, MA: Blackwell, 1994.

Tylor, Edward B. *Primitive Culture*. London: John Murray, 1871.

Vail, Leroy, ed. *The Creation of Tribalism in Southern Africa*. Berkeley: University of California Press, 1989.

Van Broeck, Jeroen. "Cultural Defence and Culturally Motivated Crimes." *European Journal of Crime, Criminal Law, and Criminal Justice* 9, no. 1 (2001): 1–31.

Volpp, Leti. "(M)isidentifying Culture: Asian Women and the 'Cultural Defense.'" *Harvard Women's Law Journal* 17 (1994): 57–101.

———. "Talking 'Culture': Gender, Race, Nation, and the Politics of Multiculturalism." *Columbia Law Review* 96, no. 6 (1996): 1573–617.

———. "Blaming Culture for Bad Behavior." *Yale Journal of Law and the Humanities* 12 (2000): 89–116.

———. "Feminism and Multiculturalism." *Columbia Law Review* 101 (2001): 1181–218.

Wagner, Roy. *The Invention of Culture*. Chicago: University of Chicago Press, 1981.

Waldron, Jeremy. "Minority Cultures and the Cosmopolitan Alternative." *University of Michigan Journal of Law Reform* 25 (1992): 751–93.

———. "What Is Cosmopolitan?" *Journal of Political Philosophy* 8, no. 2 (2000): 227–43.

Waters, Mary C. *Ethnic Options: Choosing Identities in America*. Berkeley: University of California Press, 1990.

Welchman, Lynn, and Sara Hossain. *"Honour": Crimes, Paradigms, and Violence against Women*. London: Zed Books, 2005.

Werbner, Pnina. "Global Pathways, Working-Class Cosmopolitans, and the Creation of Transnational Ethnic Worlds." *Social Anthropology* 7, no. 1 (1999): 17–35.

Wikan, Unni. *Generous Betrayal: Politics of Culture in the New Europe*. Chicago: University of Chicago Press, 2002.

Williams, Raymond. *Keywords: A Vocabulary of Culture and Society*. London: Fontana/Croom Helm, 1976.

Wright, Susan. "The Politicization of 'Culture,'" *Anthropology Today* 14, no. 1 (February 1998): 7–15.

Young, Iris Marion. *Justice and the Politics of Difference*. Princeton, NJ: Princeton University Press, 1990.

Index

abortion, 39–40, 114, 130–31, 144, 155. *See also* women

Abu-Lughod, Lila, 24, 48, 116

Ackerman, Bruce, 68–69

Adesanya, Mrs., 78, 79, 83

adoption, 54

adultery, 73, 75, 76, 84, 91. *See also* sexual relations

affirmative action, 15, 54–55, 56, 59. *See also* discrimination

Africa, 57

African Americans, 16, 54–55, 109

African Caribbeans, 57

African tribalism, 44

age: and marriage, 9, 14, 66, 78–79, 101, 120, 121–23, 122, 125, 132, 139; for occupations, 112; regulations concerning, 165, 166, 177; and sexual relations, 32, 73, 81

agency: and culture as determinative, 9, 14, 40, 51; degrees of, 104; and exit, 150; gendered understanding of, 97; in non-Western cultures, 26, 148, 150; and protection, 179; in treatment, 176; and violence against women, 149; of women, 26, 101, 150. *See also* autonomy; choice; culture(s), as determinative

Ahluwalia, Kiranjit, 86–87

Aisha (in Wikan), 74, 75

Alhaji Mohamed v. Knott [1969] 1QB 1, 78–79, 81

Amish, 16, 138, 141, 143, 152

anthropology, 16, 21, 24, 42, 43, 49, 50, 51, 62n43, 99, 135, 150

apartheid, 169

Appiah, Kwame Anthony, 16, 69

Archibugi, Daniele, 72

Arneson, Richard, 37–38

Asians, 5, 57, 87

assimilation, 4, 8, 14, 22, 64

association, freedom of, 155, 156

Australia, 3; *National Agenda for a Multicultural Society,* 3

Austria, 114

autonomy, 86, 100–106; capability of, 177; and choice, 126; and community, 105–6; context for, 105; and cultural defence, 94, 100; and cultural expectations, 131; culture as condition for, 105; and culture as determinative, 133; definition of, 101–2; degrees of, 104; despite constraints, 130; and dress, 100–101; and equality, 38–41; and equality of women, 173; and identity, 155; and influence of gender and class, 127, 128; in *Mandla v. Dowell Lee,* 107; and multiculturalism, 100, 104; and policy, 124; and religion, 100; of uncoerced adult, 125–26. *See also* agency; choice; culture(s), as determinative; self

Azam, Mohammed, 87, 88

Balibar, Etienne, 42, 56, 58

Bangladesh, 57, 123

Bangladeshis, 61, 65, 66

Barry, Brian, 5n8, 111, 138, 143n18, 146–47

Baumann, Gerd, 31, 51–52

Bedouins, 116

Begum, Shabina, 59–60

Begum, Tasleem, 90

Belgium, 115, 116, 163, 165

Benhabib, Seyla, 21, 27–28, 29, 161

Betambeau, John, 95n47

Bibi, Bashir Begum, 85–86, 88, 97

biological determination, 56

blanket prohibitions, 100–101, 114, 118, 119, 123, 124, 125, 132

border crossing, 48

Boy Scouts of America v. Dale, 155

Briggs, Jack, 94

Briggs, Zena, 94

Brubaker, Rogers, 17

Bui, Quang Ngoc, 84

burka, 8, 114

Burma, 123

Canada, 22, 65, 109n18, 122; Arbitration Act (1991), 169–70; Royal Canadian Mounted Police, 113

capacity: cultural, 106–8, 112, 128–29; economic, 108; social, 108

Lightning Source UK Ltd.
Milton Keynes UK
UKOW02f0102200116

266731UK00004B/143/P